The Oxford Introductions to U.S. Law

Constitutional Law

The Oxford Introductions to U.S. Law

Constitutional Law

MICHAEL C. DORF WITH
TREVOR W. MORRISON

Dennis Patterson, Series Editor
The Oxford Introductions to U.S. Law

OXFORD
UNIVERSITY PRESS

OXFORD
UNIVERSITY PRESS

*Oxford University Press, Inc., publishes works that further Oxford University's objective of excellence
in research, scholarship, and education.*

Oxford   New York
Auckland   Cape Town   Dar es Salaam   Hong Kong   Karachi   Kuala Lumpur   Madrid   Melbourne
Mexico City   Nairobi   New Delhi   Shanghai   Taipei   Toronto

With offices in
Argentina   Austria   Brazil   Chile   Czech Republic   France   Greece   Guatemala   Hungary   Italy
Japan   Poland   Portugal   Singapore   South Korea   Switzerland   Thailand   Turkey   Ukraine
Vietnam

Copyright © 2010 by Oxford University Press, Inc.

Published by Oxford University Press, Inc.
198 Madison Avenue, New York, New York 10016

Oxford is a registered trademark of Oxford University Press
Oxford University Press is a registered trademark of Oxford University Press, Inc.

Library of Congress Cataloging-in-Publication Data
Dorf, Michael C.
  The Oxford introductions to U.S. law. Constitutional law / Michael C. Dorf ; with
Trevor W. Morrison.
     p. cm.—(The Oxford introductions to U.S. law)
  Includes bibliographical references and index.
  ISBN 978-0-19-537003-4 (pbk. : alk. paper)
  1. Constitutional law—United States. I. Morrison, Trevor W.
II. Title. III. Title: Constitutional law.
  KF4550.D598 2010
  342.73—dc22   2010013594

1 2 3 4 5 6 7 8 9

Printed in the United States of America

Note to Readers
This publication is designed to provide accurate and authoritative information in regard to the subject
matter covered. It is based upon sources believed to be accurate and reliable and is intended to be
current as of the time it was written. It is sold with the understanding that the publisher is not engaged
in rendering legal, accounting, or other professional services. If legal advice or other expert assistance is
required, the services of a competent professional person should be sought. Also, to confirm that the
information has not been affected or changed by recent developments, traditional legal research
techniques should be used, including checking primary sources where appropriate.

*(Based on the Declaration of Principles jointly adopted by a Committee of the
American Bar Association and a Committee of Publishers and Associations.)*

You may order this or any other Oxford University Press publication by
visiting the Oxford University Press website at www.oup.com

For Sherry and Beth

Acknowledgments

AS ORIGINALLY CONCEIVED, this book was to be a work of completely joint authorship. However, long before we completed the manuscript, Trevor Morrison took a position as Associate White House Counsel in the Obama Administration, the demands of which precluded full participation in the writing. Consequently, Michael Dorf completed the job. We planned the structure and overall argument together, but Morrison was the initial author of only Chapters 5 (Separation of Powers), 9 (Congressional Enforcement of Constitutional Rights), and 10 (Beyond the Courts), with Dorf writing the balance of the book. We have nonetheless used the plural authorial voice to reflect the collaborative nature of the project.

A number of other people were instrumental in the production of this book. Dennis Patterson first suggested the project to us and we would like to also thank Lori Wood, formerly of Oxford University Press. Chris Collins succeeded her as our principal editor, and was very accommodating of our tardiness. Sherry Colb and Steven Shiffrin provided insightful comments on chapter drafts, and Benjamin Beaton and James Rumpf were terrific research assistants. We also very much appreciate the comments of several anonymous reviewers of the original proposal; we altered the organization and emphasis of the book in response to their observations. Needless to say, all errors are our own.

Contents

CHAPTER 1 **Who Decides?** 1

CHAPTER 2 **Judicial Review** 11

What Is Judicial Review and What Purpose Does
It Serve? 12
What Does the Constitution Say about Judicial
Review? 21
Writtenness 22
Supremacy 26
Articles III and VI 28
What Are the Practical Consequences of Judicial
Review? 31
Further Reading 38

CHAPTER 3 **Constitutional Interpretation** 41

Judicial Restraint 50
Natural Law and the Moral Reading 52
Representation Reinforcement 57
Originalism 61
Eclecticism 65
Further Reading 68

CHAPTER 4 **Federalism** 69

The Benefits and Costs of Federalism 71
Limits of Enumerated Powers 78

Internal versus External Commerce 79
Pretext 81
Economic Activity 82
"Etiquette" Limits on Federal Power 84
Traditional Areas of State Sovereignty 85
Commandeering 86
Sovereign Immunity 89
Clear Statement Rules 91
Federalism-Based Limits on the States 92
Further Reading 93

CHAPTER 5 **Separation of Powers 95**

The Function of Separation of Powers 97
Selected Themes in Separation of
Powers Doctrine 104
The Executive 104
The Legislature 117
The Judiciary 119
Further Reading 124

CHAPTER 6 **Equal Protection 125**

Slavery 126
From *Plessy* to *Brown* 128
Anti-Subordination or Color Blindness? 134
Tiers of Scrutiny 142
Purpose and Effect 148
Is Equality an Empty Idea? 150
Further Reading 151

CHAPTER 7 **Enumerated Rights: The First Amendment 153**

Freedom of the Press 157
Freedom of Speech 159
Free Exercise of Religion 171
No Establishment of Religion 178
Further Reading 185

CHAPTER 8 **Unenumerated Rights** 187

> The Privileges or Immunities Clause 191
> The *Lochner* Era 196
> Incorporation of the Bill of Rights 201
> The Right of "Privacy" 205
> Further Reading 215

CHAPTER 9 **Congressional Enforcement of Constitutional Rights** 217

> The State Action Requirement 218
> Defining the Rights to be Enforced 222
> Enforcement as Deterrence and Prevention,
>   within Limits 228
> Further Reading 234

CHAPTER 10 **Beyond the Courts** 235

Index 241

ONE

Who Decides?

MANY OF THE CENTRAL QUESTIONS in American constitutional law ask "who decides?" Does the Constitution's grant to Congress of the power "[t]o regulate commerce ... among the several states" include the power to proscribe the possession of marijuana grown and used for medical purposes within a single state, or does the Tenth Amendment's reservation to the states of "[t]he powers not delegated to the United States" entitle a state to legalize medical marijuana within its territory?[1] Does congressional power to declare war include the power to limit or revoke authority for military action, or does the President's status as Commander in Chief give him wide discretion to act once Congress has approved or even merely acquiesced in the commitment of armed forces to the field? When can elected bodies limit individual rights to speak, to practice religion, and to make choices about parenting and sexual relations? And most fundamentally, who decides "who decides"? In other words, in these constitutional conflicts—between the state and federal governments, between the branches of the federal government, and between government (at any level) and the individual—by what authority do unelected judges and Justices substitute their judgment about the Constitution's allocation of authority for the (implicit or explicit) constitutional judgment of elected officials?

---

1. *See* Gonzales v. Raich, 545 U.S. 1 (2005).

Constitutional law sometimes addresses questions of the proper allocation of decisional authority directly. For example, in *Nixon v. United States*[2] (not *that* Nixon), the Supreme Court held that the clause of Article I that gives the Senate "the sole Power to try all Impeachments" ordinarily precludes resort to the courts by an impeached judge who claims that the circumstances of his trial—live testimony before a committee followed by a full transcript and report to the Senate as a whole—were impermissible. The issue, the Court said, was committed to the Senate.[3]

More commonly, however, constitutional law establishes rules and standards that, at most, only indirectly answer the "who decides" question. For example, the Fourteenth Amendment's Equal Protection Clause by its terms protects all persons. Yet legislation invariably draws distinctions among persons, and so the Clause cannot possibly be interpreted to forbid all laws and policies that treat different people differently. Indeed, the courts could not even enforce a rule that required all distinctions to be justified to the judges' satisfaction, for such a rule would invite a flood of litigation. Accordingly, the Supreme Court upholds laws challenged on equal protection grounds so long as they are minimally rational—unless those laws draw distinctions on the basis of a small number of presumptively impermissible grounds, such as race, national origin, and sex.[5] In the latter circumstances, the courts apply various forms of "heightened scrutiny."

The different tiers of scrutiny roughly implement a "who decides" principle: The Supreme Court allocates to political actors primary responsibility for adjusting the benefits and burdens of ordinary legislation; however, when political actors draw distinctions on grounds (such as race or sex) that have traditionally been the basis

---

2. 506 U.S. 224 (1993).

3. *Id.* at 238.

4. *See, e.g.,* Williamson v. Lee Optical, 348 U.S. 483 (1955).

5. *Cf.* United States v. Carolene Products, 304 U.S. 144, 153 n.4 (1938).

for subjugating whole groups of people (such as African Americans or women), judges demand an extraordinarily persuasive justification for the distinction.

The mechanism of tiers of scrutiny plays an important role beyond the equal protection context, most notably in cases involving so-called "fundamental rights."[6] To recognize a right as fundamental is to allocate decisions regarding whether to exercise that right to the individual rather than to the government. Thus government action that infringes fundamental rights, like government action that uses one of the presumptively suspect classifications, triggers heightened judicial scrutiny. The judicial decision as to whether to recognize a particular fundamental right has often been controversial precisely because of the allocational stakes. When the Supreme Court says, for instance, that custodial parents have a fundamental right to decide whether and when other adults may interact with their children, it allocates power away from elected state representatives, to individual parents, and, in making the decision, to itself.[7]

To recognize that constitutional law frequently concerns the allocation of decision-making authority is not to deny that it has other concerns as well. Distinct constitutional language, with distinct history, and which calls into play distinct policy concerns, governs disputes involving federalism, separation of powers, and individual rights. Given the very broad range of subjects that constitutional law addresses, no single lens could possibly capture all the issues.

Nonetheless, in an important sense, much of every constitutional dispute really does pose the question of who decides. If the courts uphold some challenged law or program, their ruling means

---

6. *See, e.g.,* Harper v. Virginia Bd. of Elections, 383 U.S. 663 (1966); Skinner v. Oklahoma, 316 U.S. 535 (1942); *cf.* Washington v. Glucksburg, 521 U.S. 702 (1997).

7. *See* Troxel v. Granville, 530 U.S. 57 (2000).

that the person or body responsible for that law or program had the constitutional authority to decide to adopt it. If they strike down a challenged law or program, their ruling means that the responsible person or body overstepped his, her, or its bounds.

In determining whether any challenged government action exceeds constitutional limits, courts—or in the case of constitutional issues that are inappropriate for judicial resolution, political actors—must ask two kinds of questions: First, did the kind of decision taken fall within the institutional competence of the decision maker? And second, even if the decision-making entity had the affirmative authority to prescribe the challenged law or policy, did it violate some prohibitory constitutional language or doctrine? For example, a federal statute forbidding cars moving in interstate commerce from displaying bumper stickers critical of Congress would satisfy the first condition—because it regulates interstate commerce, a power specifically granted to Congress by Section 8 of Article I—but would fail the second—because it would abridge the freedom of speech in violation of the First Amendment.

The Constitution imposes structural limits on the federal government that it does not impose on the governments of the states and their subdivisions. For example, the federal government only possesses those affirmative powers delegated to it by the Constitution. As Justice Clarence Thomas aptly put it, "[t]he Federal Government and the States . . . face different default rules: where the Constitution is silent about the exercise of a particular power— that is, where the Constitution does not speak either expressly or by necessary implication—the Federal Government lacks that power and the States enjoy it."[8] Subject only to prohibitions contained in the federal Constitution and the limits imposed by their own state constitutions—which operate independently of *federal* constitutional law—the states have plenary power (sometimes called a

---

8. U.S. Term Limits, Inc. v. Thornton, 514 U.S. 779, 848 (1995) (Thomas, J., dissenting). We do not read the majority to disagree with this proposition.

general "police power") to enact legislation on whatever subjects they see fit.

Constitutional doctrines governing the allocation of authority among the different branches of government also limit the federal government but not the states. Here the structure of the federal government mirrors the structure of the Constitution itself, with separate articles establishing distinct legislative, executive, and judicial branches. The Supreme Court has accordingly invalidated lawmaking schemes that assigned legislative powers to executive actors[9] and vice versa.[10] As we shall see, the Supreme Court has struggled both in defining the distinction between different sorts of powers and in discerning where the line between permissible cooperation and unconstitutional usurpation lies. As Justice Robert Jackson famously wrote in his concurrence in the *Steel Seizure Case*, "[w]hile the Constitution diffuses power the better to secure liberty, it also contemplates that practice will integrate the dispersed powers into a workable government."[11]

We consider the doctrine of separation of powers at length in Chapter 5. Here we simply note that there *is* a relatively robust constitutional doctrine of separation of powers applicable to the federal government—one that has been invoked to invalidate, among other things, the legislative veto,[12] the Gramm-Rudman-Hollings Act (which gave a budgetary ax to the Comptroller General),[13] and the line item veto.[14] By contrast, the federal Constitution applies no such limit to the states. A state could, if it so chose, adopt a parliamentary system of government in which the leader of the majority

---

9. *See* Panama Refining Co. v. Ryan, 293 U.S. 388 (1935); A.L.A. Schechter Poultry Corp. v. United States, 295 U.S. 495 (1935).

10. *See* INS. v. Chadha, 462 U.S. 919 (1983).

11. Youngstown Co. v. Sawyer, 343 U.S. 579, 635 (1952) (Jackson, J., concurring).

12. *See Chadha*, 462 U.S. at 959 (Powell, J., concurring in the judgment).

13. Bowsher v. Synar, 478 U.S. 714 (1986).

14. Clinton v. City of New York, 524 U.S. 417 (1998).

party in the legislature is also the head of the executive branch and her ministers are also legislators.

If the Constitution imposes more structural obstacles on the federal government than it imposes on the states, it nonetheless constrains the states in important ways. Constitutional doctrines rooted in the Commerce Clause, the Privileges and Immunities Clause of Article IV, the Privileges or Immunities Clause of the Fourteenth Amendment, the Equal Protection Clause of the Fourteenth Amendment, and the unenumerated right to travel[15] limit the ability of states to discriminate against citizens, products, and services that come from other states. In addition to these and other interstate limits, perhaps the most important limit on the states is the Supremacy Clause of Article VI, which makes all valid federal law—including the Constitution itself, but also treaties and statutes—trump all contrary state law—even provisions of state constitutions.

Prior to the Civil War, the federal and state governments faced different default rules with respect to rights as well as structural provisions. The Bill of Rights applied only to the federal government,[16] with just a handful of rights articulated in Section 10 of Article I constraining the states. Since the 1960s, however, the Supreme Court has treated the Fourteenth Amendment as extending most of the protections set forth in the Bill of Rights to limit the states. Although there continue to be small differences, today, for the most part, federal, state, and local governments are held to the same standards when it comes to individual rights.[17]

Exactly what those standards are has proven extraordinarily divisive, tapping into some of the most hotly contested cultural issues of our time, including such matters as abortion, affirmative

---

15. *See* Saenz v. Roe, 526 U.S. 489 (1999); *see also* Crandell v. Nevada, 73 U.S. 35 (1867).

16. *See* Barron v. Baltimore, 32 U.S. 243 (1833).

17. *See* Duncan v. Louisiana, 391 U.S. 145, 164 (1968) (Black, J., concurring).

action, capital punishment, gun control, and prayer in the schools. Of course, the difficulty and moral divisiveness of the underlying normative questions account for most of the controversy, e.g., is a fetus a person; if so, when; and what consequences follow for regulation of abortion? Should race-conscious government decision making be permitted when purportedly undertaken for the benign purpose of remedying rather than perpetuating the subordination of racial minorities? Given the inevitability of mistakes and bias, can the state deliberately kill its citizens, and if so, under what circumstances? Does private possession of firearms promote or undermine public safety? In a country in which the overwhelming majority of the population professes religious faith, does exclusion of organized prayer from public schools promote social harmony by keeping religious divisions out of the public sphere, or does it treat religious beliefs and the people who hold them as inferior to secular beliefs and their adherents? Even if we had no Supreme Court with the power of judicial review—indeed, even if we had no Constitution—these issues would likely spark deep and acrimonious disagreement.

But of course we do have a Constitution and a Supreme Court with the power of judicial review, and when divisive social issues become constitutional questions, they are transformed. The underlying substantive issues remain salient, but they are submerged beneath a debate about what actors have the constitutional authority to decide them.

We have organized the chapters of this book around the principal doctrinal subject matter areas in constitutional law, with two exceptions. First, we have largely omitted discussion of issues of criminal procedure. Before the 1960s, the relatively small number of Supreme Court decisions involving constitutional criminal procedure were typically treated as part of the main body of constitutional law, but since the "Warren Court Revolution," the body of doctrine in this area has grown so large as to justify separate treatment in courses and books. Second, two chapters address materials that do not conventionally fall within any doctrinal area. Chapter 3 examines interpretive methodology and Chapter 10 concludes the book by briefly looking at how political actors and the People themselves address constitutional questions in contexts in which they have the final word.

The subject matter area organization of this book should make it easier to use for students whose principal exposure to the materials of constitutional law comes in such substantive bits, but it should obscure neither the cross-cutting theme of allocation of decision-making authority nor the connections between doctrinal areas. We have already noted that the Court uses different levels of scrutiny as a tool for addressing the "who decides" question in multiple contexts. It also uses and re-uses other tools as well.

For example, "neutrality" requirements appear in a wide range of subject areas. Laws challenged on free-speech grounds must generally be "content-neutral;"[18] government must be neutral with respect to different religions as well as between religion and non-religion;[19] state laws that apply neutrally among intrastate and interstate commerce are subject only to deferential judicial scrutiny;[20] race-neutral means of achieving some important government objective must be deemed inadequate before the government may use race-based means.[21] The various neutrality requirements filter out the sorts of suspect considerations that would give courts the warrant to remove a decision from the actor otherwise entitled to make it.

Requirements that various actors obey various procedural rules also serve an important "who decides?" function. Always uneasy about its own power, the Court is most comfortable in finding obligations in the Constitution where those obligations can be characterized as merely procedural rather than substantive. As a formal matter, procedural rules can be said to amount to something other

---

18. Ward v. Rock Against Racism, 491 U.S. 781, 790–92 (1989).

19. *See* Epperson v. Arkansas, 393 U.S. 97, 103–04 (1968).

20. *See* Minnesota v. Clover Leaf Creamery Co., 449 U.S. 456 (1981).

21. *See* Grutter v. Bollinger, 539 U.S. 306, 339 (2003).

than a simple value choice by the Court.[22] They can take the form of constitutional doctrine itself, as, for example, when the Court requires that government officials who demand licenses for expressive activities like parades do so only pursuant to standards clearly articulated in advance.[23]

Procedural requirements can also serve constitutional aims when they operate as sub-constitutional doctrine. For example, various clear-statement rules require Congress to state some intention expressly in order for the resulting statute to be interpreted to have far-reaching effect. The Supreme Court has used clear statement rules to protect the constitutional interests of individuals—by, for example, requiring a clear statement from Congress to restrict the jurisdiction of courts to entertain petitions for writs of habeas corpus[24]—as well as the constitutional interests of institutions—by, for example, requiring a clear statement from Congress to abrogate the states' immunity to unconsented private lawsuits.[25]

Alexis de Tocqueville famously observed, "[t]here is hardly a political question in the United States which does not sooner or later turn into a judicial one."[26] Contemporary critics of the practice of judicial review echo Tocqueville when they lament the Supreme Court's constitutionalization of some of our most important policy issues. Better, the critics say, for divisive issues to be resolved by counting the votes of the elected representatives of the People than by counting the votes of nine unelected Justices.[27]

22. *See* JOHN HART ELY, DEMOCRACY AND DISTRUST: A THEORY OF JUDICIAL REVIEW 92 (1980).

23. *See* Forsyth County, Ga. v. Nationalist Movement, 505 U.S. 123, 130–31 (1992).

24. *See* INS v. St. Cyr, 533 U.S. 289, 308–13 (2001).

25. *See* Atascadero State Hospital v. Scanlon, 473 U.S. 234, 242 (1985).

26. ALEXIS DE TOCQUEVILLE, DEMOCRACY IN AMERICA 270 (J.P. Mayer ed., George Ferguson trans., Anchor 1969) (1835).

27. *See generally* ALEXANDER BICKEL, THE LEAST DANGEROUS BRANCH: THE SUPREME COURT AT THE BAR OF POLITICS (1962).

Whatever the normative merits of the critics' case against judicial review, as a descriptive matter it seriously overstates the role of judicially enforced constitutional law on the great issues of the day. The courts have almost nothing to say about when to go to war, how to address environmental threats, how to distribute the burdens of taxation and the benefits of spending, or, more broadly, fiscal, monetary, and trade policy. The Supreme Court's willingness to let political actors resolve these questions shows that it recognizes serious limits on its own authority to decide important issues. In contrast, constitutional courts in many other countries enforce social and economic rights in ways that have a large impact on questions our Court deems beyond its ken.[28]

Still, within the realm of subject areas over which the Court does claim authority, the judicial review critics have a point. Especially in recent years, the Justices have made clear that they decide who decides.[29] The subsequent chapters of this book—and further study of the primary materials of constitutional law—will give the reader the tools to judge for herself whether the Constitution and the Court that professes to speak in its name wisely allocate the sovereign powers that We the People have granted.

---

28. *See, e.g.,* South Africa v. Grootboom, 2000 (11) BCLR 1169 (CC) (S. Afr.).

29. *See, e.g.,* Dickerson v. United States, 530 U.S. 428 (2000).

☙ TWO

Judicial Review

THE CONSTITUTION OF THE UNITED STATES nowhere expressly states that the courts have the authority to declare Acts of Congress unconstitutional. That apparent omission has sometimes been offered as the basis for a charge that the Supreme Court in *Marbury v. Madison*[1] arrogated to itself authority that the Constitution had in fact lodged in elected officials: the power to determine the meaning of the Constitution. The constitutional text is indeed ambiguous about what institution, if any, has the final say about constitutional meaning, but it is not *especially* ambiguous on this point. Other familiar features of constitutional law are based on textual reeds not much thicker than those supporting judicial review, yet enjoy widespread acceptance. For example, the First Amendment of the Constitution limits the ability of "Congress" to abridge freedom of speech and the press; yet no one today seriously argues that therefore the President or the courts are entitled to act as censors of unpopular opinions. Freedom of expression is celebrated because Americans today understand that many different governmental actors could undermine speech that the Constitution means to protect. Judicial review itself, by contrast, has long been criticized as undemocratic, or to be more precise, as "countermajoritarian."[2]

---

1. 5 U.S. (1 Cranch) 137 (1803).

2. *See* ALEXANDER M. BICKEL, THE LEAST DANGEROUS BRANCH: THE SUPREME COURT AT THE BAR OF POLITICS 16–23 (2d ed. 1986).

This chapter begins by asking why the architects of a new constitution might choose to include a mechanism of judicial review in an otherwise mostly democratic instrument. What purposes does judicial review serve, and at what price? We then turn our attention to the particular case of the American Constitution. The question of whether it in fact authorizes judicial review is important, though largely moot: There is no realistic possibility that the courts will lose the power of judicial review any time soon. Accordingly, contemporary debates about the legitimacy of judicial review are best seen as providing the theoretical underpinnings for arguments about two other sorts of questions. First, when courts do exercise the power of judicial review, what methods of interpretation should they use? Second, to what extent does judicial *review*—the power to find a law inconsistent with the Constitution in a particular case— translate into judicial *supremacy*—the power of the courts to bind political actors in other contexts? We return to these questions in subsequent chapters.

⅏ What Is Judicial Review and What Purpose Does It Serve?

The term "judicial review" refers to the power of courts to reach independent judgments about the meaning of the Constitution, and thus to set aside laws, regulations, and policies that conflict with the judicial construction of the Constitution. In many countries, the power of judicial review is centralized in a single Constitutional Court. In the United States, however, with only very minor exceptions, all state and federal courts have the power of judicial review. Thus, even a single judge on a state trial court has the power—indeed the duty—to invalidate an Act passed by Congress and signed by the President, if the judge concludes that the law violates the Constitution. Of course, such a decision would be subject to further review by state appellate judges and potentially by the United States Supreme Court, but in the meantime, in the absence of a stay, the state trial judge's ruling would have to be obeyed by the parties to the case.

Judicial review can have different implications depending upon the actors subject to it. Both state and federal courts have the authority to review executive as well as legislative action, at the national, state, and local levels. A decision by a federal court invalidating a state law or a municipal ordinance has a federalism dimension to it, while a decision by that same court invalidating an Act of Congress raises issues of separation of powers. Justice Oliver Wendell Holmes, Jr., once said that the Supreme Court's power to review state laws for unconstitutionality was substantially more important to the Union than its power to review Acts of Congress.[3] Holmes and others took this view because judicial review of state laws serves to ensure the uniformity of federal constitutional law. If the constitutional judgments of state legislatures were not subject to some form of federal review, then the Constitution might take on fifty different meanings, and one of its basic purposes—"to form a more perfect union"—would be substantially undermined. By contrast, if a different national institution, such as Congress, were the authoritative interpreter of the Constitution, then no lack of uniformity would result (at least in federal law).

Most of the critical commentary on the practice of judicial review in the United States focuses on cases involving alleged constitutional infirmities in national legislation. In such cases, the power of judicial review is the power of the courts to disregard a law passed by Congress and (absent the override of a veto) signed by the President. Although there are many examples of judicial review being used to set aside state or local law, or executive action, for the most part we will focus our discussion in this chapter on this instance of ultimate conflict: The federal courts versus Congress and the President.

---

3. Oliver Wendell Holmes, Law and the Court, *in* Collected Legal Papers 291, 295–96 (1920).

Uniformity in federal law could be ensured by treating the national legislature as the final authority on constitutional questions. Why, then, do we have judicial review? To understand the main purposes of judicial review, it may be useful to ask how a constitution can function without it. Partly under the influence of the American model, these days nearly all democratic countries have some form of judicial review. But that was not always so, and even today, some countries do not empower their courts to invalidate unconstitutional laws. Consider the Netherlands, a constitutional monarchy in which the national Parliament is the principal law-making body. The Dutch Constitution begins by reciting rights that parallel, and in important respects exceed, the rights recognized by the U.S. Constitution.[4] It also sets out modes of election, terms of office, and most of the other sorts of "structural" features we associate with a constitution. However, Article 120 of the Dutch Constitution forbids judicial review in no uncertain terms. It states that "[t]he constitutionality of Acts of Parliament and treaties shall not be reviewed by the courts."[5]

Does Article 120 render the rest of the Dutch Constitution a meaningless piece of paper? Hardly. Members of Parliament and public ministers swear allegiance to the Constitution and thus have an obligation to oppose legislation and policies that, in their view, violate the Dutch Constitution, however otherwise desirable they believe such legislation and policies to be. Government officials who disregard the Constitution face the possibility of political sanctions, including, ultimately, removal from office.

---

4. The Constitution of the Netherlands, *available at* http://www.minbzk.nl/bzk2006uk/subjects/constitution-and/4800/the_constitution_of.

5. The picture is somewhat complicated by the fact that the Netherlands is a member state of the European Union and a signatory to the European Convention on Human Rights, thus authorizing a form of international judicial review to ensure that Dutch law conforms to European standards. But that is still not judicial review under the Dutch Constitution.

The Dutch model of legislative supremacy on matters of consti-tutional interpretation places a premium on democratic values. Constitutional language is often open-ended. For example, the Fourteenth Amendment of the U.S. Constitution forbids states from denying the "equal protection of the laws," and the Eighth Amendment bans "cruel and unusual punishments." Reasonable people can disagree over whether some law does or does not pro-tect people equally, or whether some punishment is cruel and unusual. Legislative supremacists say that given such reasonable disagreement, constitutional ambiguity should be resolved by democratic means.

The argument for legislative supremacy is hardly trivial, and recent years have witnessed a revival of legal scholarship calling for the abolition of judicial review on democratic grounds. Jeremy Waldron puts the point most forcefully by noting that in hard cases, the Justices of the United States Supreme Court themselves typi-cally cannot agree, and the Court uses the same method for resolv-ing disagreement as the legislature—voting. If we are going to resolve hard constitutional questions by counting votes, Waldron asks, why should we count the votes of unelected judges rather than those of the People's representatives?[6]

Part of the answer to Waldron's question may be that we have to worry about easy cases as well as hard ones. Chief Justice John Marshall made this point in his opinion in *Marbury v. Madison*, when he asked rhetorically whether the Court would have to stand idly by were Congress to violate such unequivocal constitutional requirements as the prohibition on export duties or the rule demand-ing the testimony of two witnesses for a treason conviction.[7] If these examples seem far-fetched, consider that all around the world, dic-tators seize and hold power while claiming to respect their national

---

6. Jeremy Waldron, *The Core of the Case Against Judicial Review*, 115 YALE L.J. 1346, 1388–92 (2006).

7. 5 U.S. (1 Cranch) 137, 179–80 (1803).

constitutions, even as they blatantly ignore these documents. In late 2007, after illegally firing the Pakistan Supreme Court, Pakistani strongman Pervez Musharaff even had the temerity to invoke Abraham Lincoln in defense of the proposition that he was only trying to save his country's constitution by suspending it.[8]

One need not venture overseas to encounter examples of laws and policies that test constitutional limits. Even knowing that his policies could be challenged in court, President George W. Bush asserted sweeping powers to conduct warrantless surveillance, to detain aliens and citizens indefinitely without any obligation to provide an impartial hearing, and even to ignore statutes and treaties by torturing suspected terrorists. The Bush Administration did not stop pressing some of these extreme arguments until they were rejected by the Supreme Court.

Accordingly, judicial review may best be justified on the ground that a constitution's chief aims include limiting the power of elected officials. To give those very officials unreviewable authority to determine the limits of their own power would be to put the fox in charge of the henhouse. On this account, even clear constitutional rules are, to adapt a phrase of James Madison, mere "parchment barriers," if not enforced through institutional competition—the regime of checks and balances.[9] Judicial review secures the judiciary's place in a constitutional system of divided government and thus puts the courts in a position to ensure that the Constitution's limits are more than empty verbiage.

The advisability of judicial review thus appears to rest on a balance of risks. Without judicial review, there is a substantial danger that the political branches of government will overstep the bounds that the constitution places on their authority. With judicial review, however, there is a substantial risk that the courts will overstep

---

8. *See* David Rohde, *Pakistani Sets Emergency Rule, Defying U.S.*, N.Y. TIMES, Nov. 4, 2007, at A1.

9. THE FEDERALIST No. 48, at 308 (James Madison) (Clinton Rossiter ed., 1961).

their own bounds, by finding in the Constitution's magisterial ambiguities the license to displace policies chosen by the People's representatives with policies that the judges happen to favor.

How can a constitutional designer know which risk is greater? In the modern era, defenders of judicial review have pointed to a number of institutional characteristics of the judiciary that make it especially suited to guard against constitutional excesses by the other branches. Here we focus on two such characteristics, both of which we will explore in greater detail in subsequent chapters on constitutional interpretation and substantive doctrines.

First, democratic elections under the principle of majority rule may be an excellent means of selecting policies that best serve the public welfare, but modern constitutions—including the American Constitution since the adoption of the Fourteenth Amendment—typically include protections for minority rights. Majority voting is hardly an ideal method of protecting minority rights. True, even courts decide contested cases involving minority rights by majority vote of the judges. However, institutional safeguards—such as life tenure and salary protection for federal judges, and a judicial culture that cherishes evenhandedness—make courts less of an interested party than the elected branches in a conflict pitting the alleged rights of a minority against the will of the majority.

Second, constitutions typically protect various aspects of liberty—such as freedom of expression and the right to freedom of movement except upon conviction of a crime after a fair trial. Here, judicial review can function as an aspect of the system of checks and balances. In order to pass any law at the national level, proponents must secure majorities in both houses of Congress and must obtain the President's signature; failing the latter, they must secure two-thirds majorities in both houses. The requirements of bicameralism and presentment ensure that the government will not lightly burden the People with noxious laws. These "veto gates" bias our laws in favor of the status quo. Where fundamental liberties are involved, the additional requirement that a law survive judicial review for constitutionality adds a further bias against regulation.

Courts cannot enact affirmative legislation; they can only strike down laws passed by the legislature; and so judicial review can be expected to decrease the sum total of regulation. To put the point more positively, judicial review provides a bias towards liberty.[10]

The bias towards liberty can be double-edged, however. From the 1890s until the late 1930s, courts regularly invalidated state and federal legislation that, in the judges' view, unduly interfered with the liberty of contract and property. In the most infamous case of this era, *Lochner v. New York*, the United States Supreme Court struck down a law setting sixty hours as the maximum work week for bakers.[11] As a formal matter, the ruling did protect liberty—the liberty of bakery employees to work for more than sixty hours per week. As a practical matter, however, maximum hour legislation itself can be understood as a protection for the liberty of non-unionized workers who, lacking individual bargaining power, would otherwise have little choice but to work as many hours as employers required. By protecting the rights of contract and property, the *Lochner* Court sacrificed a substantive conception of liberty favored by the legislature for a formal conception of liberty favored by the Justices.

Although the Supreme Court overruled *Lochner* and related precedents in the late 1930s,[12] the ghost of *Lochner* has haunted constitutional law ever since. We will see in the next chapter how the dominant approaches to constitutional interpretation aim to avoid repeating the mistake of the *Lochner* era, even as they disagree about precisely what that mistake was. For present purposes, it suffices to note that *Lochner* rightly produces some skepticism about the claim that judicial review enhances liberty. One can go overboard with that sort of skepticism, however. In the *Lochner* era cases, the Supreme Court did favor a formal conception of liberty

10. *See* Richard H. Fallon, Jr., *An Uneasy Case For Judicial Review*, 121 HARV. L. REV. 1693, 1705–06 (2008).

11. 198 U.S. 45 (1905).

12. *See, e.g.*, West Coast Hotel v. Parrish, 300 U.S. 379 (1937).

over a substantive conception—favoring rights *against* government regulation rather than rights *to* government protection—but the Constitution itself exhibits such a bias in favor of negative rights over positive rights.

Some foreign constitutions create affirmative rights to government benefits, such as education, employment, and health care.[13] The U.S. Constitution does not, leaving such matters to legislative discretion. Accordingly, although one can quarrel with the particular conception of liberty that the *Lochner* Court favored, one cannot tax judicial review as such with the sin of favoring negative rights over positive rights. Indeed, people who favor inclusion of positive rights in a constitution typically mean to *expand* judicial review, rather than to shrink its domain.

Suppose one thinks that judicial review serves the egalitarian and libertarian values enshrined in the Constitution. Such a view might justify a limited form of judicial review, one that only applies when equality or liberty is at stake. As we shall see in subsequent chapters, various constitutional doctrines say something very much like that, applying exacting judicial scrutiny only where core equality or liberty concerns are at issue. But what about structural provisions of the Constitution, such as separation of powers and federalism? Do egalitarian or libertarian arguments justify judicial review to enforce these provisions?

Some constitutional scholars have argued that the courts ought not interfere with the judgments of the political branches on structural questions,[14] and the Supreme Court appeared to endorse this view in the 1980s, at least with respect to the scope of

---

13. For instance, the South African Constitution guarantees rights to housing, health care, food, water, social security, and education. S. AFR. CONST. 1996, arts. 26–27, 29.

14. *See* JESSE H. CHOPER, JUDICIAL REVIEW AND THE NATIONAL POLITICAL PROCESS (1980); Herbert Wechsler, *The Political Safeguards of Federalism: The Role of the States in the Composition and Selection of the National Government*, 54 COLUM. L. REV. 543 (1954).

congressional power.[15] More recently, however, the Court has reverted to its traditional pattern of enforcing the structural provisions with no less vigor than the individual rights provisions.[16] By confining each branch of the federal government to its proper role, and by policing the bounds between the state and federal governments, the Court exercising the power of judicial review can limit the size and scope of government. Thus, the libertarian rationale for judicial review can be, and has been, invoked to justify judicial enforcement of structural no less than rights provisions.

Indeed, the distinction between structural and rights provisions is sometimes hard to discern. Justice Anthony Kennedy, writing for the majority in a case holding that Congress had acted unconstitutionally in stripping federal courts of the power to grant writs of habeas corpus for foreign nationals detained as enemy combatants at Guantanamo Bay Naval Base, argued that the Suspension Clause—which limits the circumstances under which the privilege of the writ of habeas corpus may be suspended—serves both to limit government power and to preserve liberty.[17] Four years earlier, Justice Sandra Day O'Connor similarly defended judicial enforcement of an alleged enemy combatant's due process rights to know and contest the basis for his detention, stressing that the Constitution "most assuredly envisions a role for all three branches when individual liberties are at stake."[18] Structure and rights intertwine.

The foregoing arguments hardly exhaust the sorts of reasons one might have for favoring a constitution that includes judicial review over one that omits it. Another argument, to which we return in the next chapter, emphasizes the need for judicial review to protect the democratic process itself: Legislators, if left to their own devices, will stack the electoral deck so as to undermine the People's

15. *See* Garcia v. San Antonio Metro. Transit Auth., 469 U.S. 528 (1985).

16. *See, e.g.*, Clinton v. City of New York, 524 U.S. 417 (1998); Printz v. United States, 521 U.S. 898 (1997); New York v. United States, 505 U.S. 144 (1992).

17. Boumediene v. Bush, 128 S.Ct. 2229, 2246–47 (2008).

18. Hamdi v. Rumsfeld, 542 U.S. 507, 536 (2004).

ability to vote them out of office. Still another argument, which we will not develop at any length, points to the inevitability of at least some independent judicial construction of any constitution that serves one of the key functions that the U.S. Constitution does—establishing the mechanisms by which key government actors are chosen. Even if courts were only given the formal power to interpret statutes, they would still have to distinguish valid statutes from forgeries, and the criteria for *identifying* statutes—including the criteria for distinguishing Congress from a group of impostors—are mostly found in the Constitution.[19]

These and still other arguments show how one could plausibly think that judicial review is consistent with constitutional democracy. We do not mean to suggest that these arguments are necessarily persuasive. Critics of judicial review have their reasons for thinking that even protection of minority rights and negative liberty should be left in the hands of democratic processes. Were one writing a constitution for a new polity, or thinking about fundamental changes to the American Constitution, one would surely want to give the arguments of the judicial review critics a full airing. For understanding American constitutional law as it currently exists, however, the arguments against judicial review serve less to delegitimate the entire enterprise than to color the way in which judicial review might be practiced, a point to which we return later in this chapter and throughout the book.

⁂ What Does the Constitution Say about Judicial Review?

If judicial review can be justified as a plausible means of securing constitutional values, it does not necessarily follow that the U.S. Constitution establishes judicial review. All of the foregoing

---

19. *See* Matthew D. Adler & Michael C. Dorf, *Constitutional Existence Conditions and Judicial Review*, 89 VA. L. REV. 1105 (2003).

arguments about the virtues of judicial review could be made in the Netherlands, but they would be unavailing, given the Dutch Constitution's express disavowal of judicial review. The U.S. Constitution does not expressly disavow judicial review but neither does it expressly endorse the practice. Thus, we must ask: Does the best reading of the Constitution include a power of judicial review?

Traditional attempts to answer this question begin with *Marbury v. Madison* and Alexander Hamilton's *Federalist No. 78*, which set forth most of the arguments that John Marshall later deployed in *Marbury*. In the course of invalidating Section 13 of the Judiciary Act of 1789, Marshall offered three principal reasons for inferring the power of judicial review. Two of these, as we shall see, beg the question, but the third is sound, or at least sound enough to render judicial review a highly plausible inference from the constitutional text.

Writtenness

In *Marbury*, Chief Justice Marshall contended that the very writtenness of the Constitution entails judicial review. "To what purpose are powers limited, and to what purpose is that limitation committed to writing," he asked, "if these limits may, at any time, be passed by those intended to be restrained?"[20] Marshall was surely right that writing down the Constitution would have been at most a symbolic gesture if the limits it contains could be overridden at will. But he was equally surely mistaken in assuming that absent judicial review, Congress would have the power to override the Constitution. In a constitution without judicial review, members of Congress themselves would have both a legal and a moral duty to abide by the limits written in the Constitution. In fact, members of Congress have those duties now, though they are also subject to the external

---

20. 5 U.S. (1 Cranch) 137, 176 (1803).

constraint of judicial review. Removing judicial review would not erase their own duty of fidelity to the Constitution. It might even lead elected officials to take constitutional limits more seriously, knowing that no court would be able to clean up their mistakes.

If it seems absurd to suppose that Congress and the other actors to whom constitutional limits are addressed could be constrained by the Constitution even absent judicial review, consider an analogy.[21] Suppose a group of friends organize themselves into two teams to play a weekly game of basketball. The friends know the rules of basketball and so they make their own calls. If a player on Team A travels with the ball, a player on Team B will call her for it, and possession of the ball will go to Team B. If a Team B player fouls a Team A player, the latter will call a foul and, depending on the local convention and type of foul, either take the ball out of bounds or attempt free throws. There may be ambiguities in the rules, and so we can imagine (although it would be highly unusual in reality) that the friends bring with them a copy of the official rules of (let us say, college) basketball. These rules in fact call for the use of referees, but let us imagine that by unanimous consent, the players have agreed to disregard all rules involving referees. We can even imagine that in the copy of the rulebook used by this group, the rules that involve referees have been crossed out.

What significance can be attributed to the transition from a game in which the players rely on their collective recollection of the rules, to one in which they keep a rulebook at the ready? Most importantly, the players now have a good way to resolve disputes over what the rules are. Suppose the ball hits the top of the backboard before dropping through the basket. Is this a field goal or a turnover? In the pre-rulebook games, if the players disagreed over the answer, they would argue over who was best recalling the rule.

---

21. The example we discuss in the text is adapted from one explored in H.L.A. HART, THE CONCEPT OF LAW 138–41 (1961), although Hart was addressing the nature of adjudication in general, rather than judicial review under a constitution in particular.

By contrast, with a rulebook at courtside, they just look up the answer (and learn that the basket counts).

Clearly the decision to use a rulebook does not resolve all disputes. Many rules in basketball are notoriously difficult to apply in close cases. Should contact between an offensive player and a defensive player be ruled a charge, a block, or no foul? Was a foul committed in the act of shooting? And so on. Having a rulebook at the ready will not resolve these questions because they are not disputes over the content of the rules but over what the rules mean in practice. Still, for a complicated game such as basketball, the rulebook is useful simply as an aid to memory.

And Chief Justice Marshall's opinion in *Marbury* made just this point about the Constitution. So "that those limits" it contains "may not be mistaken, or forgotten, the constitution is written."[22] Here, then, we have a reason for writing down a constitution that is unrelated to judicial (or other external) review: to settle certain matters rather than relying on memory.

Writtenness alone does not entail judicial review, any more than by using a rulebook, our hypothetical ballplayers commit themselves to using a referee. Recall that in these players' version of the rulebook, the provisions calling for a referee have been eliminated. The rules for the friendly game of basketball are just like the Dutch Constitution: They are written down and they expressly reject any outside authority as arbiter of disputes.

To be sure, there are good reasons to use referees (and thus not to cross out the provisions setting out their duties): The players are self-interested and even if acting in good faith, they will tend to see infractions by opposing players and overlook their own; if competition becomes heated, fights may break out. Objective referees with the trust of both teams can keep tempers under control.

This argument for employing referees looks very much like a familiar argument for judicial review. Congress, too, is self-interested,

---

22. 5 U.S. (1 Cranch) at 176.

and will tend to construe the Constitution in ways that favor its own power. Likewise, a dispute between the branches of the federal government, between different States, or between the States and the federal government, could become a constitutional crisis if the actors were left to their own devices. Judicial review can tamp down the political equivalent of flaring tempers.

Still, in both contexts, the addition of an outside arbiter has costs. Our basketball players may not be able to find a competent referee, or may not want to pay one, and even if they can easily afford to do so, the addition of a referee could change the character of the game. Players who were formerly good sports about calls by opposing players may now try to deceive the referees by, for example, "flopping" when there is even incidental contact. Likewise, scholars sometimes argue that the practice of judicial review leads politicians to abdicate their responsibility to make their own judgments about constitutionality.[23] "If the bill proves to be unconstitutional," a legislator may think, "the courts will strike it down, so I can vote for the bill if I think my constituents favor it, regardless of what the Constitution says." Legislative neglect of constitutional duty may be a cost of judicial review. How to tally up the costs and benefits of judicial review (or of employing referees in a friendly game of basketball) is a difficult question, but the answer does not depend on the writtenness of the Constitution (or the rules of basketball).

Why, then, has the Constitution's writtenness often been invoked as a basis for judicial review? We think the answer may be a kind of historical guilt by association. The generation of Americans that framed the Constitution was familiar with the English constitution, which, at the time, was neither written nor provided for judicial review. Parliamentary supremacy, the framers may well have thought, was a natural consequence of an unwritten constitution,

---

23. *See* James B. Thayer, *The Origin and Scope of the American Doctrine of Constitutional Law*, 7 HARV. L. REV. 129, 155–56 (1893).

and thus, writing down a Constitution that expressly limits Congress—the American heir to Parliament—entailed judicial review. To leave issues of constitutional interpretation to Congress, in this view, would be to revert to legislative supremacy.

Thus, Marshall's opinion in *Marbury* said that if there were no judicial review, "the legislature [could] alter the constitution by an ordinary act."[24] He overlooked the possibility that before the legislature enacts a law, it makes a judgment about the law's constitutionality, perhaps because the English Parliament too was supposed to consider issues of constitutionality (under England's unwritten constitution) even under a system of parliamentary supremacy. The Constitution's writtenness does not logically entail judicial review, but the contrast it creates with the traditional understanding of the English constitution exerts a strong psychological pull in the direction of judicial review.

Supremacy

Closely related to the argument from writtenness is an argument from supremacy. Marshall stated in *Marbury* that the principle that "an act of the legislature, repugnant to the constitution, is void.... is essentially attached to a written constitution."[25] The argument from supremacy begins with the proposition, enshrined in Article VI, that the Constitution is the supreme law of the land, superior to ordinary law. Therefore, it continues, if Congress passes a law that violates the Constitution, that law is void. Accordingly, the argument concludes, courts must disregard unconstitutional laws.

Thus stated syllogistically, these steps seem almost ineluctable, until one asks how the courts are supposed to know whether an act is repugnant to the Constitution. Marshall had two answers. First, as

---

24. 5 U.S. (1 Cranch) at 177.

25. *Id.*

we have seen, he supposed an exceptionally clear case, such as a treason conviction on the testimony of one rather than two witnesses. But this sort of argument works only for clear cases, and could at most support the conclusion that the courts are empowered to disregard legislative acts that *clearly* violate the Constitution (a view championed by James Bradley Thayer in the late nineteenth century).[26]

To make his argument work for judicial review in *all* cases, Marshall added a second proposition: "It is emphatically the province and duty of the judicial department to say what the law is." This is the most famous line in the *Marbury* opinion. But what does it mean, precisely? As a statement about the function of courts in cases involving statutory interpretation, it seems to be an accurate description. In the course of resolving a case in which one party's right to relief rests upon a certain construction of a statute, the courts resolve the issue for themselves.[27] Accordingly, if Marshall was right that the Constitution should be treated just like any other law, then the judicial duty to say what the law is entails judicial review.

In a moment, we will expand on the excellent textual evidence Marshall had for concluding that, so far as enforcement goes, the Constitution is like ordinary law. But first we note that despite some of the *Marbury* opinion's rhetoric, supremacy by itself does nothing to establish judicial review. A written constitution (like the Dutch one) that vests final interpretive authority over the constitution in the legislature would still be supreme over ordinary law: In deliberations over whether to pass a bill, the argument that the bill conflicts with the constitution would, if accepted, provide dispositive

---

26. Thayer, *supra* note 23, at 17–20.

27. This statement needs to be qualified in modern cases in which an administrative agency is charged with implementing a statute, *see* Chevron v. National Resources Defense Council, 467 U.S. 837 (1984), but that concern did not exist in Marshall's day, and we can bracket it here. *See also* Henry P. Monaghan, Marbury *and the Administrative State*, 83 COLUM. L. REV. 1 (1983).

grounds for rejecting the bill, no matter how desirable as a matter of policy the bill was thought to be.

Supremacy simply means that the Constitution—however its meaning is ascertained in uncertain cases—prevails over subconstitutional law. The real question in *Marbury* was: What institution has the authority to decide what the Constitution means where the text, or its application to a particular case, is unclear? One highly plausible answer is: the courts and ultimately the Supreme Court. Another plausible answer, however, is: Congress and the President. Given the theory of popular sovereignty that underwrites both the content of the Constitution and the mechanism by which it was adopted, it would hardly be anomalous for final authority to decide its meaning to be vested in the elected branches of the national government.

Articles III and VI

Although writtenness and supremacy only make judicial review plausible, a closer reading of the constitutional text does provide stronger grounds for inferring a power of judicial review. Article III, Section 2 of the Constitution extends federal judicial power "to all cases, in law and equity, arising under th[e] Constitution. . . ." Marshall asked rhetorically: "Could it be the intention of those who gave this power, to say that, in using it, the constitution should not be looked into?"[28] If the federal courts had to accept the judgment of Congress on questions of constitutionality, then there would be no point to conferring jurisdiction for cases arising under the Constitution. The fact of congressional enactment would resolve all constitutional doubts, and cases challenging the validity of federal statutes would reduce to trivially easy cases of statutory interpretation. Yet Article III, Section 2 separately confers on the federal courts the power to hear

---

28. *Marbury*, 5 U.S. (1 Cranch) at 179.

all cases arising under "the laws of the United States," so the reference to cases arising under the Constitution must be given some additional content, lest it be rendered redundant.

There is still further textual evidence that the Constitution contemplated judicial review. The text of the Supremacy Clause of Article VI is peculiar. After declaring the supremacy of federal law generally, and of the Constitution above all other law, it adds "and the judges in every state shall be bound thereby, anything in the Constitution or laws of any State to the contrary notwithstanding," explicitly instructing state judges to set aside laws that, in their judgment, violate the Constitution. It is possible to read too much into this provision. *All* government officials, at every level and at every branch, are bound by the Constitution and valid laws enacted pursuant to it, and so state judges would be obliged to follow the Constitution even if the Supremacy Clause had omitted this specific invitation. Still, the singling out of state judges suggests that they have a special duty to enforce the Constitution. And that special duty looks just like the power of judicial review in *Marbury*.

Now notice what happens when we combine Articles III and VI. Article III gives the Supreme Court appellate jurisdiction, as to law and fact, over federal constitutional questions. It also gives Congress the option of creating no lower federal courts (under what is known as the "Madisonian Compromise"). So suppose that Congress had created no lower federal courts. The Supreme Court would then only be able to hear appellate cases coming out of the state courts— and the latter, by virtue of the Supremacy Clause, are expressly instructed to set aside unconstitutional state laws.[29] In reviewing state court decisions under the Constitution, the United States Supreme Court would have the same responsibility of judicial review as they do.

29. This paragraph and the next rely on an argument developed in Herbert Wechsler, *Toward Neutral Principles of Constitutional Law*, 73 HARV. L. REV. 1, 3–5 (1959).

The foregoing is a very strong, although not quite airtight, textual argument for judicial review. One small hole concerns the instruction to state court judges to set aside unconstitutional *state* laws without mentioning any parallel authority to set aside *federal* laws. It is possible to argue that the omission entails a lack of judicial authority to invalidate federal laws as unconstitutional. In this view, consistent with the statement by Justice Holmes about the relative importance of the powers to set aside state and federal laws, Congress would be the final authority on the constitutionality of federal laws. Nonetheless, this seems to read too much into the text of the Supremacy Clause. The command to state judges more likely focuses on state law to emphasize that under the Constitution, state judges owe their first responsibility to federal law, including the federal Constitution.

A second, arguably more serious, difficulty with the argument from the texts of Articles III and VI concerns congressional power to adjust the jurisdiction of the federal courts. Article III permits Congress both to decide whether to create lower federal courts and to make "Exceptions" to and "Regulations" of the Supreme Court's appellate jurisdiction. Suppose Congress were to "except" from the Court's jurisdiction all cases posing constitutional objections to federal statutes. Throughout American history, scholars have debated whether such an effort to circumvent judicial review would itself be constitutional. One school of thought—traceable to a powerful argument by Justice Joseph Story—argues that such a large "exception" would be inconsistent with Article III's vesting in the federal courts the power to hear *all* federal question cases.[30] But this argument itself has its difficulties, most importantly the fact that the very first Judiciary Act, passed in 1789 closely on the heels of

---

30. *See* Martin v. Hunter's Lessee, 14 U.S. (1 Wheat.) 304, 328–31 (1816); *see generally* RICHARD H. FALLON, JR., ET AL., HART AND WECHSLER'S THE FEDERAL COURTS AND THE FEDERAL SYSTEM 288–302 (6th ed. 2009).

ratification, would have been unconstitutional under Justice Story's theory.

The precise scope of congressional power to tinker with judicial review has generated a substantial body of academic literature.[31] The problem, however, may be more theoretical than real. Although Presidents and members of Congress from time to time assert their authority to limit the jurisdiction of the federal courts, no effort to cut back substantially on the power of judicial review itself has come close to succeeding. That fact itself is telling. Even if we judge the textual authority for a power of judicial review to be merely strong rather than overwhelming, the practice is now very widely accepted.

※ What Are the Practical Consequences of Judicial Review?

What follows from a holding by the Supreme Court (or other court) that a law is unconstitutional? Courts and commentators (including us) sometimes refer to judicial opinions as "invalidating" laws. In some countries, constitutional courts officially have this power: A law that has been declared unconstitutional is wiped off the books. In the United States, however, despite occasional talk about an unconstitutional law as a legal "nullity,"[32] judicial review is more modest. An American court exercising the power of judicial review simply sets aside the unconstitutional law or the unconstitutional application of the law, but the law remains on the books, and typically may be enforced in other contexts. Even when a court finds that a law is "facially" unconstitutional, that ruling is, strictly speaking,

---

31. *See, e.g.,* Gerald Gunther, *Congressional Power to Curtail Federal Court Jurisdiction: An Opinionated Guide to the Ongoing Debate*, 36 STAN. L. REV. 895 (1984).

32. *See, e.g.,* Branch v. Smith, 538 U.S. 254, 281 (2003).

only binding on the parties to the case. To be sure, the court's ruling will be an enforceable precedent in later cases, but only to the extent that later decisions give the ruling precedential effect.

The strong preference in the U.S. legal system for as-applied rather than facial litigation[33] is connected to an important restriction on the jurisdiction of federal courts. Article III extends the federal judicial power to "cases and controversies." Case law reads these words as establishing a number of important limits on the contexts in which federal courts can resolve legal issues. In all federal court cases (including those seeking to vindicate constitutional and sub-constitutional interests), plaintiffs must establish Article III standing: a concrete injury in fact, traceable to the defendant's allegedly unlawful conduct, and redressable by a favorable ruling. Federal courts can issue anticipatory or declaratory relief from future wrongs, but only if the harm is imminent. These and other limitations on the jurisdiction of the federal courts implement a principle that forbids the judiciary from issuing advisory opinions in merely hypothetical cases. By contrast, constitutional courts in other countries and state courts in some American states do have the power to issue advisory opinions in "abstract" cases.[34] State courts that issue advisory opinions can even do so in cases involving federal constitutional issues.[35] The constitutional limit on federal advisory opinions is a product of the limited jurisdiction of the federal courts set out in Article III, and therefore not applicable to state courts, regardless of the subject matter.

Throughout American history, political actors have seized upon the limited nature of the judicial power to assert authority for a right or even a duty of independent interpretation of the Constitution.

---

33. *See, e.g.*, Sabri v. United States, 541 U.S. 600, 608–10 (2004).

34. *See* Helen Hershkoff, *State Courts and the "Passive Virtues": Rethinking the Judicial Function*, 114 HARV. L. REV. 1833 (2001); Osmar J. Benvenuto, *Reevaluating the Debate Surrounding the Supreme Court's Use of Foreign Precedent*, 74 FORDHAM L. REV. 2695, 2730 n.282 (2006).

35. *See, e.g.*, R.I. Depositors Econ. Prot. Corp. v. Brown, 659 A.2d 95 (R.I. 1995).

Most famously, campaigning against Stephen Douglas, Abraham Lincoln denounced the *Dred Scott* case—which held that African Americans were not citizens and which struck down the Missouri Compromise[36]—and contended that it was not yet settled law. Many years later, President Reagan's Attorney General, Edwin Meese, would cite Lincoln's statements as authority for the view that courts cannot resolve questions of constitutionality outside the scope of contested cases: political actors and voters remain free to reach their own judgments.[37] This idea that each branch or department of government is entitled to draw its own constitutional conclusions sometimes goes under the name of "departmentalism."[38]

The Supreme Court itself has generally taken a contrary, and self-serving, view. The high-water mark of judicial supremacy came in *Cooper v. Aaron*.[39] After the Governor of Arkansas abetted the efforts of the Little Rock schools to resist the Court's desegregation mandate of *Brown v. Board of Education*,[40] the Justices unanimously and emphatically asserted their own authority. *Marbury*, the Court said,

> declared the basic principle that the federal judiciary is supreme in the exposition of the law of the Constitution, and that principle has ever since been respected by this Court and the Country as a permanent and indispensable feature of our constitutional system. It follows that the interpretation of the Fourteenth Amendment enunciated by this Court in the *Brown* case is the supreme law of the land....[41]

---

36. Dred Scott v. Sandford, 60 U.S. (19 How.) 393 (1857).

37. Edwin Meese III, *The Law of the Constitution*, 61 TUL. L. REV. 979, 985 (1987).

38. *See* LARRY D. KRAMER, THE PEOPLE THEMSELVES 105–11 (2004).

39. 358 U.S. 1 (1958).

40. 347 U.S. 483 (1954).

41. *Cooper*, 358 U.S. at 18.

Given the historical context, the Court's equation of the Constitution with its interpretations thereof was a wholly sympathetic attempt to stamp out open rebellion. Nonetheless, the rhetoric of *Cooper* is surely an overstatement.

As *Marbury* itself acknowledged, the courts do not involve themselves in so-called "political questions," issues that are constitutional in nature but committed to the political branches. Thus, for example, when the House and Senate considered, respectively, whether to impeach and remove President Clinton for perjury and obstruction of justice arising out of the Monica Lewinsky affair, they had to decide the constitutional question of whether Clinton's conduct amounted to, in the words of Article II, Section 4, "high Crimes and Misdemeanors." The Supreme Court had made clear in an earlier case that this question was a matter for the House and Senate alone to decide.[42] Contrary to the broadest reading of *Cooper*, the Representatives and Senators were entitled to—indeed they had little choice but to—make their own judgments about constitutional meaning.

In theory, departmentalism and judicial exclusivity lie at opposite ends of a spectrum, but in practice they do not lead to very different results. An Administration that takes the departmentalist view will nonetheless find it necessary, as a matter of prudence, to accept the authority of the courts. Otherwise, it will find its policies subject to repeated reversal by the courts, and repeated defiance will come to threaten the rule of law itself.[43] Lincoln recognized as much, calling defiance of settled judicial precedent a form of "revolution."

At the same time, true judicial exclusivity does not exist in the American constitutional system. In addition to deciding officially non-justiciable political questions, political actors have substantial latitude to make independent constitutional decisions, especially when doing so would entail reading a particular constitutional

---

42. Nixon v. United States, 506 U.S. 224 (1993).

43. *See, e.g.*, Stieberger v. Bowen, 801 F.2d 29 (2d Cir. 1986).

provision more restrictively than the courts have done. For example, a President will sometimes veto a bill that he knows the Supreme Court would uphold but that he thinks is unconstitutional. Thus, in *McCulloch v. Maryland*, decided in 1819, the Justices upheld the power of Congress to create a national bank.[44] Nonetheless, thirteen years later, President Andrew Jackson vetoed a bill to renew the bank partly on policy grounds and partly on the ground that it amounted to an "invasion[] of the rights and powers of the several States."[45] Did Jackson thereby exceed the scope of his authority? Only an extremely aggressive version of judicial supremacy would suggest as much. Even if Jackson had vetoed the bill exclusively on constitutional grounds, most commentators then and now would not view such a move as a defiance of the power of judicial review. It is one thing for a President (or, as in *Cooper*, a Governor) to defy a judicial determination that a particular action is unconstitutional; it is quite another for him to stay his hand on constitutional grounds even though the courts would uphold the action.

The point just made is worth emphasizing. Put simply, the power of political actors in the American system to "over-enforce" the Constitution should not be confused with a power to defy the courts. If the Supreme Court says that the guarantees of the Fourteenth Amendment's Equal Protection Clause do not limit private actors—as it said in the nineteenth century[46]—that ruling does not prevent Congress from passing a law forbidding private employment discrimination by enterprises engaged in interstate commerce. The Supreme Court ruling in this instance sets a floor, rather than a ceiling, and additional protection pursuant to one of the enumerated powers of Congress is thus permissible. By contrast, if the Court says that the First Amendment invalidates a law

---

44. 17 (4 Wheat.) U.S. 316 (1819).

45. Veto Message to the Senate (July 10, 1832), in 2 MESSAGES AND PAPERS OF THE PRESIDENTS, 1789–1908, at 576, 590 (James D. Richardson ed., 1908).

46. The Civil Rights Cases, 109 U.S. 3 (1883).

prohibiting "indecent" pictures on the Internet, Congress cannot grant greater protection to children by reenacting the law. The effort to give children additional protection *from* such speech would abridge adults' First Amendment right *to* speak by sharing indecent but non-obscene photographs.[47]

Sometimes Congress or a state legislature might nonetheless enact a law that it knows to be unconstitutional under the Court's precedents in an effort to get the Court to reconsider these precedents. Such enactments and reenactments are certainly legitimate, given that the Court does, from time to time, reconsider its precedents. If a constitutional decision by the Supreme Court forever precluded legislation in violation of that decision, there would be no way to test the continuing vitality of the Court's doctrines. However, the final say with respect to this sort of conflict remains with the Court.

Furthermore, the power of independent political authority to interpret the Constitution can be abused. To a substantially greater extent than any of his predecessors, President George W. Bush used signing statements—statements made in connection with the President's signing of a bill into law—to frustrate the will of Congress in the guise of constitutional interpretation. To take one notorious example, after Congress passed a bill that appeared to bar all torture by U.S. personnel, President Bush signed it with the proviso that his Administration would construe the ban "in a manner consistent with the constitutional authority of the President . . . as Commander in Chief."[48] That may sound innocuous, but because the Bush Administration thought that Congress lacked the authority to impose certain limits on the President's authority to interrogate detainees, this signing statement was widely regarded as expressing his intent to ignore, by effectively rewriting, the very law

---

47. *See* Ashcroft v. ACLU, 542 U.S. 656 (2004); Reno v. ACLU, 521 U.S. 844 (1997).

48. Elisabeth Bumiller, *For President, Final Say on a Bill Sometimes Comes after the Signing*, N.Y. TIMES, Jan. 16, 2006, at A11.

he was signing. Nonetheless, any power can be abused. The Bush Administration's bold use of signing statements does not by itself show that the President should have no independent role in constitutional interpretation.

Even the more modest accounts of judicial review in the United States accord to our courts substantially greater finality than in some other legal systems. It is noteworthy that within the last generation, the two legal systems with which the United States has the most in common—those of Canada and the United Kingdom—have embraced judicial review with an important limitation. The Canadian Charter of Rights and Freedoms, adopted in 1982, and the United Kingdom's Human Rights Act, adopted in 1998, both protect rights that substantially parallel the rights contained in the American Constitution. In Canada, the "Notwithstanding Clause" of the Charter permits the provincial and national parliaments to disregard key Charter provisions, and the judicial interpretations thereof, for a period of up to five years, if they declare their intention to do so in the relevant legislation.[49] Likewise, under the Human Rights Act, the courts may make "declarations of incompatibility" between ordinary legislation and the rights protected by the European Convention on Human Rights, but the authority to set the legislation aside ultimately remains with political actors.[50]

As a historical matter, the "softer" style of judicial review we see in Canada and the United Kingdom was partly a reaction to the perceived excesses of judicial review in the United States. By giving the legislature the final authority to pass on constitutionality, Canada and the United Kingdom substantially undercut the claim that judicial review amounts to usurpation of the legislative role.

---

49. Canadian Charter of Rights and Freedoms, Part I of the Constitution Act, 1982, being Schedule B to the Canada Act 1982, ch. 11, § 33 (U.K.), *available at* http://laws.justice.gc.ca/en/charter/index.html.

50. Human Rights Act, 1998, c. 42, § 4, sched. 1 (Eng.), *available at* http://www.opsi.gov.uk/ACTS/acts1998/ukpga_19980042_en_1#pb2-l1g4.

Interestingly, in Canada, the Notwithstanding Clause has become almost taboo: It has never been invoked by the national parliament and only rarely used (after an initial blanket invocation by Quebec) by the provinces. This seems the best of both worlds: The possibility of legislative override ensures the legitimacy of judicial review, while the prestige of the Supreme Court of Canada and the Canadian Charter ensure that legislators do not lightly invoke the Notwithstanding Clause.

However, before one concludes that Canadian-style judicial review is superior to its much older American cousin, one should ask whether American courts could have accomplished what they did if the United States Constitution contained a notwithstanding clause. Would Southern States have invoked it to resist the desegregation mandate of *Brown v. Board of Education*? Would newspaper reporters and editors be languishing in prison under seditious libel laws? Constitutional regimes must be evaluated in context and as a whole. If the Notwithstanding Clause works well in Canada, it would not necessarily succeed in the United States.

In any event, for good or ill, the American Constitution has long been understood to give the Supreme Court the final word on justiciable constitutional matters. Accordingly, in the United States, the debate over how to reconcile judicial review with democracy has not been an argument over *whether* to have judicial review. *Marbury* settled that question. The American debate for over two centuries has been primarily about *how* judicial review should be exercised. In other words, by what methods should the Constitution be interpreted? The next chapter takes up that question.

𝄞 Further Reading

ALEXANDER M. BICKEL, THE LEAST DANGEROUS BRANCH: THE SUPREME COURT AT THE BAR OF POLITICS (2d ed. 1986).
Richard H. Fallon, Jr., *An Uneasy Case For Judicial Review*, 121 HARV. L. REV. 1693 (2008).

BARRY FRIEDMAN, THE WILL OF THE PEOPLE (2009).

LARRY D. KRAMER, THE PEOPLE THEMSELVES (2004).

Michael W. McConnell, *The Story of* Marbury v. Madison: *Making Defeat Look Like Victory*, *in* CONSTITUTIONAL LAW STORIES 13 (Michael C. Dorf ed., 2d ed. 2009).

MARK TUSHNET, TAKING THE CONSTITUTION AWAY FROM THE COURTS (1999).

William W. Van Alstyne, *A Critical Guide to* Marbury v. Madison, 1969 DUKE L.J. 1.

Jeremy Waldron, *The Core of the Case Against Judicial Review*, 115 YALE L.J. 1346 (2006).

THREE

Constitutional Interpretation

IN *MCCULLOCH V. MARYLAND*, Chief Justice Marshall famously cautioned that "we must never forget it is a *constitution* we are expounding."[1] He thus suggested that there is something about constitutions that calls for a particular set of interpretive tools, or at least a different usage of the standard interpretive tools. Why might that be so?

We can readily understand why interpretation of a *legal* text would differ from interpretation of language in other contexts. If someone wants to interpret a poem, a painting, or some other work of art in an idiosyncratic fashion, that is her own business. Perhaps she wants to stage a performance of Richard Wagner's *Götterdämmerung* using modern costumes and scenery suggesting that the opera is an allegory about the decline of American power. You could point out to her that this is not how Wagner intended the opera to be performed, but she certainly knows that already. Her interpretation is simply that: *her* interpretation. If audience members find that the opera so staged speaks to them, it is surely pedantry to insist that they have somehow "missed the point." They have gotten *a* point from the opera, and who are you to begrudge them that?

By contrast, interpretation of legal texts is an inherently social exercise. A judge or labor arbitrator who chooses to read the Wagner Act (named for a different Wagner) as a metaphor for the Russian

---

1. 17 U.S. (4 Wheat.) 316, 407 (1819) (emphasis in original).

Revolution truly has missed the point, unless he confines his metaphorical reading to his spare time. Legal texts—wills, contracts among private parties, legislation, administrative regulations, constitutions, and so forth—set out legal rights and duties. How government officials interpret legal texts necessarily affects the content of these legal rights and duties, and therefore, we have legitimate grounds for criticizing their idiosyncratic interpretations of legal texts. This is not to say that everybody agrees about how exactly legal interpretation should best be conducted. On the contrary, it has long been a source of intense disagreement among judges, scholars, and others. However, that disagreement is bounded by certain assumptions about the nature of the enterprise, assumptions that need not apply to interpretation of art, literature, and music.

Accordingly, we would have no difficulty understanding what Marshall would have meant had he said something like "we must never forget it is a *legal text* we are interpreting." Such a statement would serve as a reminder that legal interpretation differs from other forms of interpretation.

Yet Marshall's famous line in *McCulloch* draws a distinction *within* the domain of legal texts. He tells us that certain types—constitutions—call for a different method of interpretation than do other types. That notion is immediately problematic because, as we saw in Chapter 2, much of Marshall's argument for judicial review in *Marbury v. Madison* rested on the proposition that the Constitution—while higher law in the sense that it trumps contrary, sub-constitutional, law—is ordinary law in the sense that judges can construe and apply it.[2] Did Marshall pull a fast one? How can the Constitution be ordinary law for purposes of justifying judicial review, but extraordinary law for purposes of selecting a mode of interpretation?

In the context of the *McCulloch* decision itself, there is a relatively straightforward answer, but to understand what Marshall meant by that answer requires that we look more closely at the case.

---

2. 5 U.S. (1 Cranch) 137, 177–79 (1803).

At issue in *McCulloch* was whether Congress had the power to charter a national bank, even though Article I, Section 8 does not expressly grant Congress any such power. The issue had been hotly contested from the earliest days of the Republic, when President George Washington asked two of his cabinet secretaries to offer competing views. Treasury Secretary Alexander Hamilton said Congress had the authority to charter the bank. Hamilton pointed to the variety of economic powers given to Congress by Article I, Section 8, such as the power to tax, to spend, to borrow money, and to regulate interstate commerce.[3] These powers could not be exercised effectively, Hamilton argued, without assuming the existence of other powers needed to carry them out. A national bank, while not strictly essential to the exercise of the economic powers expressly granted to Congress, was nonetheless "necessary and proper" for their implementation.[4]

Taking the other side, Secretary of State Thomas Jefferson argued that the bank was invalid. To protect state sovereignty, Jefferson noted, the Constitution conferred on the federal government only limited, specifically enumerated powers. Inferring additional powers in the way that Hamilton proposed would, according to Jefferson, render the national government effectively omnipotent.[5]

In the next chapter, we shall return to the substantive issue of federalism raised by the bank question, but for present purposes it suffices to note that when the issue came before the Supreme Court a generation later, the Court accepted Hamilton's view: The enumerated powers, Chief Justice Marshall said in *McCulloch*, include

3. Alexander Hamilton, Opinion on the Constitutionality of the Bank (Feb. 23, 1791), *in* 3 THE FOUNDERS' CONSTITUTION 247, 248–49 (Philip B. Kurland & Ralph Lerner eds., 1987).

4. *Id.* at 249.

5. Thomas Jefferson, Opinion on the Constitutionality of the Bill for Establishing a National Bank (Feb. 15, 1791), *in* 3 THE FOUNDERS' CONSTITUTION, *supra* note 3, at 245, 246–47.

implied powers.[6] Why? Marshall answered that a constitution only sets forth the broad outline of government. In characteristically colorful language, he declared: "A constitution, to contain an accurate detail of all the subdivisions of which its great powers will admit, and of all the means by which they may be carried into execution, would partake of the prolixity of a legal code, and could scarcely be embraced by the human mind."[7]

To the extent that Marshall was making a claim about all constitutions, history has proven him wrong. Many constitutions in fact do "partake of the prolixity of a legal code." The Constitution of Alabama is the most notorious. The world's longest, it contains hundreds of amendments, including Amendment 351, which authorizes the legislature to enact a special tax to fund measures to control "mosquitoes, rodents and other vectors of public health" in one particular county. Likewise, the Constitution of India contains hundreds of articles and is many, many times longer than the Constitution of the United States.

To be fair, when Marshall wrote for the Court in *McCulloch*, India had no constitution. The 1819 Constitution of Alabama, adopted less than a year after *McCulloch* was decided, looked much like the federal one. We should understand Marshall to be making both a general claim about the best way to write a constitution—"keep it short"—and a specific claim about the actual U.S. Constitution, which happens to be short: In light of the Constitution's brevity, interpreters will need to do some reading between the lines. And that is just what the Court did in *McCulloch*. It found that congressional power to create a bank could be inferred from other, express powers.

Granting that *McCulloch* authorizes constitutional interpreters to read between the lines, we still have a difficult question: How, exactly, should that task be accomplished? Here, *McCulloch* could

---

6. *McCulloch*, 17 U.S. at 408–09.

7. *Id.* at 407.

be read in two very different ways. On its face, the case appears to authorize an expansive approach to interpretation across the board. Under this first reading, wherever the Constitution speaks in general terms, courts would be warranted in finding unspoken assumptions and implications. We will call this the "inference-authorizing" view of *McCulloch*.

An alternative reading would emphasize that the case was about congressional power. The Court did not hold, after all, that Congress was *required* to create a bank, but only that Congress was *permitted* to do so. Under this second reading, Congress is the institution authorized to fill in the blanks between the enumerated powers. This reading of *McCulloch* makes it a case about deference: Within the broad outline of the Constitution, the elected branches of government get to make specific policy decisions, such as whether to have a national bank. We will call this the "deference-granting" view.

In *McCulloch* itself, both readings lead to the same result: Congress can charter a bank. However, the difference between the two approaches becomes clear if we imagine a case that involves a question of individual rights rather than congressional power. Suppose Congress passes a law forbidding the posting of indecent photographs on Internet websites, and suppose further that a defendant invokes the First Amendment as a defense to prosecution under the statute.[8] The First Amendment, ratified in 1791, of course contains no express references to the Internet or photographs, neither of which had been invented yet. Should its protections for "speech" and "the press" nonetheless be construed as implying protection (at least presumptively) for all forms of communication, including new technology?

Under the inference-authorizing view of *McCulloch*, the First Amendment's protections for "speech" and "the press" could be understood as identifying a value of free expression that receives

---

8. *Cf.* Reno v. ACLU, 521 U.S. 844 (1997).

protection regardless of the precise medium through which communication occurs. That is not to say, of course, that all communicative acts would be constitutionally protected. For example, terrorists have no First Amendment right to blow up a building to make a point. However, the mere fact that some expressive act is not specifically enumerated in the First Amendment would not be enough to prevent a judge from deciding that such an act is constitutionally protected.

Under the deference-granting view, however, a rights case differs crucially from a powers case. A judicial decision accepting that Congress can charter a bank, or maintain an air force even though the Constitution refers only to land and naval forces, leaves in place a decision taken through the national democratic process. By contrast, a judicial decision that "freedom of speech, or of the press" extends to television, the Internet, and other media not specifically mentioned in the 1791 text, takes some decisions out of the hands of the People's representatives. It makes the courts, rather than Congress or state legislatures, the final authority on what regulations of these media are permissible. Under the deference-granting view of *McCulloch*, acceptance of the proposition that Congress has broad latitude to adjust policy to changing times does not entail acceptance of the quite different proposition that the Court will use its own powers of constitutional inference to block legislation that does not expressly contradict the text.

Did the Marshall Court subjectively intend the inference-authorizing or the deference-granting view? Perhaps the most we can say is that the Court had no occasion to distinguish these views, given the nature of the case before it. We do know that Marshall was not opposed to striking down federal laws—as in *Marbury*—or state laws—as in the 1810 case of *Fletcher v. Peck*[9]—when a legislature violated what he thought was the best reading of the Constitution.

---

9. 10 U.S. (6 Cranch) 87 (1810).

In any event, the precise intentions of the *McCulloch* Court are not especially important for understanding the stakes in debates about constitutional interpretation, nor do the precise terms "inference-authorizing" or "deference-granting" even appear in the relevant literature. We have introduced them here simply to aid readers in understanding how constitutional interpretation might differ from other kinds of legal interpretation. The key point is that it potentially differs in two, almost contradictory ways. Under the inference-authorizing view, the Constitution's brevity leaves to all interpreters, including in proper cases, *the courts*, the task of filling in the gaps. Under the deference-granting view, courts are only warranted to override legislative decisions where the Constitution speaks in express terms: Constitutional gap-filling is left to elected officials.

The Supreme Court has never fully resolved the tension between the two readings of *McCulloch*. Certainly the Court has applied the inference-authorizing method to rights cases, but when it has done so most openly, it has been subject to withering criticism from both dissenting Justices and outside commentators.[10] Conservatives routinely denounce judicial decisions protecting abortion[11] and gay rights,[12] as well as those limiting the death penalty[13] and school prayer.[14] Meanwhile, liberals denounce judicial decisions restricting

---

10. *See, e.g.*, John Hart Ely, *The Wages of Crying Wolf: A Comment on* Roe v. Wade, 82 YALE L.J. 920 (1973).

11. *See, e.g.*, Planned Parenthood of Southeastern Pa. v. Casey, 505 U.S. 833, 979 (1992) (Scalia, J., dissenting).

12. *See, e.g.*, Lawrence v. Texas, 539 U.S. 558, 586 (2003) (Scalia, J., dissenting).

13. *See, e.g.*, Kennedy v. Louisiana, 128 S.Ct. 2641, 2665 (2008) (Alito, J., dissenting).

14. *See, e.g.*, Santa Fe Indep. Sch. Dist. v. Doe, 530 U.S. 290, 318 (2000) (Rehnquist, C.J., dissenting).

race-conscious government programs[15] and gun control,[16] as well as those protecting states' rights.[17] The charge, whether from the right or the left, is that the Justices are simply imposing their own values, rather than faithfully interpreting the Constitution.

We think this charge is almost universally unfair. Liberal Justices who think the Constitution protects abortion rights really do think that, just as conservative Justices who think the Constitution forbids most race-based affirmative action really do think that. We have no reason to suppose that any Justice secretly says to himself or herself "I know the Constitution really permits abortion restrictions, but I'm going to lie and vote to rule that it does not, because I want to impose my own values on the country."

Nonetheless, anyone remotely familiar with the work of the Supreme Court knows that positions on what the Constitution means tend to come in clusters that pretty closely track ideological views on salient political issues. It cannot be simply a coincidence that the same Justices who think the Constitution denies legislatures control over abortion rights also think the Constitution permits much affirmative action and gun control—and vice versa. Moreover, empirical scholarship using statistical models of judicial behavior shows that a Justice's ideology as measured on the left/right political spectrum is an excellent predictor of how that Justice will vote in constitutional cases that implicate left/right ideological divisions.[18] Accordingly, anybody approaching the question of how

---

15. *See* Parents Involved in Cmty. Schs. v. Seattle Sch. Dist. No. 1, 551 U.S. 701, 861–63 (2007) (Breyer, J., dissenting).

16. *See* District of Columbia v. Heller, 128 S.Ct. 2783, 2868 (2008) (Breyer, J., dissenting).

17. *See, e.g.,* Kimel v. Fla. Bd. of Regents, 528 US 62, 96 (2000) (Stevens, J., dissenting in part).

18. *See* JEFFREY A. SEGAL & HAROLD J. SPAETH, THE SUPREME COURT AND THE ATTITUDINAL MODEL REVISITED 86–114, 312–56 (2002); Jeffrey A. Segal, Lee Epstein, Charles M. Cameron & Harold J. Spaeth, *Ideological Values and the Votes of U.S. Supreme Court Justices Revisited,* 57 J. POL. 812, 817–19, 822 (1995).

the Supreme Court ought to interpret the Constitution should begin with a healthy dose of skepticism about the entire enterprise. If we are trying to predict how Justices will actually vote, knowing what those Justices think about how to interpret the Constitution will generally be less helpful than knowing where they fall on the ideological spectrum.

But what if you *are* a judge or Justice—or, more likely, a lawyer appearing before a court—charged with making a constitutional decision? Surely you as a lawyer cannot say to the court: "Do the liberal (or conservative) thing here, your honor." Instead, you will try to show how *the Constitution* actually requires the result that favors your client. You will need an argument, in other words, about how the Constitution should be interpreted. Even if you are a complete cynic about what actually drives judicial decision making in constitutional cases, you cannot put your cynicism in a brief.

Moreover, complete cynicism is unwarranted. Ideology may explain a great deal, but it does not explain everything. Sometimes judges and Justices vote "against type" because they are persuaded by the force of legal arguments that the Constitution requires something different from what they would favor as a matter of policy.[19] More generally, a judge or Justice approaching the job in good faith will want to do all he or she can to control for ideological bias. This is especially true in the vast majority of cases decided not by courts of last resort, such as the Supreme Court, but by trial and intermediate courts, whose members are more tightly constrained by precedent and more disciplined by the prospect of reversal on appeal.

We can understand various theories of constitutional interpretation as providing different answers to the question of how a judge distinguishes between outcomes she favors on political grounds and those she favors because the Constitution commands them. To be sure, that is not *all* that is at stake in debates over

---

19. See Michael C. Dorf, *Whose Ox is Being Gored? When Attitudinalism Meets Federalism*, 21 ST. JOHN'S J. LEG. COMMENT. 497 (2007).

constitutional interpretation. For example, most methods of constitutional interpretation can be employed by elected officials no less than by judges—and elected officials have no reason to fret over the fact that their constitutional views track their political views. Still, the debate over constitutional interpretation has largely been shaped by anxieties over the proper role of the courts, especially the Supreme Court.

Accordingly, in the balance of this chapter, we briefly present five leading approaches to constitutional interpretation by the courts. We do not claim that these are the only five approaches, nor do we attempt to argue that any one of them is the "best." Rather, we show how different methods of constitutional interpretation attempt to resolve the tension between the two views of *McCulloch*. That tension, moreover, is not simply a product of Marshall's opinion, but is inherent in American constitutional adjudication: The Constitution, as higher law, places some policies out of bounds, but its terse language leaves open many questions about just where the boundary lines lie. Judges turn to theories of constitutional interpretation to explain how and why their decisions speak not for themselves, but for the Constitution itself.

✸ Judicial Restraint

Judges sometimes say that they believe in "judicial restraint,"[20] a philosophy often defined in opposition to "judicial activism." Neither term has any precise content, although in constitutional discourse, judicial activism is frequently a label used by people who disagree with particular decisions as a shorthand for the claim that the judges who made these decisions improperly substituted their own

---

20. *See, e.g.*, District of Columbia v. Heller, 128 S.Ct. 2783, 2846 n.39 (2008) (Stevens, J., dissenting); Boumediene v. Bush, 128 S.Ct. 2229, 2282 (2008) (Roberts, C.J., dissenting).

policy judgment for that of the legislature. Someone who practices judicial restraint, by contrast, only finds that laws or policies are unconstitutional if clearly compelled to do so by the Constitution.[21]

Yet all judges, regardless of the methods of constitutional interpretation to which they subscribe, believe that they can only hold laws or policies invalid on constitutional grounds. What, then, distinguishes judicial restraint from other interpretive methodologies? Partly the answer is simply a modest attitude. A practitioner of judicial restraint tries very hard not to find unconstitutionality. Where the constitutional text admits of more than one interpretation, a restrained judge grants significant weight to the interpretation given to it (whether explicitly or implicitly) by officials accountable to the People. As we noted in Chapter 2, James Bradley Thayer articulated this view in the late nineteenth century,[22] and virtually all commentators on constitutional law have endorsed some version of it.

If judicial restraint sounds appealing in theory, in practice judges have had difficulty abiding its tenets, for judicial restraint—like judicial activism—is often in the eye of the beholder. Conservative Justices who condemn decisions striking down abortion regulations or the application of the death penalty accuse their liberal colleagues of judicial activism,[23] just as liberal Justices condemn their conservative colleagues for the same sin when the latter strike down race-based affirmative action programs or laws that intrude on states' rights.[24] One is tempted to caution both sides against

---

21. *See, e.g.,* ALEXANDER M. BICKEL, THE LEAST DANGEROUS BRANCH 34–46 (1962).

22. James B. Thayer, *The Origin and Scope of the American Doctrine of Constitutional Law,* 7 HARV. L. REV. 129, 144 (1893).

23. *See, e.g.,* Stenberg v. Carhart, 530 U.S. 914, 955 (2000) (Scalia, J., dissenting).

24. *See, e.g.,* United States v. Morrison, 529 U.S. 598, 651 n.19 (2000) (Souter, J., dissenting); United States v. Lopez, 514 U.S. 549, 611 (1995) (Souter, J., dissenting).

throwing stones. A judge who restrains himself against striking down laws only when he agrees with the policy behind those laws is not practicing judicial restraint in any meaningful sense.

More charitably, we might say that judicial review is a bit like eating potato chips. A judge can swear to himself that he will only strike down laws that are blatantly unconstitutional, but once he gets started with judicial review he may find it impossible to stop himself. By self-consciously espousing judicial restraint, a judge at least makes himself aware of his potential bias, and that awareness may aid in combating the bias.

Restraint, however, is not complete deference. Even practitioners of judicial restraint believe that some laws are invalid, and thus judicial restraint usually acts as a supplement to other methods of constitutional interpretation.

⅏ Natural Law and the Moral Reading

In the 1798 case of *Calder v. Bull*, Supreme Court Justices Chase and Iredell exchanged pointed dicta over the question of whether the judiciary has the power to invalidate laws that violate no provision of the Constitution. Justice Chase, announcing the Court's opinion, appeared to equate constitutional limits with natural justice.[25] We say "appeared to" because Justice Chase then looked to positive law and English practice to inform his understanding of the "express compact and [the] republican principles" that stood behind any valid legislative act.[26] In any event, Justice Iredell, who agreed with the result in the case (upholding a Connecticut law), was troubled

---

25. 3 U.S. (3 Dall.) 386, 399, 400 (1798) (Iredell, J.) (disagreeing that inconsistency with "natural justice" could void a law).

26. *Id.* at 388 (Chase, J.).

by what he took to be Justice Chase's suggestion that natural justice alone could invalidate a legislative act. Iredell wrote:

> The ideas of natural justice are regulated by no fixed standard: the ablest and the purest men have differed upon the subject; and all that the court could properly say, in such an event, would be, that the Legislature (possessed of an equal right of opinion) had passed an act which, in the opinion of the judges, was inconsistent with the abstract principles of natural justice.[27]

Ever since, Iredell's views have been understood as canonical. The courts have no authority to strike down laws other than as inconsistent with some provision of the Constitution.

Yet if *Calder v. Bull* eliminated natural justice as a freestanding basis for judicial review, principles of natural justice and natural law (terms we will treat as synonymous although they have been used to connote somewhat different ideas) have nonetheless played a substantial role in American constitutional law. To be sure, "natural law" is much like "judicial activism," a term applied as a criticism of someone else's judicial philosophy. Thus, in the 1960s, Justice Hugo Black famously accused the Court of following natural law when it found constitutional rights in the Due Process Clause— such as the right of married couples to use contraception—that he thought his colleagues were simply making up.[28] Ever since, no Justice has expressly affirmed a belief in natural law, as then-Judge Clarence Thomas learned during his confirmation hearings for the Supreme Court: Thomas had to disavow a speech he had given years earlier in which he praised someone else's article on natural law.[29]

---

27. *Id.* at 399 (Iredell, J.).

28. Griswold v. Connecticut, 381 U.S. 479, 511–12, 514–16 (1965) (Black, J., dissenting).

29. Nomination of Judge Clarence Thomas to be Associate Justice of the Supreme Court of the United States: Hearings before the Senate Comm. on the Judiciary, 102nd Cong., 127–29, 146–48 (1991).

Yet despite express disavowals, something like natural law arguably informs much of the Court's jurisprudence interpreting open-ended constitutional provisions. Consider the Eighth Amendment's prohibition on cruel and unusual punishments. In the 2008 case of *Kennedy v. Louisiana*, the Court held that the death penalty may not be imposed for the crime of raping a child.[30] The Court treated the Eighth Amendment's language as calling for an evaluation of evolving standards in society (as measured by, among other things, positive law) as well as the Justices' "own independent judgment."[31] Although purporting to explain how they reached decisions only in Eighth Amendment cases, this methodology is quite common in the work of the Court: In attempting to determine how to apply such terms as "unreasonable" (in the Fourth Amendment), "due process" (in the Fifth and Fourteenth Amendments), and "equal protection" (in the Fourteenth Amendment), the Justices look to combine evidence of the terms' historical usage, current social attitudes, the Court's precedents, and the particular Justices' own notions of justice.

Indeed, Ronald Dworkin has argued at length that this process is *the* central method of Anglo-American adjudication, including constitutional adjudication. According to Dworkin, judges in constitutional (and other) cases look for the interpretation that best fits the existing law, where "best" takes its meaning from principles of political morality.[32] If this seems unduly highfalutin, you can understand Dworkin's view as more or less equating constitutional adjudication with the common law method. Faced with a new case, a judge using the common law method looks for analogies to prior cases; where competing analogies are available, the judge looks for the one that best fits; and "best" necessarily will depend in some measure on the

---

30. 128 S.Ct. 2641, 2646 (2008).

31. *Id.* at 2649–51.

32. RONALD DWORKIN, LAW'S EMPIRE 254–58 (1986); RONALD DWORKIN, A MATTER OF PRINCIPLE 143–44 (1985).

judge's values. Dworkin calls this approach the "moral reading" of the Constitution.[33]

Consider the question the Supreme Court faced in the 2007 case of *Parents Involved in Community Schools v. Seattle School District No. 1*: whether a public school district could voluntarily use students' race as part of an effort to ensure that no particular school deviated too far from the racial composition of the district as a whole.[34] The prior cases pointed in two directions. The Court's civil-rights era decisions held that race-conscious student assignments could be ordered as a remedy for past unconstitutional segregation and said in dicta that voluntary race-based integration of this sort was permissible;[35] yet those cases pre-dated a line of affirmative action cases requiring that all classifications based on race be justified by exacting standards.[36] Thus, in interpreting the Fourteenth Amendment's Equal Protection Clause, the Court had to decide whether the Seattle case was more like the civil-rights era desegregation cases or more like the later affirmative action cases. The Justices disagreed. The five most conservative Justices favored the affirmative action analogy, and invalidated the Seattle system (and one from the Louisville area in a companion case); the four most liberal Justices followed the desegregation analogy. Nobody cited Professor Dworkin, much less natural law, but an outside observer would not need much training in political science to see that values—perceptions of natural justice, if you will—played a key role in the case.

Given the prevalence of close Supreme Court cases that divide along ideological lines, and given the extensive use of common law

---

33. RONALD DWORKIN, FREEDOM'S LAW: THE MORAL READING OF THE AMERICAN CONSTITUTION 2–15 (1996).

34. Parents Involved in Cmty. Schs. v. Seattle Sch. Dist. No. 1, 551 U.S. 701, 709–11 (2007).

35. *See* Swann v. Charlotte-Mecklenburg Bd. of Ed., 402 U.S. 1, 16 (1971).

36. *See, e.g.,* Grutter v. Bollinger, 539 U.S. 306, 326 (2003); Adarand Constructors, Inc. v. Pena, 515 U.S. 200, 224 (1995).

reasoning in such cases, Dworkin's notion of a moral reading is one quite plausible description of what the Justices are up to in difficult constitutional cases. Yet the very accuracy of this description would appear to call into question the legitimacy of the methodology and constitutional adjudication more broadly. If, in most hard cases, constitutional adjudication boils down to the judges' values, then why do we need judicial review at all? Why not simply let the People's elected representatives make the value judgments?

Dworkin has an answer to this question. He says that even though judges disagree in hard cases, there really are right answers in those cases. The right-answers thesis is in turn connected to a meta-ethical view that Dworkin also holds, called moral realism.[37] Moral realists believe that morality is real,[38] and their claims certainly make better sense of how most of us talk about morality than do the claims of moral relativists, expressivists, and skeptics. If you think (as we certainly hope you do) that slavery, murder, and rape are wrong, then you likely think that they *really* are wrong, not that you don't like slavery, murder, and rape in the way that you don't like the taste of asparagus. If moral realism is right, then there are right answers to moral questions, and so finding the right moral reading of the Constitution is not simply a matter of subjective values.

We will not attempt to resolve whether moral realism is right, because even if it is, the moral reading remains problematic. Knowing that there is a right answer to the question of whether voluntary race-conscious student assignments violate equal protection does not tell us what institution is best situated to find that right answer: local school boards, state legislatures, Congress, or the courts?

---

37. Ronald Dworkin, *Objectivity and Truth: You'd Better Believe It*, 25 PHIL. & PUB. AFF. 87, 117 (1996).

38. *See id.* at 127–28.

By virtue of their legal training and the independence bestowed by life tenure and salary protection, judges may be better situated to answer some sorts of questions than politicians are. One might even argue that they are better situated than politicians to answer moral questions.[39] But in a generally democratic society, that is at best an awkward argument. That awkwardness probably explains why Justices who employ natural law and the moral reading—and they all can be said to do so on occasion—rarely do so openly.

℀ Representation Reinforcement

If a judge had to choose between morality (or any other set of substantive norms) and deference to political actors as an across-the-board approach to constitutional interpretation, she would have to betray one or the other primary value in the exercise of judicial review. Yet the judge need not make such an all-or-nothing choice. She might choose instead to defer to political actors in some cases, while following her own interpretive instincts in other cases. The hard question would then be when to defer and when not to defer. The representation-reinforcing approach to constitutional interpretation—sometimes called "process theory"[40]—provides an elegant answer. For the most part, it observes, the Constitution entrusts questions of policy and value to elected officials, and so in the ordinary course, judges should defer to the decisions of such elected officials; however, where someone invokes the Constitution to complain that the democratic process itself has been corrupted, then the outputs of that process do not deserve deference.[41]

---

39. *See, e.g.,* CHRISTOPHER L. EISGRUBER, CONSTITUTIONAL SELF-GOVERNMENT 58–59 (2001).

40. *See, e.g.,* Michael J. Klarman, *The Puzzling Resistance to Political Process Theory*, 77 VA. L. REV. 747 (1991).

41. *Id.* at 749.

The kernel of the representation-reinforcement approach was set out in a footnote in the 1938 case of *United States v. Carolene Products Co.*[42] In the course of upholding a federal law regulating the content of milk products in interstate commerce, the Court tentatively identified areas in which deference to the legislature would be unjustified: (1) laws challenged as violating specific provisions of the Bill of Rights, including those incorporated against the states by the Fourteenth Amendment; (2) laws that "restrict[] those political processes which can ordinarily be expected to bring about repeal of undesirable legislation," including restrictions on voting, freedom of expression, and political association; and (3) laws that, as a result of prejudice, disadvantage religious, national, or racial minorities.[43]

This was a remarkably prescient footnote. It roughly foretold the Supreme Court's agenda through the 1960s, and to an important extent, still accounts for a large swath of constitutional doctrine. At least with respect to individual rights (as opposed to government powers), official doctrine holds that courts should defer to legislative judgment absent one or more of the considerations set forth in the *Carolene Products* footnote.[44] As elaborated at length in John Hart Ely's extraordinarily influential 1980 book, *Democracy and Distrust*, judicial review—the substitution of the judges' understanding of the Constitution for the understanding of elected officials—can only be justified where: (1) the Constitution is clear; (2) the political game is rigged; or (3) prejudice has so infected the political process that the same groups are consistently shut out.[45]

---

42. 304 U.S. 144 (1938).

43. *Id.* at 152 n.4.

44. ERWIN CHEMERINSKY, CONSTITUTIONAL LAW: PRINCIPLES AND POLICIES 678 (3d ed., 2006).

45. JOHN HART ELY, DEMOCRACY AND DISTRUST: A THEORY OF JUDICIAL REVIEW 101–04 (1980).

Despite its powerful theoretical roots and its ongoing importance, representation reinforcement nonetheless can be criticized
in a number of ways. First, although Ely argued that the Constitution's
central value is democracy—and thus that judicial review faces a
countermajoritarian difficulty—the point is hardly obvious.
Progressives from the late nineteenth century and into the early
twentieth complained bitterly that the Constitution was insuffi-
ciently democratic,[46] and today some scholars argue that the
Constitution is essentially libertarian.[47] If one is inclined to see
things this way, then one can turn the matter on its head and argue
that the non-exercise of judicial review frequently poses a "counter-
libertarian" difficulty. Even if one is not prepared to go quite that far,
there remains the sense that the Constitution serves multiple,
sometimes conflicting values, and that a form of judicial review that
singles out process values will unfairly cheat substantive values.[48]

Second, the strategy of distinguishing islands of robust judicial
review amidst a sea of deference to legislatures only works so long
as the sea is substantially larger than the islands. Yet the area falling
outside the presumption of constitutionality recognized in the
Carolene Products footnote encompasses many of the most contentious questions courts face, including affirmative action, gay rights,
school prayer, pornography, and so on. Even the abortion right,
which Ely himself originally thought an unwarranted constitutional
inference by the Burger Court because it is a substantive

46. William E. Scheuerman, *Constitutionalism in an Age of Speed*, 19 CONST.
    COMMENT. 353, 353 (2002).

47. *See, e.g.,* RANDY BARNETT, THE STRUCTURE OF LIBERTY (1998).

48. *See* JAMES E. FLEMING, SECURING CONSTITUTIONAL DEMOCRACY 19–36
    (2006).

right unconnected to clear constitutional text or the political process,[49] can be, and has been, recharacterized as protecting women's equal political participation within the representation-reinforcement framework.[50] If so many of the hot-button constitutional issues that come before the courts arguably fall outside the area of deference to elected officials, then representation reinforcement simply shifts the terms of debate within the practice of judicial review; it does not much cabin that practice.

Third, the Supreme Court's 2000 decision in *Bush v. Gore*[51] severely unsettled the assumption that the Court could act as a neutral referee in disputes over the ground rules of democracy. Such disputes are not only "political" in the same sense as disagreements over the constitutionality of abortion restrictions or affirmative action; they can appear to be nakedly partisan. The perception among many observers that the Justices voted in *Bush v. Gore* based on their preferences as between the two candidates was no less a blow to the legitimacy of judicial review than its most controversial decisions in substantive areas. Process theorists, in this view, were naive to suppose that political actors would be more willing to accept the courts' judgments about their electoral prospects than they would be willing to accept judicial rulings about the substantive legislation they enacted.

Even with the foregoing flaws, representation reinforcement remains influential in Supreme Court doctrine. It may not serve as the all-encompassing interpretive approach of any Justice, but instead tempers the judgments the Court might otherwise reach. When employing process theory, the Court hesitates before exercising the power of judicial review. In order to displace the substantive judgments of elected officials in any given case, the Justices

---

49. Ely, *supra* note 10, at 933, 943–44.

50. *See* Reva B. Siegel, *Sex Equality Arguments for Reproductive Rights: Their Critical Basis and Evolving Constitutional Expression*, 56 EMORY L.J. 815 (2007).

51. 531 U.S. 98 (2000).

must assure themselves that there exists some sound reason to distrust the political process.

⁓ Originalism

Judges who call themselves "originalists" believe that the Constitution means today what it meant when it was originally ratified. For the body of the Constitution, the operative date is 1789, for the Bill of Rights it is 1791, and for the Fourteenth Amendment it is 1868. What makes the Constitution higher law, in the first place, the originalist says, is the fact that it was adopted by the People, and it therefore should be interpreted in accordance with how the People understood it when they adopted it.[52] When a law violates the Constitution's original meaning, the originalist says, striking down that law does not substitute the *judge's* views for those of the People; rather, it applies the true meaning of the Constitution, adopted by a rigorous super-majoritarian process, to displace an unconstitutional law adopted by a merely majoritarian process.[53]

Originalism comes in two principal forms. Some originalists equate constitutional meaning with the "original intent" of either the framers or the ratifiers of the Constitution.[54] Yet that notion has been subject to extensive criticism. Even the relatively small group of men who met in Philadelphia in 1787 were not of one mind on what every contestable provision of the Constitution meant, and they deliberately met in secret. James Madison, who was the document's principal author, took the most extensive notes of the

52. ROBERT H. BORK, THE TEMPTING OF AMERICA: THE POLITICAL SEDUCTION OF THE LAW 145–47 (1990).

53. John O. McGinnis & Michael B. Rappaport, *Our Supermajoritarian Constitution*, 80 TEX. L. REV. 703, 802–05 (2002).

54. *See, e.g.*, Edwin Meese III, *Interpreting the Constitution, in* INTERPRETING THE CONSTITUTION: THE DEBATE OVER ORIGINAL INTENT 13, 16 (Jack N. Rakove ed., 1990).

Constitutional Convention,[55] but delayed publishing them for half a century, by which time constitutional law developed in part based on other, less authoritative, accounts of the Convention.[56] Contemporary sources, such as the Federalist Papers and the writings of Anti-Federalists, are somewhat suspect because they were expressly polemical. Moreover, as Madison himself argued, because the state ratifying conventions were necessary for the Constitution to become law, the understandings of the Constitution evinced at those conventions provide "a better standard by which to judge original intent than even the Philadelphia convention. . . ."[57] Yet there is no straightforward method of identifying and aggregating the intentions of the people who attended the ratifying conventions.

These and other difficulties have led many originalists to abandon original intent in favor of "original public meaning."[58] The real authors of the Constitution, according to this view, were the People whose representatives ratified it, and thus the goal of constitutional interpretation should be to retrieve the original generally understood meaning of the words that were ratified, including any relevant terms of art.[59] Original-public-meaning originalism is less vulnerable than is original-intent originalism to the problems of attributing intentions to a collective body, because original-public-meaning originalism has no interest in intentions as such. Thus, where an original-intent originalist might give great weight to Madison's Convention notes or accounts of the state ratifying conventions, an original-public-meaning originalist would look to

55. JAMES MADISON, THE DEBATES IN THE FEDERAL CONVENTION OF 1787 (Gaillard Hunt & James Brown Scott eds., 1920).

56. *See* Donald O. Dewey, *James Madison Helps Clio Interpret the Constitution*, 15 AM. J. LEG. HIST. 38, 44–45 (1971).

57. DREW R. MCCOY, THE LAST OF THE FATHERS: JAMES MADISON AND THE REPUBLICAN LEGACY 75–76 (1989).

58. *See* Vasan Kesavan & Michael Stokes Paulsen, *The Interpretive Force of the Constitution's Secret Drafting History*, 91 GEO. L.J. 1113, 1114 (2003).

59. RANDY BARNETT, RESTORING THE LOST CONSTITUTION 89–93 (2004); ANTONIN SCALIA, A MATTER OF INTERPRETATION 38 (1997).

such sources only as an indication of what the salient language meant, supplementing them with citations of dictionaries of the period.

A lively intra-originalist debate exists over whether original-public meaning originalism is superior to original-intent originalism, including a debate over whether it is even possible to talk about the meaning of words independent of the intentions of the speaker.[60] For present purposes, we can put that debate aside and focus on three difficulties faced by both forms of originalism.

First, it is hardly self-evident that the Constitution derives its current legal force from its ratification in 1789 (and thereafter for amendments). Certainly no one alive today voted in any election necessary to ratify the original Constitution, and by modern standards, the electorate of the time was woefully undemocratic: enslaved African Americans, women, and most white men without property were ineligible to vote. One might accordingly conclude that, with the exception of recent amendments, the Constitution derives its current legal force from the fact that Americans today more or less accept the legitimacy of the Constitution.[61] And if contemporary consent validates the Constitution, then perhaps contemporary understandings of the Constitution's language should prevail over contrary original understandings.

Second, a jurisprudence of original understanding could be enormously disruptive to the existing legal order because, in important respects, much well-accepted constitutional doctrine violates the original understanding. An originalist Supreme Court might have to declare all federal administrative agencies unconstitutional; it might also have to renounce its decisions holding that the Bill of Rights limits the states (rather than just limiting the federal government).

---

60. *See* Larry Alexander & Salkrishna Prakash, *"Is that English You're Speaking?" Why Intention Free Interpretation is an Impossibility*, 41 SAN DIEGO L. REV. 967, 976 (2004).

61. Richard H. Fallon, Jr., *Legitimacy and the Constitution*, 118 HARV. L. REV. 1787, 1802–06 (2003).

As a practical matter, it is inconceivable that the Supreme Court would take such measures, and so pure originalism would, at the very least, need to include a substantial exception for settled non-originalist practice.

Third, the original understanding can be highly indeterminate. Sometimes indeterminacy results from changed circumstances. Is a thermal imaging scan a "search" within the meaning of the Fourth Amendment, thus requiring a warrant based on probable cause?[62] No one alive and speaking English (or any other language) in 1791 or 1868 had occasion to address that question.

Originalism can also yield indeterminate answers to old questions. Consider, for example, the question of whether the Second Amendment protects a private right to possess firearms for personal use against criminals. In the 2008 case of *District of Columbia v. Heller*, all nine Justices relied extensively on evidence of the original understanding.[63] Five Justices found such a right; four Justices dissented; and the division tracked ideological lines. It is possible that all the dissenters, or all of the Justices in the majority, were using the historical materials dishonestly, but it is more plausible that the historical materials alone simply did not answer the question. Given that Americans argue intensely over the meaning of statutes enacted in the very recent past, it should hardly be surprising that there is disagreement over the original meaning of constitutional provisions adopted many generations ago.

Despite these and other shortcomings, originalism remains a powerful force in constitutional interpretation. For some, like Supreme Court Justice Antonin Scalia, it is "the lesser evil."[64] Justice Scalia acknowledges some of the flaws of thoroughgoing originalism, but thinks that these flaws are less serious than those of rival interpretive methods.

---

62. Kyllo v. United States, 533 U.S. 27 (2001).

63. 128 S.Ct. 2783 (2008).

64. Antonin Scalia, *Originalism: The Lesser Evil*, 57 U. CIN. L. REV. 849 (1989).

Meanwhile, even judges who do not consider themselves originalists will usually consider the original understanding of a constitutional provision as one factor in deriving a current interpretation.[65] After all, even if the Constitution derives its ultimate legitimacy from contemporary popular acceptance, what We the People accept today includes not just its text considered in isolation, but also the history that led to its adoption (as well as the post-ratification history). Add to that the almost-mythic regard in which our constitutional culture holds the framers, and one can see why the original understanding plays an important role in constitutional law.

🎜 Eclecticism

Although individual Supreme Court Justices from time to time vow allegiance to one or another of the theoretical approaches discussed above, the Court as a whole has never endorsed a single interpretive methodology. In part this reflects the dynamics of a multi-member body, but more fundamentally, it reflects the complexity of life and the breadth of subjects regulated by the Constitution. How could any interpretive approach be satisfactory in all contexts? Constitutional theorists who emphasize the impracticability of any single approach are eclectics.[66]

Judges are drawn to eclecticism in part by the nature of the job. Then-Judge John Roberts said in answer to a question from Senator Orrin Hatch during his Supreme Court confirmation hearing, "I do not have an overarching judicial philosophy that I bring to every case. . . . I tend to look at the cases from the bottom up rather than the top down."[67] Judges in a common-law system, Roberts explained,

---

65. *See, e.g., Heller*, 128 S.Ct. at 2831–42 (Stevens, J., dissenting).

66. *See, e.g.,* PHILIP BOBBITT, CONSTITUTIONAL INTERPRETATION 8–10 (1991).

67. Nomination of Judge John Roberts to be Chief Justice of the Supreme Court of

do best by staying close to the facts, leaving theory mostly for the academics.

Over the range of constitutional cases, one sees substantial evidence of eclecticism, with different rulings emphasizing, to greater or lesser degrees: text; original understanding; post-ratification history; precedent; moral principle; and prudential consideration of the likely consequences of a decision. An opinion will be especially persuasive if it successfully argues that most or all of these factors point in the same direction.

But what should an eclectic judge do when different factors point in different directions, or when sound arguments can be made in different directions within a single "modality" of constitutional meaning?[68] Richard Fallon has considered this question at some length. He argues that under such circumstances, the judge revisits her initial conclusions in an effort to make the different sorts of arguments cohere, that is, to line up in one direction.[69] What is the "glue" that makes the arguments hang together better for one result rather than another? Recall that Dworkin says principles of political morality do this work, but if that is the case, then eclecticism turns out to be no different from the moral reading. Moreover, what if no amount of pushing and pulling can force the arguments in the same direction? Fallon then says that judges have implicitly adopted a hierarchy of forms of argument, with text prevailing over original understanding, in turn prevailing over theory, and so forth.[70] Yet it is hardly clear that this hierarchy holds across different judges or even across different cases decided by the same judge.

---

the United States: Hearings before the Senate Comm. on the Judiciary, 109th Cong., 159 (2005).

68. BOBBITT, *supra* note 66, at 11–22.

69. Richard H. Fallon, Jr., *A Constructivist Coherence Theory of Constitutional Interpretation*, 100 HARV. L. REV. 1189, 1237–51 (1987).

70. *Id.* at 1243–48.

Accordingly, another leading constitutional eclectic, Philip Bobbitt, contends that the conscience of the judge leads him to choose which modality to favor in any given case.[71] That may well be an accurate description of what judges in fact do, but it hardly amounts to a theory of interpretation, for different judges will interpret the obligations of conscience differently.

In the end, eclecticism may devolve into a kind of crude celebration of judicial discretion, although this view too has its champions, most prominently federal appellate judge Richard Posner. Judge Posner contends that in the sorts of constitutional cases that reach the Supreme Court, the formal legal materials and conventional modes of argument rarely dictate one answer or another.[72] Hence, Posner argues, within the range of outcomes that could plausibly be defended with conventional legal arguments, the judge should pick the one that, all things considered, will lead to the best result.[73] Indeed, if one accepts Posner's strongly skeptical premises, it would appear that this is what judges inevitably do, regardless of what they say they are doing.

* * *

We have suggested that each of the leading approaches to constitutional interpretation is flawed or incomplete. It does not follow, however, that constitutional interpretation is impossible or a sham. Many constitutional questions have clear answers. The President must be at least 35 years old, Senators serve for six-year terms, and a treason conviction requires the testimony of two witnesses or a confession in open court. Any plausible theory of interpretation will affirm these results precisely because the constitutional text leaves so little room for interpretation. The sorts of cases likely to reach the courts are precisely those in which there is room for interpretation— in other words, hard cases. Pretty much by definition, no method of

---

71. Bobbitt, *supra* note 66, at 155–62.

72. *See* RICHARD A. POSNER, HOW JUDGES THINK 269–323 (2008).

73. RICHARD A. POSNER, LAW, PRAGMATISM, AND DEMOCRACY 57–96 (2003).

interpretation will render a hard case easy, except by glossing over just those aspects of the case that make it hard.

Key features of the U.S. Constitution have remained essentially unchanged for over two centuries, a period of time during which the U.S. population has grown from about four million to over 300 million, while the country and the world have undergone enormous economic, social, and technological change. It should hardly be surprising that scholars and judges disagree over how to answer the constitutional questions thrown up by efforts to govern this complex and fractious society. The great surprise is that the Constitution—including the institution of judicial review—works at all. Does the Constitution owe its longevity to the foresight of its authors, to the flexible interpretation it has been given over the years, or to both? Any answer we give will be controversial, and we are tempted to say that that too, is part of the genius of the American constitutional system.

✺ Further Reading

CHARLES L. BLACK, JR., STRUCTURE AND RELATIONSHIP IN CONSTITUTIONAL LAW (1969).

PHILIP BOBBITT, CONSTITUTIONAL INTERPRETATION (1991).

RONALD DWORKIN, FREEDOM'S LAW: THE MORAL READING OF THE AMERICAN CONSTITUTION (1996).

JOHN HART ELY, DEMOCRACY AND DISTRUST: A THEORY OF JUDICIAL REVIEW (1980).

Antonin Scalia, *Originalism: The Lesser Evil*, 57 U. CIN. L. REV. 849 (1989).

LAURENCE H. TRIBE & MICHAEL C. DORF, ON READING THE CONSTITUTION (1991).

FOUR

Federalism

THE PRINCIPAL AIM OF THE CONSTITUTIONAL CONVENTION of 1787 was to
revise the Articles of Confederation so as to strengthen the national
government. The Constitution that emerged achieved this end by
granting to the national government broad powers to act directly
on the People, thereby freeing it from dependence on the states. At
the same time, however, the interests of the states were protected
through the structure of the national government. The chief mechanisms included, and include to this day: representation of each state
on an equal-voting basis in the Senate; Presidential elections via an
Electoral College chosen on a state-by-state basis; the requirement
that constitutional amendments be ratified by a super-majority of
states; and the prohibition on amending the structure of the Senate
without unanimous consent of the states. In light of these and other
"political safeguards of federalism,"[1] is there any need for the
Supreme Court to provide additional protection for the states by
second-guessing Congress's judgment that particular laws are
within the scope of federal power? The Supreme Court itself has
vacillated in answering this question of who (Congress or the
Supreme Court) decides who (the federal government or the states)
decides particular policy questions.

---

1. Herbert Wechsler, *The Political Safeguards of Federalism: The Role of the States
   in the Composition and Selection of the National Government*, 54 COLUM. L. REV.
   543 (1954).

This chapter begins with an overview of the costs and benefits of American federalism. We then turn our focus to two sorts of mechanisms for restricting the powers of Congress beyond the safeguards built into the structure of the federal government: first, subject matter limits on particular powers, such as the power to regulate interstate commerce, that leave some activities beyond the domain of national lawmaking; and second, "etiquette" limits that admit congressional subject matter competence but invalidate particular means by which Congress exercises its powers, such as subjecting states to lawsuits for monetary damages. The Supreme Court's vacillation in the federalism area has reflected ambivalence over how robustly it should enforce these two kinds of limits.

That vacillation is understandable because neither of the Court's two polar approaches to federalism questions is truly satisfactory, and it is exceedingly difficult to identify and maintain a stable resting point between the poles. Taken to its logical extreme, the "political safeguards" view—which would render federalism cases essentially non-justiciable—makes a mockery of the maxim that the federal government has only limited powers. Yet the Court's efforts to fashion doctrines that protect state sovereignty invoke categories that bear little relation to facts on the ground, as in its distinction between "economic" and "noneconomic" activity.[2] For that matter, the Court has sometimes moved far beyond the constitutional text, as in the extension of the Eleventh Amendment's express prohibition on out-of-state citizens suing states in federal court to also bar in-state citizens suing states in state court.

This chapter concludes with a brief exploration of the limits that principles of federalism place on the states. The avoidance of inter-state trade wars was one of the chief goals of the Philadelphia Convention of 1787, and the Constitution has been enormously successful in knitting the United States into a single

---

2. United States v. Morrison, 529 U.S. 598, 613 (2000).

continent-sized economy. In this respect, at least, the Constitution did create a "more perfect Union."

ⅶ The Benefits and Costs of Federalism

Under a unitary system of government, sovereignty resides in a central government. Smaller jurisdictions, such as cities or counties, may have local responsibilities, but the central government retains the ultimate power to shift those responsibilities. By contrast, in a federal system, ultimate authority is divided between the national government and smaller jurisdictions like states or provinces. France, Israel, and the United Kingdom are examples of unitary states, while Canada, Germany, and the United States have federal systems. In practice, the terms "unitary" and "federal" are better understood as ideal types or extreme points on a spectrum, as nominally unitary states often include substantial quasi-permanent devolution of power and local autonomy.

With that caveat in mind, we can still fruitfully ask why constitution writers might prefer one ideal type over the other. Justice Sandra Day O'Connor listed the following benefits of federalism in her opinion in *Gregory v. Ashcroft*, a statutory interpretation case with constitutional overtones:

> [Federalism] assures a decentralized government that will be more sensitive to the diverse needs of a heterogeneous society; it increases opportunity for citizen involvement in democratic processes; it allows for more innovation and experimentation in government; and it makes government more responsive by putting the States in competition for a mobile citizenry.[3]

Let us briefly consider each of these claims.

---

3. 501 U.S. 452, 458 (1991).

The argument that decentralized government is more responsive to diverse needs rests in part on the assumption that remote bureaucratic regimes do not take local concerns seriously. That assumption seems reasonable. For example, if you want a traffic light installed at a dangerous intersection, you would expect your local city council representative to be easier to reach than the national transportation secretary. Yet that is hardly a fair comparison. For one thing, federalism does not necessarily mean localism. Large American states like California, New York, and Texas govern many more people than small unitary governments, like that of New Zealand. (One of the authors lived in New Zealand in the late 1980s, and at the time the Prime Minister's home telephone number was listed in the Wellington phone book; the other author's father grew up in Wellington, and was more likely to meet the Prime Minister at a neighborhood grocery than ever to meet the mayor of the North American city where he now lives.) If you had to call the California Department of Transportation to report a dangerous intersection, you might find it no more responsive than its federal counterpart. Or perhaps you might find that some large jurisdiction—whether state or national—is in fact very responsive. Efforts in recent decades to "reinvent government," so as to make it more user-friendly, show that large size need not entail unresponsiveness.[4] To the extent Justice O'Connor was right that smaller jurisdictions are more responsive to their citizens' needs than are large jurisdictions, she was at best only right on average; responsiveness does not necessarily follow from decentralization.

However, when Justice O'Connor combines the notion of a mobile citizenry with responsiveness to a heterogeneous society, she invokes a powerful justification for federalism. The basic idea is that people will vote with their feet—that is, migrate to states that suit

---

4. *See, e.g.,* DAVID E. OSBORNE & TED GAEBLER, REINVENTING GOVERNMENT: HOW THE ENTREPRENEURIAL SPIRIT IS TRANSFORMING THE PUBLIC SECTOR (1992).

their policy preferences—and thus more people will satisfy more of their policy preferences under federalism than if they were subject to uniform national policies.[5] The familiar notion that the United States consists of "red states" and "blue states" provides anecdotal evidence for a phenomenon that more serious studies also show to be real.[6]

Yet if regulatory competition with respect to heterogeneously distributed preferences is a benefit of federalism, the possibility of a "race to the bottom" is a potential cost. Profit-driven enterprises generally prefer to minimize their tax bills and regulatory oversight. Thus, states seeking employment for their citizens have an incentive to offer tax breaks and weak regulation in order to lure businesses away from sister states. Locating the relevant taxing and regulatory powers at the national level avoids this risk of interstate competition, although the international mobility of capital often means that the national government faces similar competitive pressures from other sovereigns.

Justice O'Connor is plainly right that federalism affords more opportunities for democratic participation, simply by increasing the number of offices open to election. In addition, the smaller constituencies usually associated with smaller states—especially the smallest states—enable state legislators to spend more time listening to the concerns of interested citizens. But again, it is important to remember that even in democratic countries with unitary governments, citizens typically elect important local executive and legislative bodies.

---

5. *See generally* Charles M. Tiebout, *A Pure Theory of Local Expenditures*, 64 J. POL. ECON. 416 (1956).

6. *See, e.g.*, Margaret F. Brinig & F.H. Buckley, *The Market for Deadbeats*, 25 J. LEGAL. STUD. 201, 209–14, 231–32 (1996) (finding evidence of migration due to welfare payment differences); Jonathan Tilove, *The New Map of American Politics*, AM. PROSPECT, May–June 1999, at 34, 35 (describing emigration of white conservatives from California to Rocky Mountain states); *see also* David E. Bernstein, *The Law and Economics of Post-Civil War Restrictions on Interstate Migration by African-Americans*, 76 TEX. L. REV. 781, 840–46 (1998) (discussing postbellum migration of African Americans).

Justice O'Connor was hardly the first to associate federalism with innovation and experimentation. Justice Louis Brandeis famously referred to the states as experimental laboratories.[7] It is much less risky to execute a policy experiment only in, say, Wisconsin, than to shift national policy. If the state policy fails, much less will have been invested and many fewer people will be affected. Additionally, both positive and negative results come to light much more quickly if fifty states experiment simultaneously than if the national government tries one approach at a time.

Yet even the virtues of experimentation may not be so clearly tied to federalism as such. Astute legislators in a unitary regime can look to innovations by other countries in much the same way that states look to their sister states. Moreover, a unitary state can authorize pilot programs at the local or regional levels. In this regard, some skeptics argue that all the ostensible benefits of federalism can be obtained via policy-by-policy decentralization under a unitary government.[8]

Whether the skeptics are right is a difficult question to answer in the abstract, but one we can put to the side here because of its artificiality. The original Constitution certainly would not have been ratified had it abolished the states. Indeed, even with its protections for the states, it was barely ratified over the objections of Anti-Federalists who thought it already went too far in empowering the national government. Barring a revolution, the United States will retain a federalist government indefinitely, precisely because the founding generation so valued the states as to make the Senate's role all but impossible to change.[9] Thus, the choice in American constitutional cases has never been one of decentralization versus

---

7. New State Ice Co. v. Liebmann, 285 U.S. 262, 311 (1932) (Brandeis, J., dissenting).

8. *See* Edward L. Rubin & Malcolm Feeley, *Federalism: Notes on a National Neurosis*, 41 U.C.L.A. L. Rev. 903 (1994).

9. *See* U.S. Const. art. V ("[N]o Amendment . . . [shall deprive a] state, without its Consent . . . of it's [sic] equal Suffrage in the Senate.").

federalism, but rather a question of how much and what kind of decentralization federalism requires and permits.

To Justice O'Connor's catalogue of federalism's virtues, we should add one that the Founders probably thought most important of all: Federalism serves a libertarian function by limiting the power that accumulates in the hands of any single institution. Here is how *The Federalist Papers* describe the dual operation of federalism and the separation of powers:

> In the compound republic of America, the power surrendered by the people is first divided between two distinct governments, and then the portion allotted to each subdivided among distinct and separate departments. Hence a double security arises to the rights of the people. The different governments will control each other, at the same time that each will be controlled by itself.[10]

The framers' assumption that federalism prevents tyranny has become practically an article of faith in American constitutionalism, although evidence for the proposition is limited. Weimar Germany was a federal republic, and it descended into the worst tyranny in human history. Would Nazism have been stopped had the Weimar *Länder* (states) been more powerful? Was the elimination of a Prussian Social Democratic counterweight to Nazism at the national level the crucial move in securing Hitler's rise?[11] If so, does that fact vindicate or undermine the claim that federalism prevents tyranny? Judges and scholars who claim that federalism prevents tyranny do not typically examine these questions empirically.

In any event, there is one important sense in which federalism risks *fostering* tyranny, at least relative to unitary government. In what was perhaps the most far-sighted work of political science of

---

10. THE FEDERALIST No. 51, at 323 (James Madison) (Clinton Rossiter ed., 1961).

11. *See* Andrzej Rapaczynski, *From Sovereignty to Process: The Jurisprudence of Federalism After Garcia*, 1985 SUP. CT. REV. 341, 389 n. 119.

its day, James Madison's *Federalist No. 10* explained why we are more likely to find the tyranny of the majority in a small republic than in a large one. In a small polity, a single faction—such as farmers desiring easy credit, or a religious sect seeking tax revenues—can come to dominate politics and consistently impose its will on the minority. By contrast, in a large heterogeneous republic, no single interest group should be able to control the levers of power, and thus compromise with other interest groups will be essential. As Madison put it:

> The smaller the society, the fewer probably will be the distinct parties and interests composing it; the fewer the distinct parties and interests, the more frequently will a majority be found of the same party; and the smaller the number of individuals composing a majority, and the smaller the compass within which they are placed, the more easily will they concert and execute their plans of oppression. Extend the sphere and you take in a greater variety of parties and interests; you make it less probable that a majority of the whole will have a common motive to invade the rights of other citizens; or if such a common motive exists, it will be more difficult for all who feel it to discover their own strength and to act in unison with each other.[12]

In Chapter 6, we will explore the limits of this analysis, but for now it suffices to note its accuracy, broadly speaking. If maintaining the states as the federal government's robust rivals for power has, on the whole, preserved liberty by limiting the power of the national government to oppress, that same allocation of power has also empowered state and local majorities to oppress state and local minorities.

We see the dark side of the *Federalist No. 10* dynamic most clearly in the great American struggle for racial equality. Prior to the Civil War, states' rights served as a rallying cry for the preservation

---

12. THE FEDERALIST No. 10, at 83 (James Madison) (Clinton Rossiter ed., 1961).

of slavery. After the Civil War and throughout the civil rights movement of the twentieth century, it was a focal point for the preservation of Jim Crow. Although the federal government was hardly a
paragon of enlightenment during this period, federal policy was
consistently more progressive on race than that of the state
governments that most vociferously insisted on their constitutional
prerogatives. Madison's logic in *Federalist No. 10* suggests that the
historical association between states' rights and oppression of
minorities was not accidental.

Although robust protection for states' rights may generally elevate libertarian values over egalitarian ones, it does not necessarily
elevate conservative values over liberal ones. Consider two twenty-
first-century Supreme Court cases, both presenting conflicts
between liberal/libertarian state policies and conservative federal
ones. In the face of federal prohibitions, California and Oregon
asserted power to legalize medical marijuana and physician-assisted suicide, respectively. The federal marijuana ban prevailed
over California's law,[13] while Oregon's physician-assisted suicide
measure was permitted, albeit on statutory and administrative
grounds, rather than constitutional ones.[14]

State courts can also act as a libertarian counterweight to the
federal government. As the Supreme Court's individual rights jurisprudence grew more conservative in the 1970s and 1980s, the liberal Justice William Brennan called on state courts to interpret their
state constitutions to grant their citizens rights that had been
rejected by the United States Supreme Court under the federal
Constitution.[15] Brennan recognized that in this regard, federalism
can indeed provide a double security for liberty.

This analysis suggests we cannot simply assume that conservatives will favor, and liberals will oppose, states' rights. Indeed, in the

---

13. Gonzales v. Raich, 545 U.S. 1, 32–33 (2005).

14. Gonzales v. Oregon, 546 U.S. 243, 275 (2006).

15. *See* William J. Brennan, Jr., *The Bill of Rights and the States: The Revival of State
Constitutions as Guardians of Individual Rights*, 61 N.Y.U. L. Rev. 535 (1986).

political sphere, it sometimes appears as though preferences with respect to federalism are entirely opportunistic—with politicians and voters favoring the allocation of power to whichever level of government is most likely to produce their favored policy outcomes. That should hardly be surprising. Imagine the attack ads against a member of Congress who votes against the Gun Free School Zones Act and the Violence Against Women Act. He would have real difficulty explaining in a sound bite that he opposes both guns in schools and violence against women, but thinks these issues would be better addressed at the state level. Both of these laws were adopted by near-unanimous votes in both houses of Congress—and both were later struck down by the Supreme Court on federalism grounds.[16]

The apparent unwillingness of Congress to reject popular measures on federalism grounds is powerful evidence that politics alone does not safeguard the Constitution's reservation of some powers to the states. Let us now take a closer look at the courts' efforts to fill the gap.

✄ Limits of Enumerated Powers

We saw in Chapter 3 that in *McCulloch v. Maryland* the Supreme Court afforded Congress considerable scope to legislate pursuant to the powers enumerated in Article I, Section 8.[17] In addition to invoking the interpretive principles discussed above, we note here that the *McCulloch* Court also turned to the so-called "Sweeping Clause," which gives Congress the authority "[t]o make all Laws which shall be necessary and proper for carrying into Execution the [enumerated] Powers [of Congress], and all other Powers vested by

---

16. *See* United States v. Lopez, 514 U.S. 549 (1995); United States v. Morrison, 529 U.S. 598 (2000).

17. 17 U.S. (4 Wheat.) 316 (1819).

th[e] Constitution in the Government of the United States, or in any Department or Officer thereof." Maryland argued that a national bank was not strictly "necessary" for the federal government, but Chief Justice Marshall opined that as used in Article I, necessary means "convenient," not "indispensable."[18] He explained further that the Sweeping Clause's location in Section 8's list of powers, rather than in Section 9's list of limitations on Congress, revealed that it expanded rather than contracted congressional power.[19]

Note, however, that the Court in *McCulloch* did not take the view that it lacked authority even to examine an Act of Congress challenged as beyond the powers enumerated in the Constitution. Marshall accepted, as he would later write in the case of *Gibbons v. Ogden*, that "enumeration presupposes something not enumerated."[20] For much of constitutional history and to this day, the key federalism cases have posed the question of what Congress cannot regulate. Focusing initially on congressional power to regulate interstate commerce, here we examine three lines that the Court has attempted to draw.

Internal versus External Commerce

Article I empowers Congress to "regulate Commerce ... among the several States." In *Gibbons*, the Court asserted, logically enough, that this power does not reach "the exclusively internal commerce of a State."[21] What commerce fits that description? *Gibbons* itself shows the problematic nature of the distinction. At issue were New York State's efforts to grant an exclusive license to conduct steamboat business in the state's waters, in the face of a federal law

---

18. *McCulloch*, 17 U.S. (4 Wheat.) at 35.

19. *Id.* at 38.

20. 22 U.S. (9 Wheat.) 1, 195 (1824); *see also McCulloch*, 17 U.S. (4 Wheat.) at 32.

21. 22 U.S. (9 Wheat.) at 195.

that granted additional licenses. Even the intrastate portions of interstate transactions, the Court held, were part of interstate commerce, and thus regulable by Congress. "Commerce among the States," Marshall wrote, "cannot stop at the external boundary line of each State, but may be introduced into the interior."[22]

Marshall's inference that the Commerce Clause reaches beyond mere border crossings was eminently practical, but it also foretold the demise of "interstateness" as a basis for limiting congressional power. By the middle of the nineteenth century, the second industrial revolution was well on its way to transforming communications and transportation, so much so that today it is difficult to imagine a commercial activity that is not connected to the interstate market.

To be sure, for a brief period the Court did try to revive the intrastate/interstate line by distinguishing manufacturing—which was ostensibly intrastate—from interstate distribution.[23] But the distinction crumbled in the face of economic reality. Coal mined in Pennsylvania and iron ore mined in Minnesota might be shipped by rail to Ohio to be turned into steel, then to Michigan to be incorporated into automobiles, which would then be sold nationally. Whether combined under the umbrella of a vertically integrated corporation or accomplished through market transactions, each stage in this process is part of the same economic chain. Thus under the logic of *Gibbons*, the whole enterprise could be regulated by Congress. Tellingly, even after what some have described as a "federalism revolution" in the Supreme Court,[24] only one Justice, Clarence Thomas, has seriously suggested reviving the distinction between intrastate and interstate commerce.[25]

---

22. *Id.* at 194.

23. *See, e.g.,* Hammer v. Dagenhart, 247 U.S. 251, 272 (1918).

24. *See, e.g.,* Erwin Chemerinsky, *The Federalism Revolution*, 31 N.M. L. REV. 7 (2001).

25. *See, e.g.,* United States v. Lopez, 514 U.S. 549, 584–85, 602 (1995) (Thomas, J., concurring).

Pretext

In *McCulloch*, Chief Justice Marshall suggested another distinction between permissible and impermissible regulation. He indicated that Congress may not, "under the pretext of executing its powers, pass laws for the accomplishment of objects not intrusted to the government."[26] This idea held sway for a time as well, with the Court invalidating laws—such as the one forbidding the interstate transportation of goods manufactured using child labor—that, while taking the form of interstate commercial regulation, in fact aimed at a perceived evil occurring purely intrastate.[27] Yet that line failed as well.

To the extent that the pretext category relied on the intrastate/interstate line, it succumbed to the pressures described above. To the extent that it relied on a motive test, it lacked any justification. Why must Congress, in regulating interstate commerce, be concerned only about commerce per se? Congress enacts laws governing labor, health and safety, the environment, and virtually every other subject it regulates under the commerce power in order to address the ill effects of various commercial activities on people. In doing so, it often relies on values that go beyond such narrowly economic notions as wealth maximization. As the Court explained in upholding the public accommodations provisions of the 1964 Civil Rights Act, "[t]hat Congress was legislating against moral wrongs in many of these areas rendered its enactments no less valid."[28] Given the inevitable normativity of legislation, a pretext test that rules out moral concerns is unworkable.

---

26. McCulloch v. Maryland, 17 U.S. (4 Wheat.) 316, 423 (1819).

27. *Hammer*, 247 U.S. at 271–72 (invalidating Keating-Owen Child Labor Act).

28. Heart of Atlanta Motel, Inc. v. United States, 379 U.S. 241, 257 (1964).

Economic Activity

The distinction that modern Commerce Clause doctrine draws, at least for now, is between "economic" and "noneconomic" activity. Congress may regulate the former but the Court has raised serious questions about the latter, even if the noneconomic activity has interstate commercial effects.[29] Although it has not categorically ruled out congressional regulation of noneconomic activity, it appears to regard such regulation as at least presumptively invalid, noting that "thus far in our Nation's history our cases have upheld Commerce Clause regulation of intrastate activity only where that activity is economic in nature."[30] The Court's cases do not entirely make clear why they settle on this line, except perhaps to say that *some* line is necessary to maintain the distinction between what is enumerated and what is not, and that every other line to have been previously tried had failed.

Will the economic/noneconomic distinction survive? To date, only two Supreme Court cases have used this line to strike down Acts of Congress as beyond the scope of the Commerce Clause. The Court held in 1995 and 2000, respectively, that neither possession of a firearm in the vicinity of a schoolyard[31] nor gender-motivated violence[32] constitutes economic activity. Neither case provided clear guidance about what activities count as economic, although in upholding the application of a federal prohibition on growing marijuana in 2005, the Court invoked Webster's Dictionary to define economic activity as "the production, distribution, and consumption of commodities."[33]

---

29. *See* United States v. Morrison, 529 U.S. 598, 611, 617–19 (2000).
30. *Id.* at 613.
31. *Lopez*, 514 U.S. at 567.
32. *Morrison*, 529 U.S. at 613.
33. Gonzales v. Raich, 545 U.S. 1, 25–26 (2005).

Yet that definition is both under-inclusive and over-inclusive. Surely Congress can and does regulate the provision of services as well as commodities. And if the definition is meant to exclude "noneconomic" activity, it is difficult to understand why mere consumption of commodities should count. As defined in the marijuana case, a woman eating a tomato from her garden is engaged in economic activity, whereas a man babysitting for money is not. These classifications make no sense on their own, much less as an interpretation of the Commerce Clause.

A cynic might be tempted to observe that the author of the foregoing definition of "economic," Justice John Paul Stevens, had earlier voted to uphold the Gun Free School Zones Act and the civil remedy provision of the Violence Against Women Act. Could he have deliberately chosen a wobbly definition so as to undermine the entire enterprise of distinguishing economic from noneconomic activity? Even if so, none of the Justices who favor robust judicial protection for states' rights has yet articulated an alternative definition.

Moreover, it seems extraordinarily unlikely that the Supreme Court will further cut back in any substantial way on the scope of activities that Congress may regulate. For one thing, the Court's own Commerce Clause precedents establish that Congress may, by including a "jurisdictional element" in a statute, convert an otherwise impermissible regulation into a valid law.[34] For example, after the Court invalidated the original Gun Free School Zones Act, Congress amended the statute to provide that the relevant crime now consists in knowing possession of "a firearm that has moved in or that otherwise affects interstate or foreign commerce."[35] With this additional formal requirement, the lower courts have upheld the law.[36]

---

34. *See Lopez*, 541 U.S. at 561–62 (citing United States v. Bass, 404 U.S. 336 (1971)).

35. 18 U.S.C. § 922(q)(2)(A).

36. *See, e.g.*, United States v. Danks, 221 F.3d 1037, 1038–39 (8th Cir. 1999).

Finally, even in those rare instances in which a subject falls outside the scope of the Commerce Clause as understood by the Supreme Court, Congress may still be able to regulate it pursuant to some other enumerated power. First, as discussed in Chapter 9, Congress has the power to pass laws enforcing the Fourteenth Amendment, although since 1997 the Court has narrowed its understanding of that authority in some respects.[37] Additionally, however, Congress's power to spend money remains a potent source of authority. Subject only to the most theoretical limits, Congress can condition the grant of funds to the states on state compliance with federal mandates. Thus, even if we assume that Congress could not, under the Commerce Clause (as influenced by the Twenty-First Amendment) enact a national drinking age, Congress was able to accomplish much the same objective by conditioning federal highway grants to states on their adopting a minimum drinking age of 21.[38]

✷ "Etiquette" Limits on Federal Power

Perhaps because of the Court's difficulties in identifying discrete fields that are beyond the power of Congress to regulate, much federalism doctrine takes the form of what might be called "etiquette" limits on federal power.[39] Instead of finding that the predicate of some federal law falls outside the substantive scope of any congressional power, courts may invalidate a particular law because it operates in an impermissible manner. Such etiquette restrictions often aim to protect states' dignitary interests, although some

---

37. *See, e.g.,* Bd. of Trs. of the Univ. of Ala. v. Garrett, 531 U.S. 356 (2001); Morrison, 529 U.S. at 617–19; City of Boerne v. Flores, 521 U.S. 507 (1997).

38. *See* South Dakota v. Dole, 483 U.S. 203 (1987).

39. *See* Mathew D. Adler & Seth F. Kreimer, *The New Etiquette of Federalism: New York, Printz, and Yeskey,* 1998 SUP. CT. REV. 71.

doctrines also invoke fiscal considerations. Here we take note of four sorts of etiquette restrictions.

Traditional Areas of State Sovereignty

The Supreme Court did not permit the federal government to "directly displace the States' freedom to structure integral operations in areas of traditional governmental functions,"[40] but abandoned the rule after eight years. In the leading case of *National League of Cities v. Usery*, the Court invalidated a federal law extending minimum wage and maximum hour protections to state and local government employees. The Court acknowledged that private sector employees doing the exact same jobs—working for a mass transit system—would be engaged in interstate commerce, and thus regulable by Congress. Nonetheless, the Court held that states (and their subdivisions) as such were immune to federal regulation.

After diligently attempting to apply the distinction between immune and regulable state activities in subsequent cases, the Justices eventually gave up the effort as "unsound in principle and unworkable in practice."[41] Given changes in the economy and social relations, there is no particular reason to privilege "traditional" from new government functions. Moreover, immunity from regulation gave the states an incentive to provide services that, absent the distorting effect of the Supreme Court's rule, might be provided more effectively through the market. Finally, there was the problem of the constitutional text. The enumerated powers themselves—including the Commerce Clause—draw no distinction between commerce in which the state engages versus commerce in which only private

---

40. Nat'l League of Cities v. Usery, 426 U.S. 833, 852 (1976), *overruled by* Garcia v. San Antonio Metro. Transit Auth., 469 U.S. 528 (1985).

41. *Garcia*, 469 U.S. at 531, 546–57.

actors engage. And the Tenth Amendment seems to confirm that federal regulation of the states stands on the same footing as federal regulation of private actors. It only reserves to the states "[t]he powers not delegated to the United States." Thus, if a power is delegated by the Commerce Clause (or another provision), it cannot be reserved to the states by the Tenth Amendment.

Commandeering

Nonetheless, the Justices in the majority in *National League of Cities* were right, were they not, to worry about Congress reaching too deeply into the administration of state government? The system of federalism assumes, after all, that states will function as at least quasi-sovereign entities. Suppose the federal government were, under the guise of regulating interstate commerce, to tell a state where to locate its capital, or what laws to pass? As to the former question, even in overruling *National League of Cities*, the Court left open the possibility that it might invalidate such an extreme directive, though it also suggested that this was an impractical worry.[42] As to the latter question, a more recent line of cases in fact forbids Congress from "commandeering" state legislative and executive powers.[43]

Like the now-discarded doctrine of *National League of Cities*, the cases that prohibit Congress from directing states to pass laws or to enforce federal laws rest on an uncomfortable textual foundation. Indeed, the Court acknowledged that "there is no constitutional text speaking to" the commandeering question,[44] although only after rejecting what may be the strongest textual basis for the

---

42. *See id.* at 556 (citing Coyle v. Oklahoma, 221 U.S. 559 (1911)).

43. *See* Printz v. United States, 521 U.S. 898 (1997); New York v. United States, 505 U.S. 144 (1992).

44. *Printz*, 521 U.S. at 905.

rule: the provision of Article IV guaranteeing each state a republican form of government. An order from Congress to a state legislature to pass a law, thus rendering the state legislature a mere puppet, hardly seems consistent with state self-government. Nevertheless, in *New York v. United States*, the majority rejected the Guarantee Clause challenge because the federal law at issue left the state legislature with sufficient control over its own agenda to qualify as a republican form of government.[45]

The Justices have accordingly sought support for their prohibition on commandeering "in historical understanding and practice, in the structure of the Constitution, and in" their own cases.[46] Whether the Court has correctly read those sources is contestable, as evidenced by the 5–4 margins in the two relevant cases. As Justice Breyer argued in his dissent in *Printz v. United States*, it is hardly clear that a rule barring commandeering enhances rather than diminishes the power of the states. If Congress cannot direct the states to enforce federal law, then it must create a federal bureaucracy to do the job, and states will lose the ability to shape the law's execution.

Even if the anti-commandeering rule can be justified in principle, the ease with which it can be circumvented limits its practical effect. Congress may not order a state legislature to enact a law or a state executive to enforce one, but it can offer federal funds to states on the condition that they take such actions. To be sure, "bribing" state governments to achieve national ends requires that Congress offer a sufficiently large inducement, so fiscal constraints may limit the ability of Congress to evade the anti-commandeering rule via the spending power.

However, Congress can also direct state policy through "conditional preemption," which requires Congress to allocate no money

45. 505 U.S. at 185–86.

46. *Printz*, 521 U.S. at 905.

at all.[47] Suppose, for example, that Congress wants state officials to enforce federal drug laws. It could not directly require them to do so without running afoul of the anti-commandeering principle. Nonetheless, the Court's cases suggest that Congress could instead pass a law preempting the drug laws of any state that refuses to enforce the federal drug laws. So long as the forbidden state regulation falls within the extremely broad category of interstate commerce (or within some other enumerated power), Congress may preempt—that is, forbid—state regulation. The only apparent limit on congressional ability to circumvent the anti-commandeering principle via conditional preemption is the willingness of a state, to its own detriment, to call Congress's bluff.

The ease with which Congress can evade the anti-commandeering principle has led some commentators to call for tighter restrictions on the spending power and conditional preemption, but these restrictions would themselves raise hard questions. For instance, one proposal would limit Congress to attaching conditions to funds that "reimburse" states for the costs of participating in federal programs, rather than attaching collateral conditions to the receipt of federal funds in the first instance.[48] That is attractive in principle, but in practice the distinction may be impossible to maintain, because money is fungible. Congress may legitimately worry that its efforts to fund one state project free up state funds for other projects Congress does not want to subsidize. Nor is it entirely clear that the courts could fashion and enforce a doctrine that distinguished between permissible and impermissible conditional preemption without passing judgment on the underlying congressional policy decisions. Accordingly, the anti-commandeering rule for now remains a largely symbolic limit.

---

47. *See, e.g., New York*, 505 U.S. at 167; Hodel v. Va. Surface Mining & Reclamation Ass'n, 452 U.S. 264, 288 (1981).

48. Lynn A. Baker, *Conditional Federal Spending After* Lopez, 95 COLUM. L. REV. 1911 (1995).

Sovereign Immunity

Article III of the original Constitution permitted federal courts to hear "controversies . . . between a State and Citizens of another State." In the 1793 case of *Chisholm v. Georgia*, the Supreme Court took the text at face value, holding that this provision permitted a federal court to hear a suit by South Carolina citizen against the state of Georgia for money owed.[49] The decision was widely unpopular, and the Eleventh Amendment was quickly proposed and ratified to displace *Chisholm's* rule. Its text forbids only federal court suits "commenced or prosecuted against one of the United States by Citizens of another State, or ... Foreign State," but the Amendment has been interpreted to stand for a much broader principle—namely that the states enjoy immunity from private lawsuits for money damages unless they have given their consent to be sued.[50] Thus, a provision that by its terms only controls lawsuits in *federal* courts by citizens of *other* states has also become a source of the judge-made rule barring damages actions in *federal or state* court by the state's *own* citizens.

We say "a" source rather than "the" source because the Supreme Court's cases describe state sovereign immunity as a tacit principle of the constitutional structure as a whole, including both the Tenth and Eleventh Amendments. But while that move perhaps plugs a hole in the Eleventh Amendment's text, it hardly explains why immunity from unconsented lawsuits is the sort of hallmark of sovereignty that the Union's federal design must have preserved. Critics of the sovereign immunity doctrine, including dissenting Justices, object that it originates in the principle that the King, being the source of the law, cannot violate the law, and that this notion has no place in a republican system of government.[51]

---

49. 2 U.S. (2 Dall.) 419 (1793).

50. *See* Alden v. Maine, 527 U.S. 706, 712 (1999).

51. *See, e.g., id.* at 801–03 (Souter, J., dissenting); Seminole Tribe of Fla. v. Florida, 517 U.S. 44, 103 n.2 (1996) (Souter, J., dissenting).

The Court's cases do not offer much of a normative justification for state sovereign immunity, typically asserting that the doctrine was assumed when the Constitution was adopted (or at least when the Eleventh Amendment was ratified) and thus is simply part of the bargain struck at the Founding. Academic defenders of the doctrine have noted, however, that it does serve at least one salutary purpose: Under a longstanding exception, private parties may sue state officers to enjoin future violations of law,[52] and, it has been argued, current doctrine thereby channels litigation toward fixing ongoing problems rather than providing compensation for completed wrongs.[53] At least some would argue that this is a desirable allocation of judicial resources and state expenditures. Yet whatever the merits of that particular argument, it would be difficult to imagine a persuasive normative case for the Supreme Court's sovereign immunity doctrine as a whole, which includes a remarkable array of exceptions and exceptions to the exceptions.

In any event, we group sovereign immunity doctrine under the heading of etiquette rules because it does not formally limit the substance of what Congress may do.

For example, Congress can require states to respect private copyrights. It can authorize public and private prospective enforcement of those private copyrights. It can authorize the imposition of civil fines or other monetary remedies in enforcement actions against the state by the federal government. It can authorize copyright damages actions against local officials whose authority ultimately comes from state law. It cannot, however, authorize private suits for money damages against unconsenting states themselves. Perhaps any of these individual rules could be defended on functional grounds, but taken together it is not clear that they advance any substantively meaningful set of values.

---

52. *Ex parte* Young, 209 U.S. 123 (1908).

53. *See* John C. Jeffries, *The Right-Remedy Gap in Constitutional Law*, 109 YALE L.J. 87, 90, 105–10 (1999).

Clear Statement Rules

The final federalism-based etiquette rule we will consider is the requirement that when Congress passes legislation that goes to the edge of its substantive powers relative to the states (or that simply implicates important state interests), it must do so clearly.[54] In this context and elsewhere, a judicially imposed clear statement rule has two main functions. First, it has an evidentiary cast. If the political safeguards of federalism are working well, then Congress will not want to push its power to the limit, and a rule construing vague language as preserving state prerogatives would therefore better capture congressional intent than would a neutral approach. And even if statutory interpretation pursuant to a clear statement rule does not at first reflect the true intent of Congress, over time it will, as members of Congress and their staff learn to be clear if they want to shift power away from the states.

Second, a clear statement rule has a substantive bias. A presumption against the exercise of federal power places the burden of overcoming legislative inertia on those favoring federal regulation. Thus, at least in principle, clear statement rules combine the best aspects of the two polar views we have been exploring: The Court neither abdicates its responsibility to enforce federalism norms, nor prevents Congress from fully employing its powers when it truly wishes to do so.

Nonetheless, the Court has adopted clear statement rules in only some federalism-related contexts, and their actual effect on ultimate outcomes is far from certain. Here as in so many areas of the Court's federalism jurisprudence, the doctrine seems at once noble and Sisyphean: Even as the Court accepts (however grudgingly) that the balance of power has shifted dramatically from the states to Congress since the Founding, a majority of Justices

---

54. *See* Gregory v. Ashcroft, 501 U.S. 452, 464 (1991).

continue to look for ways to pay symbolic homage to the principle of dual sovereignty.

✹ Federalism-Based Limits on the States

The most contentious federalism questions on the Supreme Court docket concern the allocation of powers between the national government, on one hand, and the states, on the other. Thus far, we have seen how these issues of "vertical" federalism have led the Justices to announce a variety of largely ineffectual doctrines for cabining federal power. The Constitution also speaks to the allocation of power *among* the states, and such "horizontal" federalism has been quite successful. For the most part, states do not engage in trade wars with one another.

Part of the credit belongs to the Court. Since relatively early in the nation's history, the Justices have recognized a *negative*, or *dormant*, aspect to the Commerce Clause:[55] Even absent a statute enacted by Congress, some matters are beyond the power of the states to regulate (unless authorized to do so by Congress), because they fall in a zone presumptively reserved for national legislation. The so-called Dormant Commerce Clause is an awkward textual inference. Article I, Section 8 confers powers on Congress, rather than expressly limiting the states. Nonetheless, the modern interpretation of the Dormant Commerce Clause is true to the general spirit of American federalism. It principally forbids states from enacting laws that discriminate against out-of-state goods and services. Likewise, a variety of doctrines implementing Article IV and the Fourteenth Amendment further limit the states' ability to draw distinctions based on state citizenship.[56]

---

55. *See, e.g.,* Cooley v. Bd. of Wardens, 53 U.S. (12 How.) 299 (1851).

56. *See, e.g.,* Saenz v. Roe, 526 U.S. 489 (1999); Hicklin v. Orbeck, 437 U.S. 518 (1978).

The Court's willingness to protect the ability of Idaho potato farmers to compete fairly even in other potato-producing states partly explains the successful integration and specialization of the American economy. However, the Court does not deserve all of the credit, for nothing in dormant Commerce Clause doctrine or any other judicially enforceable doctrine forbids states from providing discriminatory subsidies to their own industries.[57] Although states do promote their own industries through tourism advertising, infrastructure development, and other means, we rarely see anything like the subsidies that are deployed in international trade wars. Governors and state legislators simply do not see the advantage in treating their sister states as rival mercantile powers in the way that national political figures sometimes do. Although we cannot quantify the effect with any precision, we would guess that a shared commitment to the principles of Union contained in the Constitution deserves considerable credit for this success.

✍ Further Reading

Mathew D. Adler & Seth F. Kreimer, *The New Etiquette of Federalism*: New York, Printz, *and* Yeskey, 1998 SUP. CT. REV. 71.
Michael C. Dorf, *Instrumental and Non-Instrumental Federalism*, 28 RUTGERS L.J. 825 (1997).
Lawrence Lessig, *Translating Federalism*: United States v. Lopez, 1995 SUP. CT. REV. 125.
Edward L. Rubin & Malcolm Feeley, *Federalism: Notes on a National Neurosis*, 41 U.C.L.A. L. REV. 903 (1994).
David L. SHAPIRO, FEDERALISM: A DIALOGUE (1995).
Herbert Wechsler, *The Political Safeguards of Federalism: The Role of the States in the Composition and Selection of the National Government*, 54 COLUM. L. REV. 543 (1954).

---

57. *See* West Lynn Creamery, Inc. v. Healy, 512 U.S. 186, 199 (1994).

FIVE

Separation of Powers

THE BASIC CONCEPT OF SEPARATION of powers is familiar to most high school civics students: The Constitution controls the exercise of governmental power by dividing it across three distinct departments—the legislature, the executive, and the judiciary. As James Madison famously put it, this division reflects the framers' view that "[t]he accumulation of all powers, legislative, executive, and judiciary, in the same hands, whether of one, a few, or many, and whether hereditary, self-appointed, or elective, may justly be pronounced the very definition of tyranny."[1] But the separation of powers does not mean their complete isolation from one another. To the contrary, the complement to separated power is the idea of checks and balances, in which governmental powers are not just separated but also offsetting. In short, the Constitution both disperses the functions and powers of the federal government and provides each branch with the ability and inclination to constrain the others.

The framers did not conceive of a compound government with separated functions out of nothing. Early articulations of kindred ideas may be found in the work of classical thinkers like Aristotle, Polybius, and Cicero. More immediately, the tumult of the seventeenth century in England—finally culminating in the establishment of parliamentary supremacy after the Glorious Revolution—provided the backdrop for the two works on political theory most familiar to the framers of the United States Constitution,

---

1. THE FEDERALIST No. 47, at 301 (James Madison) (Clinton Rossiter ed., 1961).

John Locke's *Two Treatises of Government*[2] and the Baron de Montesquieu's *The Spirit of the Laws.*[3] Both writers advocated forms of disaggregated government, Locke stressing in particular the need for an independent judiciary and Montesquieu, though French, championing what he understood to be the English system as the standard against which modern governments should be measured. More than anyone before him, Montesquieu stressed the need to disaggregate government's three basic tasks—"that of enacting laws, that of executing the public resolutions, and of trying the causes of individuals."[4]

Historical pedigree aside, however, by themselves these twin concepts—separation of powers and checks and balances—are little more than slogans. Merely embracing the separation of powers does not enable one to locate the outer boundaries of each branch's authority in closely contested cases, nor does it provide a metric for sorting all possible government functions into one branch or another. Similarly, the idea of checks and balances does not itself specify what a proper balance would entail in any concrete sense, nor does it provide a means of telling whether particular checks are functioning as they should. Some commentators have therefore argued that these two concepts are insusceptible of principled application, and that separation of powers law should instead be organized around other considerations.[5]

We do not go that far. We do agree, however, that whatever work these concepts do depends ultimately on the specific institutional arrangements they are thought to endorse or prohibit. And we agree that the general terms "separation of powers" and "checks and

---

2. JOHN LOCKE, TWO TREATISES OF GOVERNMENT (Peter Laslett ed., Cambridge Univ. Press 1988) (1690).

3. CHARLES DE SECONDAT, BARON DE MONTESQUIEU, THE SPIRIT OF THE LAWS (Anne M. Cohler et al. eds. & trans., Cambridge Univ. Press 1989) (1748).

4. *Id.* bk. XI, ch. 6, at 157.

5. *See, e.g.,* M. Elizabeth Magill, *Beyond Powers and Branches in Separation of Powers Law,* 150 U. PA. L. REV. 603 (2001).

balances" do not, by themselves, dictate any particular arrangements in hard cases. Still, judicial precedents and the established practices of the political branches have embraced certain approaches to these overarching concepts.

For example, one significant fault line, between "formalism" and "functionalism," maps fairly well to the twin ideas of separation and balancing—formalists stress the need to keep the branches separate lest one intrude unduly on the prerogatives of another; functionalists stress the importance of overall balance in our constitutional structure, and the need for each branch to be in a position to check the others.

The functionalist account, moreover, has spawned perhaps the most influential approach to the questions of executive power that are at the heart of separation of powers doctrine. According to that approach, the system of checks and balances is furthered by viewing the executive and legislative powers as overlapping in important respects, with courts best advancing those checks by deferring more to the executive when it acts pursuant to congressional authorization, and less when it contravenes congressional prohibitions. Underlying this framework is a particular conception of how the system of checks and balances should work.

So although we agree that the general concepts of powers and balances are of limited practical utility by themselves, we do think it is possible to identify certain themes in the way these concepts have been deployed over time. This chapter explores those themes. As an introduction to that discussion, we examine the benefits that are meant to flow from our system of separated powers.

𝍖 The Function of Separation of Powers

The basic function of the separation of powers and its complement, checks and balances, can be understood in at least two ways: as preservation of individual liberty, and as protection against arbitrary inequality in government. But how, exactly, are these ends supposed to be achieved?

It is easy enough to see how an expansive vision of overall government power could come at the price of individual liberty: Broader government power means the government may interpose itself in more areas of people's lives. Thus, at least insofar as liberty is understood in negative terms—that is, freedom *from* certain kinds of government intrusions—increases in overall government power may bring decreases in liberty. By itself, however, the idea of separation of powers does not entail any particular commitment to the overall extent of government authority. At least in theory, a government of divided power might be quite authoritarian in the aggregate, while a government of unified power might be quite modest in overall scope. How, then, is the idea of separated power meant to preserve liberty? Additionally, how can it protect against the arbitrariness entailed in, for example, government action that unduly imposes or exacerbates political, social, or other inequalities?

There are at least two answers. First, dividing government power can constrain the production of law. In the American context, this is perhaps most evident in the various "veto gates" the Constitution establishes in the process for making federal statutes. In order to become a law, a bill must pass both houses of Congress and then be signed by the President. If any one of those institutions withholds its support, the bill generally dies. The only exception is that if the President vetoes a bill, it returns to Congress and can only become law if two-thirds of each house re-passes it. The veto-override provision is thus explicitly supermajoritarian. Yet in a sense, bicameralism and presentment function like supermajoritarian requirements even in the absence of the veto-override. Because the House, Senate, and Presidency are structured so dissimilarly, and because the constituencies for each are so different, political scientists have observed that the effect of requiring the assent of all three institutions is akin to requiring a supermajority in a unicameral system.[6]

---

6. *See* JAMES M. BUCHANAN & GORDON TULLOCK, THE CALCULUS OF CONSENT 234–36 (1962); William H. Riker, *The Merits of Bicameralism*, 12 INT'L REV. L. & ECON. 166, 167–68 (1992).

Moreover, in addition to the constitutionally specified requirements of bicameralism and presentment, internal House and Senate rules (passed pursuant to a constitutional grant of power to each House to "determine the Rules of its Proceedings") give committees and subcommittees the ability to delay or even kill proposed legislation without there ever being a full vote. These arrangements multiply the number of effective veto gates in the legislative process— multiply, that is, the number of places where a bill can be defeated even when a majority of legislators support it.

The overarching point here is that by giving multiple actors a hand in the lawmaking process, the Constitution makes it more difficult to enact federal law. And that constraint enhances individual liberty—at least from a libertarian point of view, which generally treats the expansion of government itself as an encroachment upon freedom. This idea is complementary to the liberty protections entailed in the theory of enumerated and therefore limited federal power. Whereas the latter is supposed to safeguard liberty by limiting the substantive scope of federal legislation, the former does the same by erecting procedural obstacles to the production of legislation within those substantive areas.

This same feature can also be seen as protecting against substantively arbitrary or inequitable government. Simply put, the supermajoritarian constraints on federal lawmaking make it harder not just to enact federal laws in general, but also to enact unjust, arbitrary, or inequitable laws in particular. At least in theory, each veto gate in the federal legislative process can function as a check against arbitrariness; by increasing the number of actors that must separately concur in the legislation before it becomes operative, the constitutional structure increases the number of actors that must become captured (or at least distracted) before arbitrary, partial, or otherwise inequitable measures can become law.

Yet there are important potential downsides to the Constitution's constraints on federal lawmaking, downsides that the libertarian point of view in particular tends to overlook. Without attempting to boil all libertarianism down into a single sentence, it is fair to say that it often evaluates exercises of government power against an implied alternative of either no or minimal government. That is, libertarianism frequently treats the very exercise of government power as an increase in the size of the state and thus a step away from the libertarian ideal of minimal government. From this perspective, any constraint on the lawmaking process looks like an unalloyed good. But the actual status quo is pervasive, not minimal, law—at least some of which may well be oppressive, inequitable, or otherwise odious. Our point is really the obverse of the one we made in the preceding paragraph. There, we said that the constitutional constraints on the lawmaking process make it harder to enact oppressive law. The other side of that coin is that to the extent the law *now in effect* is oppressive, those same constraints make it more difficult to change the law for the better. The separation of powers, in other words, entrenches the status quo, *whatever it is*. This is not to deny the potential value in the Constitution's constraints on the production of federal law, but it is to say that any concrete assessment of that value requires attention to the actual state of the law at the relevant point in time.

There is a second way that the separation of powers is meant to promote liberty and guard against arbitrariness, distinct from its constraints on lawmaking. This benefit is captured in Madison's injunction that "[a]mbition must be made to counteract ambition."[7] Proceeding from Montesquieu's premise that "[t]he accumulation of all powers . . . in the same hands . . . [is] the very definition of tyranny,"[8] Madison urged that "the great security against a gradual concentration of the several powers in the same department consists in giving to those who administer each department the necessary constitutional means and personal motives to resist encroachments of the others."[9] In the first part of his argument,

---

7. THE FEDERALIST NO. 51 (James Madison), *supra* note 1, at 322.

8. THE FEDERALIST NO. 47 (James Madison), *supra* note 1, at 301.

9. THE FEDERALIST NO. 51 (James Madison), *supra* note 1, at 321–22.

Madison thus claimed that if the same person or entity wields the authority to make, enforce, and adjudicate the law, the concentration of power will tend towards tyranny. But how, exactly? In part, the answer is that procedural safeguards like bicameralism and presentment will lose their bite. The government-constraining effects of multiple veto gates lose their effectiveness if the veto-wielding entity is the same at every step. Put another way, the concentration of all aspects of governmental power can lead to a gradual expansion of the government (and law) itself. Another part of the concern is that the harm flowing from an excess of ambition among those in government will spread far and wide. In a government where the legislative, executive, and judicial functions are all concentrated in the same hands, the private ambitions—as well as biases, ignorance, and even ineptness—of those hands will be undiluted. All the powers given over to the government can become the instruments for the pursuit of a single private agenda, thus increasing the risk of arbitrariness, partiality, and inequity in government.

In response to these concerns, Madison conceived of the separation of powers not as eliminating politicians' and other government officials' private ambitions, but as using those ambitions to check one another. The levers of power would be arranged so that the self-interest of each branch's members would align with the protection of that branch's institutional prerogatives. Legislative, executive, and judicial officials would thus have the private motivation to protect their respective branches from the encroachments of the other two, preventing those branches from consolidating power. In this way, "the private interest of every individual [would] be a sentinel over the public rights."[10]

Madison's vision of the separation of powers, and in particular his idea of ambition checking ambition, remains hugely influential today. Yet there are reasons to question it. As Daryl Levinson and Richard Pildes have pointed out, Madison's theory omits a critical

---

10. *Id.* at 322.

institution that has come to dominate many aspects of modern politics and government: national political parties.[11] The framers generally despised political parties. And more than that, they simply did not anticipate the nature of the democratic contestation that would develop within the electoral system prescribed by the Constitution. Yet very early in the history of the Union, the dominant determinant of political cooperation and competition became not the particular branch of government in which an official served, but the political party of which he was a member. Personal ambition was aligned not with the institutional prerogatives of the branch but with the electoral fortunes of the party.

The Madisonian idea of ambition checking ambition may work very differently in a world where principal loyalties are to party rather than to branch. This is especially true in times of "unified government," when Congress and the White House are both controlled by the same party. As the effective head of his party, the President is typically in a position to exert great influence over the legislative agenda of his fellow party members in Congress. This obviously has greatest consequence when those fellow members are in the majority. Far from being driven by personal ambition to assert congressional prerogatives and interests against the executive, members of the House and Senate majorities are more likely to view party loyalty as crucial to their own career success, and to understand such loyalty to consist in pursuing the policy objectives of their party leader, the President. Of course, the extent of a President's influence over his fellow party members in Congress will vary with his own popularity, the time remaining in his administration, and variations in local electoral preferences. But in the main, party discipline tends to minimize inter-branch contestation in times of unified government.

In contrast, something closer to the Madisonian vision is more likely to obtain during periods of "divided government," when the

---

11. *See* Daryl J. Levinson & Richard H. Pildes, *Separation of Parties, Not Powers,* 119 HARV. L. REV. 2312, 2313 (2006).

White House is controlled by one party and one or both of the legislative chambers is controlled by the other. (We say "the other," not "another," because in practice American politics has long been a two-party affair.) When party rivalry can be expressed via legislative checking of the executive and vice versa, those checks are more likely to be utilized. Yet there are reasons to doubt the efficacy of Madison's theory even in periods of divided government. For one thing, internal Senate rules make it possible for the minority party to hold up legislation and other business via a filibuster, which can only be broken if three-fifths of those present vote to invoke cloture (which is to say, limit debate and ensure that an up-or-down vote is held on the matter). Assuming perfect party discipline on the issue, this means that the majority needs to occupy at least 60 seats—a hard-to-achieve supermajority—in order to overcome an obstructionist minority attempting to shield the President from debilitating congressional legislation. Even in divided government, then, Madisonian checks are difficult to implement. (Of course, the filibuster cuts the other way during periods of unified government, by enabling the congressional minority to frustrate legislative initiatives favored by both the President and the majority. In this way, the filibuster creates some checking opportunities during periods of unified government just as it blunts them in periods of divided government.) In any event, our principal point here is that in modern American politics, the extent to which formal inter-branch checks operate as Madison envisaged often depends on something he appears not to have anticipated: party alignment.

This reality notwithstanding, much separation of powers law continues to operate in the Madisonian paradigm. The formal, judge-articulated doctrine is very often premised on the idea that institutional rivalry among the branches—especially between the executive and legislature—is the core mechanism through which the Constitution's horizontal structural commitments are realized. Thus, judicial doctrine often seeks ways to facilitate that inter-branch checking and then to defer to the arrangements that result. Some, including Levinson and Pildes, argue that this is fundamentally misguided. Achieving the basic aims of the separation of powers, they argue, requires supplementing the Madisonian vision with "an understanding of the actual mechanisms of political competition."[12] For example, they call for the adoption of measures that would encourage divided government, that would grant certain "opposition rights" to the legislative minority party in times of unified government, and that would insulate the unelected administrative bureaucracy from partisan pressure.[13] These and other proposals raise fascinating questions of institutional design and democratic theory, but so far they remain only proposals—with relatively little chance of implementation. Thus, we will not dwell on them here. Instead, the balance of this chapter examines the dominant themes in separation of powers doctrine as it exists today.

※ Selected Themes in Separation of Powers Doctrine

Separation of powers law addresses the distribution of authority across, and the relationships among, the three branches. Any given separation of powers issue, however, tends to focus on one branch in particular. Our discussion of these themes in separation of powers law is thus organized around the three branches themselves. We first discuss presidential power, then move to questions of the aggrandizement or delegation of legislative power, and finally take up the judiciary's articulation of its own role in the three-branch system.

The Executive

Many issues falling under the separation of powers rubric focus on the scope of the authority constitutionally granted to the President,

---

12. *Id.* at 2385.

13. *Id.* at 2368–79.

and its relationship to the potentially overlapping power of Congress to legislate in the same areas.

The principal sources of executive power within Article II are all rather open-ended as a textual matter. The Vesting Clause provides that "[t]he executive Power shall be vested in a President of the United States of America." When contrasted with the first clause of Article I, which provides that "[a]ll legislative Powers *herein granted* shall be vested in a Congress of the United States," the Article II version seems to suggest that "the executive Power" has a content of its own, apart from the specific responsibilities mentioned elsewhere in Article II. Yet the precise nature of that power is nowhere specified in the Constitution. Similarly, although Article II makes the President "Commander in Chief of the Army and Navy," Article I grants to Congress the power "to declare War," "[t]o raise and support Armies," "[t]o provide and maintain a Navy," and "[t]o make Rules for the Government and Regulation of the land and naval Forces." Again, nothing in the text of the Constitution specifies the precise content or boundaries of these powers, nor does its language determine the relationship between presidential and congressional authority over military matters. Reflecting on this sort of textual uncertainty, Justice Robert Jackson famously lamented that "[j]ust what our forefathers did envision, or would have envisioned had they foreseen modern conditions, must be divined from materials almost as enigmatic as the dreams Joseph was called upon to interpret for Pharaoh."[14]

Judicial precedent is also rather sparse. To quote Justice Jackson again, "[a] judge . . . may be surprised at the poverty of really useful and unambiguous authority applicable to concrete problems of executive power as they actually present themselves."[15] In part, this is a consequence of the fact that many constitutional conflicts between the executive and legislative branches are unlikely to

---

14. Youngstown Sheet & Tube Co. v. Sawyer, 343 U.S. 579, 634 (1952) (Jackson, J., concurring).

15. *Id.*

produce judicially cognizable cases. Especially in areas touching upon foreign affairs and military power, the Article III limits of jurisdiction and justiciability (which we discuss briefly later in this chapter) and the courts' overarching disinclination to insert themselves into such matters combine to produce a real paucity of on-point judicial precedents. Perhaps more than in any other area of constitutional law, then, established patterns and practices by the executive and legislative branches provide much of the substance of the law in this area.

For example, although from the text of the Constitution one might think that a formal congressional declaration of war is required before the President may send the military into hostilities, long-established practice suggests otherwise. Congress has often passed measures taking the form of "authorizations for the use of force" instead,[16] and today there is no serious argument that such instruments are insufficient to provide whatever legislative authorization the President requires to use military force. This is just one illustration of the more general view that, in the words of Justice Felix Frankfurter, "[i]t is an inadmissibly narrow conception of American constitutional law to confine it to the words of the Constitution and to disregard the gloss which life has written upon them."[17]

But to say the judicial precedents on the scope of executive power are sparse is not to say they are nonexistent. Though relatively few in number, some of the Supreme Court's cases in this area exert a powerful influence beyond their precise terms, shaping our understanding of the separation of powers more broadly, and in particular of the relation between the executive and the legislative branches. Undoubtedly the most significant of these is

---

16. *See, e.g.,* Authorization for Use of Military Force, Pub. L. No. 107-40, 115 Stat. 224 (2001); The Joint Resolution to Promote the Maintenance of International Peace and Security in Southeast Asia (Gulf of Tonkin Resolution), Pub. L. No. 88-408, 78 Stat. 384 (1964) (repealed 1971).

17. *Youngstown,* 343 U.S. at 610 (Frankfurter, J., concurring).

Youngstown Sheet & Tube Company v. Sawyer,[18] the so-called *Steel Seizure Case*. The case involved a challenge to President Truman's order directing the Secretary of Commerce to take control of the nation's major steel mills to avert a nation-wide steelworker strike. The events took place during the Korean War, and Truman defended his order on the ground that the strike would have held up vital war supplies and thus jeopardized national security. The Supreme Court, however, held the seizure unlawful. Writing for the majority, Justice Black employed a formal approach to the issue. Stating that "[t]he President's power, if any, to issue the order must stem either from an act of Congress or from the Constitution itself," Black first noted that no statute authorized the order.[19] Turning next to the Constitution, he rejected the idea that Article II anywhere granted the President the power because, at bottom, the decision to seize the mills is "a job for the Nation's lawmakers, not for its military authorities."[20] Instead of "direct[ing] that a congressional policy be executed in a manner prescribed by Congress," Truman's order "directs that a presidential policy be executed in a manner prescribed by the President."[21] It was thus a fundamentally legislative act, and for the President to undertake it on his own was for him to arrogate to himself a power belonging to Congress.

Although Justice Black wrote the majority opinion in the case, a concurring opinion by Justice Jackson has become far more influential over time and has since been repeatedly embraced by Court majorities.[22] Unlike Justice Black's opinion, which viewed the decision to seize the mills as categorically legislative and thus beyond

---

18. 343 U.S. 579 (1952).

19. *Id.* at 585.

20. *Id.* at 587.

21. *Id.* at 588.

22. *See, e.g.,* Medellin v. Texas, 128 S.Ct. 1346, 1368–71 (2008); Mistretta v. United States, 488 U.S. 361, 381, 386, 408 (1989); Dames & Moore v. Regan, 453 U.S. 654, 668–69 (1981).

the bounds of Article II, Justice Jackson's approach was more functional, stressing not the boundaries of the three branches but the overlapping and checking role that each plays with respect to the others. With respect to executive power, his key insight was simple: "Presidential powers are not fixed but fluctuate, depending upon their disjunction or conjunction with those of Congress."[23]

To elaborate that insight, Jackson articulated his now-famous three-tiered scheme of presidential power. First, "[w]hen the President acts pursuant to an express or implied authorization of Congress, his authority is at its maximum, for it includes all that he possesses in his own right plus all that Congress can delegate."[24] In such circumstances, if the President's action is held unconstitutional, "it usually means that the Federal Government as an undivided whole lacks power."[25] That is, the principal remaining constitutional constraints in such cases are the Constitution's individual rights provisions, which preclude certain kinds of government action altogether, whether undertaken by the executive on its own or in concert with the legislature. (Note, though, that Jackson in the above-quoted passage said "usually," not "always." We take his hedge to be a reference to the "non-delegation doctrine," which we discuss at greater length in the next section on legislative power.)

Moreover, it may be possible to read Justice Jackson's description of this first tier to suggest that, at least in times of heightened national security concern—as in *Youngstown* itself—the Constitution's individual rights-based constraints apply less stringently when the executive acts with legislative authorization. Had the seizure order at issue in *Youngstown* been issued pursuant to an act of Congress, Jackson stated that it "would [have] be[en] supported by the strongest presumptions and the widest latitude of judicial interpretation, and the burden of persuasion would rest

---

23. *Youngstown*, 343 U.S. at 635 (Jackson, J., concurring).

24. *Id.*

25. *Id.* at 636–37.

heavily upon any who might attack it."²⁶ In this, Jackson may have been suggesting that in times of national distress or emergency, the courts will be especially reluctant to invalidate government action in the name of individual rights, provided the action is a product of cooperation between the political branches. That, in fact, is how the Supreme Court has often proceeded in times of national crisis—neither endorsing broad theories of unilateral executive power directly under Article II of the Constitution nor taking government actions off the table as categorically violative of individual rights guarantees, but substantially deferring to executive action taken pursuant to congressional authorization.²⁷ This approach creates an incentive, of course, for the executive to seek congressional input and agreement before it acts.

In contrast to cases of congressional authorization, the bottom tier of Jackson's framework encompasses presidential actions that are "incompatible with the expressed or implied will of Congress."²⁸ In those circumstances, the President's "power is at its lowest ebb, for then he can rely only upon his own constitutional powers minus any constitutional powers of Congress over the matter."²⁹ The only way for a court to uphold executive action of this sort is to "disabl[e] the Congress from acting upon the subject. Presidential claim to a power at once so conclusive and preclusive must be scrutinized with caution, for what is at stake is the equilibrium established by our constitutional system."³⁰

Jackson's framework does not specify precisely what matters the Constitution commits exclusively to the President and thus

---

26. *Id.* at 637.

27. *See generally* Samuel Issacharoff & Richard H. Pildes, *Between Civil Libertarianism and Executive Unilateralism: An Institutional Process Approach to Rights During Wartime*, 5 THEORETICAL INQUIRIES L. 1, 5, 9–30 (2004).

28. *Youngstown,* 343 U.S. at 637 (Jackson, J., concurring).

29. *Id.*

30. *Id.* at 637–38 (internal citation omitted).

insulates from congressional regulation. However, a number of the Court's cases before and after *Youngstown* have identified foreign affairs as an area in which the President is, in at least some respects, the nation's "sole organ."[31] The textual basis for this conclusion is hardly dispositive. As we noted above, Article II's Vesting Clause does not define "the executive Power," nor does it establish which, if any, of those powers are regulable by Congress. Instead, the argument in favor of presidential primacy has been more pragmatic and functional: To be effective, the nation must speak with only one voice in diplomacy and other matters of foreign affairs; compared to Congress, the executive has greater expertise, flexibility, ability to keep secrets, and capacity to act quickly as needed in such matters; thus, the President must be granted at least some measure of exclusive authority in foreign affairs. On this reasoning, Congress lacks the power to tell the President to recognize or not to recognize a particular foreign regime, or to tell him which members of a foreign government he may negotiate with, or to dictate the timing, modes, or substantive goals of his (or his subordinates') diplomatic efforts.

Nevertheless, the mere fact that a particular case implicates matters of foreign affairs is not enough to displace congressional power. *Youngstown* itself makes that clear. The connection between national steel production and the Korean War obviously brought matters of external sovereignty into play, yet Jackson stressed that "Congress ha[d] not left seizure of private property an open field but ha[d] covered it by three statutory policies inconsistent with this seizure,"[32] and he vindicated those policies by concurring in the Court's decision striking down the seizure order. More broadly, the text of the Constitution grants Congress a central role in certain foreign-related areas. Article I, Section 8, for example, gives

---

31. Haig v. Agee, 453 U.S. 280, 291 (1981) (quoting United States v. Curtiss-Wright Export Co., 299 U.S. 304, 319 (1936) (quoting remarks in 1800 by then-Rep. John Marshall in the U.S. House of Representatives)); *see also* Amer. Ins. Ass'n v. Garamendi, 539 U.S. 396, 424 (2003).

32. *Youngstown*, 343 U.S. at 639.

Congress the power to regulate commerce with foreign nations, and the Court has depicted Congress, not the President, as having primacy in that area.[33]

Perhaps the most important area of external sovereignty as to which the constitutional text divides authority is military affairs. Together, Article II's Vesting and Commander in Chief Clauses undoubtedly grant the President some measure of exclusive authority not subject to congressional regulation. For example, once a war is declared, matters of battlefield tactics (whether to attack on the east or west flank; whether to deploy the Army Rangers or the Marines) are dominantly within the President's control. Still, it is only relatively recently that presidential administrations have relied on the Commander in Chief Clause to assert exclusive presidential authority over a broad range of military affairs.[34]

These assertions of preclusive presidential authority reached their high water mark (at least to date) under President George W. Bush, in the context of the "war on terror." The Bush Administration contended that statutory provisions as diverse as prohibitions on the use of torture and restrictions on warrantless wiretapping are (or might be) unconstitutional if applied against actions ordered by the President as Commander in Chief.[35] Those arguments met with

33. *See* Barclays Bank v. Franchise Tax Bd. of Cal., 512 U.S. 298, 328–31 (1994).

34. *See* David J. Barron & Martin S. Lederman, *The Commander in Chief at the Lowest Ebb—Framing the Problem, Doctrine, and Original Understanding*, 121 HARV. L. REV. 689, 696–97 (2008); David J. Barron & Martin S. Lederman, *The Commander in Chief at the Lowest Ebb—A Constitutional History*, 121 HARV. L. REV. 941, 946–50 (2008).

35. *See, e.g.,* Statement on Signing the Department of Defense, Emergency Supplemental Appropriations to Address Hurricanes in the Gulf of Mexico, and Pandemic Influenza Act, 2006, 41 WEEKLY COMP. PRES. DOC. 1918, 1919 (Dec. 30, 2005) (responding to McCain Amendment); Letter from William E. Moschella, Assistant Attorney Gen., U.S. Dep't of Justice, to Pat Roberts, Chairman, Senate Select Comm. on Intelligence, et al. (Dec. 22, 2005) (regarding FISA and warrantless wiretapping); Memorandum from Jay S. Bybee, Assistant Attorney Gen., Office of Legal Counsel, to Alberto R. Gonzales, Counsel to the President (Aug. 1, 2002) (regarding standards of conduct rising to the level of torture under 18 U.S.C. § 2340A).

widespread criticism, and for good reason.[36] Among the arguments'
other flaws, they have tended to treat authorities recognizing presidential power to act in the absence of any action by Congress as
though they support the President's authority to act contrary to
existing legislation. Yet if Justice Jackson's framework teaches nothing else, it is that "[p]residential powers are not fixed but fluctuate,"
depending on what, if anything, Congress has done in the area.[37]
Under that understanding, presidential power to act in the absence
of congressional regulation simply does not mean presidential
power to act in the face of such regulations.

The Supreme Court stressed this precise point in *Hamdan v.
Rumsfeld* in the course of invalidating the system of military commissions that President Bush had established for the purposes of
trying enemy combatants for violating the law of war. Without
addressing whether the President has the "independent power,
absent congressional authorization, to convene military commissions," the Court stressed that "he may not disregard limitations
that Congress has, in proper exercise of its own war powers, placed
on his powers."[38] And so the Court struck down the presidentially
convened commissions precisely because they conflicted with statutory limitations that Congress had put in place.[39] Moreover,
although the Supreme Court has not had occasion to address the
Bush Administration's arguments on torture or wiretapping, the
only government actions it has upheld in the war on terror have
been those that were authorized by Congress.[40] Ultimately, then,
while there is certainly no consensus as to the precise scope of the

36. *See, e.g.*, Harold Hongju Koh, *A World Without Torture*, 43 COLUM. J. TRANSNAT'L
L. 641 (2005); W. Bradley Wendel, *Legal Ethics and the Separation of Law and
Morals*, 91 CORNELL L. REV. 67 (2005); Adam Liptak, *Legal Scholars Criticize
Memos on Torture*, N.Y. TIMES, June 25, 2004, at A14.

37. *Youngstown*, 343 U.S. at 635 (Jackson, J., concurring).

38. 548 U.S. 557, 593 n.23 (2006).

39. *Id.* at 575–76.

40. *See* Hamdi v. Rumsfeld, 542 U.S. 507 (2004).

President's exclusive authority as Commander in Chief, some positions—like the notion that Congress cannot prohibit the torture of those the government detains—can be ruled out as beyond the pale.

In between Justice Jackson's two polar categories is a middle one, encompassing cases where "the President acts in absence of either a congressional grant or denial of authority."[41] Such cases occupy a "zone of twilight in which [the President] and Congress may have concurrent authority, or in which its distribution is uncertain."[42] Jackson did not offer much direction about how to resolve cases falling in this zone, except to say that "congressional inertia, indifference or quiescence may sometimes, at least as a practical matter, enable, if not invite, measures on independent presidential responsibility," and that "[i]n this area, any actual test of power is likely to depend on the imperatives of events and contemporary imponderables rather than on abstract theories of law."[43]

Although the reference to "contemporary imponderables" provides no real help to courts seeking to decide cases according to Jackson's framework, these passages do reveal something important about Jackson's view of the cases within this middle category. Put simply, the most reliable constraint on presidential overreaching in this category is not judicial review but congressional action. In matters over which both the executive and legislative branch have some authority, "congressional inertia, indifference, or quiescence" may enable the President to occupy the field by a kind of adverse possession. When the executive acts in areas in which the legislature could too, it falls to the legislature to preserve its prerogatives. "The tools belong to the man who can use them," Jackson said, quoting Napoleon.[44] He thus "ha[d] no illusion that any decision by this Court can keep power in the hands of Congress if it is not wise

41. *Youngstown*, 343 U.S. at 637.

42. *Id.*

43. *Id.*

44. *Id.* at 654.

and timely in meeting its problems."[45] In *Youngstown* itself, Jackson and the rest of the majority resisted a generalized presidential "emergency power" strong enough to contravene legislative restrictions, stressing instead that "power to legislate for emergencies belongs in the hands of Congress."[46] Yet in the same sentence he stressed that "only Congress itself can prevent power from slipping through its fingers."[47]

In a sense, Jackson's emphasis on the importance of congressional "self-help" is another way of stating that when Congress has left an area unregulated, courts will generally defer to long-running executive practice. Justice Frankfurter's concurring opinion in *Youngstown* stressed this very point. As he put it, "a systematic, unbroken, executive practice, long pursued to the knowledge of the Congress and never before questioned, . . . may be treated as a gloss on 'executive Power' vested in the President."[48] This view, moreover, flows directly from the Madisonian model. Recall that as Madison saw it, the core mechanism of the separation of powers was ambition checking ambition—each branch protecting its own institutional powers and prerogatives against intrusions by the other two. Madison understood such checking to be particularly important between the political branches. By the same token, when one of those branches consistently acquiesces in the actions of the other, the Madisonian presumption is that those actions must not offend the acquiescing branch's core prerogatives, and thus are at least presumptively consistent with the separation of powers.

Of course, none of this is to say that the courts will enforce no constitutional limits on executive action in Jackson's "zone of twilight." When the President goes significantly beyond historical practices and acts on matters typically thought to fall within the

---

45. *Id.*

46. *Id.*

47. *Id.*

48. *Id.* at 610–11 (Frankfurter, J., concurring).

legislative competence, the courts may step in. Such intervention may be especially likely if the courts see no good reason why the President could not work with Congress to achieve the results he seeks. Moreover, as the Court has made clear in later cases applying Jackson's basic *Youngstown* framework, the three tiers of executive action are probably best viewed not as distinct "pigeonholes" but rather as different "point[s] along a spectrum running from explicit congressional authorization to explicit congressional prohibition."[49] Viewed this way, the middle part of the spectrum is not confined only to those cases where Congress has taken literally no action, but also includes cases where Congress has passed laws in the general area but not sufficiently on point to count as strong authorization or prohibition. In such cases, the Court will look to such laws for a "loos[e] sense" of whether Congress has tacitly acquiesced in or resisted the executive action in question.[50] In the latter case, the courts are more likely to remand the President to Congress for more explicit authorization.

One final point about the idea of congressional acquiescence bears emphasizing here. Under Jackson's *Youngstown* framework, the principal danger to be guarded against is an ever-encroaching executive branch that threatens to displace legislative power unless Congress asserts itself. On this view, congressional acquiescence can be seen as a kind of realization of the threat. It means ceding ground to the President, a gradual advance of the executive and retreat of the legislature. But that is only part of the story. In some cases, it may be in Congress's own self-interest to remain silent on the issue in question, precisely in the hope that its silence will be treated as acquiescence and thus enable the executive action to proceed.

Suppose, for example, that the President wants to send troops on a peacekeeping mission that could engulf the nation in a war if

---

49. Dames & Moore v. Regan, 453 U.S. 654, 669 (1981).

50. *Id.* at 677.

active fighting breaks out. Some in Congress might agree that the peacekeeping mission is consistent with the national interest, but also worry about the threat of war. Knowing the history of Presidents sending troops on comparable missions without explicit legislative authorization, Congress might choose not to act. If the mission proves unsuccessful or simply unpopular at home, Congress can disclaim responsibility. It can try to pin the whole mission on the President, claiming that he acted on his own without waiting for congressional input. Yet if Congress thought there was a real risk of the mission going badly in the first place, perhaps it should have taken action to prohibit it. Congress might not have wanted to take that step, however, out of fear that it might pay a political price for appearing weak on national defense. Hence the double attractiveness of doing nothing. By remaining silent, Congress may be able to avoid two potential political penalties—one for resisting the President on matters of national security and another for complicity in a military mission gone bad.[51]

Seen in this light, treating congressional inaction as implicit authorization threatens to diminish congressional accountability. It allows Congress to confer a measure of authority without actually doing so, and later to claim opposition even though it also never really did that. One response to this problem would be for courts to treat the absence of legislation on point as literal silence, not acquiescence implying authorization. Yet silence itself cannot reliably constrain the executive. Ultimately, as Justice Jackson emphasized, the courts cannot preserve legislative power that Congress itself is not prepared to use. So even if congressional silence counts neither for nor against the President, over time the repeated actions of the executive in the face of congressional silence provide a basis for courts to uphold each succeeding executive action. The branch best able to stem this rising tide of executive precedent is Congress,

51. *See generally* Jide Nzelibe, *Are Congressionally Authorized Wars Perverse?*, 59 STAN. L. REV. 907 (2007).

even though it may sometimes lack the ambition that Madison expected.

The Legislature

Just as presidential separation of powers issues tend to revolve around the relationship between the political branches, so too do the issues centering on the legislative power. Without purporting to survey all such issues (many of which relate more to courses on administrative law than those on basic constitutional law), we will discuss one that undergirds much of the modern administrative state: whether Congress may delegate something resembling lawmaking power to some part of the government outside the legislative branch. On this issue, as with many others we will leave untouched in this chapter (like legislative limitations on the appointment and removal of federal officers), the Supreme Court's dominant approach has been a functional one, stressing the importance of workable checks and balances over any need to maintain absolute separation of powers.

The Supreme Court's "nondelegation doctrine" dictates that "Congress generally cannot delegate its legislative power to another Branch,"[52] in light of Article I, Section 1's provision that "[a]ll legislative Powers herein granted shall be vested in a Congress of the United States." Thus stated, the doctrine might seem to suggest a rather formal approach: Examine the power in question, determine if it is legislative, and, if so, strike down the delegation as invalid. That is not, however, how the Court has applied the doctrine. Instead, the Court has construed Article I, Section 8's Sweeping Clause as empowering Congress to enlist the assistance of the other branches—in particular the executive branch—in effectuating its legislative aims. As the Court has explained, its approach "has been driven by a practical understanding that in our increasingly complex

---

52. Mistretta v. United States, 488 U.S. 361, 371–72 (1989).

society, replete with ever changing and more technical problems, Congress simply cannot do its job absent an ability to delegate power under broad general directives."[53] That basic view underlies much of the rise of the administrative state over the last three-quarters of a century. Congress can make broad policy judgments about what ends to pursue, but it often requires the assistance of the relevant administrative agency, with its ability to marshal scientific and other technical expertise, both to select the means that are best adapted to those ends and to determine what concrete outcomes are consistent with Congress's overall aims.

Applying this practical, functional approach, the Court has not struck down a delegation of congressional power since 1936.[54] The doctrine's only real substantive requirement is that Congress articulate in the legislation some "intelligible principle" to guide the agency or other delegee.[55] And the Court has kept the threshold for satisfying that requirement extremely low. For example, it upheld a provision directing the Environmental Protection Agency to set standards for the permissible levels of certain air pollutants, and requiring only that the standards "protect the public health with an adequate margin of safety."[56]

Moreover, the Court has also treated statutory gaps and ambiguities as a kind of implicit delegation of interpretive authority to the relevant administrative agency. In perhaps its most significant administrative law decision of the last fifty years, the Court in *Chevron U.S.A. Inc. v. Natural Resources Defense Council, Inc.* instructed that in a case challenging an agency's interpretation of a

---

53. *Id.* at 372.

54. Carter v. Carter Coal Co., 298 U.S. 238 (1936); *see also* A.L.A. Schechter Poultry Corp. v. United States, 295 U.S. 495 (1935).

55. J.W. Hampton, Jr. & Co. v. United States, 276 U.S. 394, 409 (1928).

56. Whitman v. American Trucking Ass'ns, 531 U.S. 457, 476 (2001) (quoting 42 U.S.C. § 7409(b)(1)).

statute it administers, the reviewing court should treat statutory silence or ambiguity on the specific point in issue as an implicit delegation of authority to the agency.[57] A court's job is not to determine the all-things-considered best reading of the statute on the point in question, but simply to determine whether the agency's interpretation is "reasonable" and hence within the terms of the implied statutory delegation.[58] Courts preserve their own role in this scheme by being reluctant to conclude that a statute is truly silent or ambiguous on the relevant question. Statutory ambiguity for these purposes is that which remains even after the court has brought all ordinary tools of statutory interpretation to bear. In those cases of persistent ambiguity, however, Congress may generally cede authority to the agency to fill in the statutory gaps without violating the nondelegation constraint.

At bottom, the nondelegation doctrine leaves disposition of the legislative power largely up to Congress. Provided Congress places some modest limits on its delegation of lawmaking power, the courts will not intervene. In the main, it is for Congress to decide how best to divide the lawmaking function between itself and the administrative state.

The Judiciary

Although the separation of powers is commonly associated with the relationship between the executive and the legislature, it has obvious ramifications for the judiciary as well. Questions about the nature and scope of judicial review, for example, cannot be answered without some reference to the Constitution's overall distribution of authority among the three branches. And limits on that authority—including justiciability doctrines like standing, mootness, ripeness,

---

57. 467 U.S. 837, 843–44 (1984).

58. *Id.* at 845.

the political question doctrine, and the bar on advisory opinions—all in some way reflect views about the relations between the judiciary and the other branches.

Consider standing doctrine, which limits who may sue in the federal courts. Although some standing requirements are said to be merely "prudential," the Supreme Court has identified certain other elements that are constitutionally compelled: "A plaintiff must allege personal injury fairly traceable to the defendant's allegedly unlawful conduct and likely to be redressed by the requested relief."[59] These requirements are "built on a single basic idea—the idea of separation of powers."[60] The core concern is that if the federal courts are not confined to the adjudication of disputes involving concrete, individualized injuries, they might become venues for a general superintendence of the executive branch. In the Court's words, "[t]o permit Congress to convert the undifferentiated public interest in executive officers' compliance with the law into an 'individual right' vindicable in the courts is to permit Congress to transfer from the President to the courts the Chief Executive's most important constitutional duty, to 'take Care that the Laws be faithfully executed.'"[61] Thus, standing doctrine ensures that the judicial power is confined to resolving concrete disputes, not overseeing the executive function generally.

Of course, this division between individual dispute resolution and broad superintendence of government is an oversimplification. The proliferation of class actions and other multi-party devices, as well as the potential for broad equitable relief in institutional reform litigation affecting entities like public schools, hospitals, and prisons, all reveal the reality of modern litigation to be far more complex than simple, individualized dispute resolution. Moreover, although the injuries that spring most readily to mind when one

---

59. Allen v. Wright, 468 U.S. 737, 751 (1984).

60. *Id.* at 752.

61. Lujan v. Defenders of Wildlife, 504 U.S. 555, 577 (1992).

thinks of a plaintiff's concrete "injury in fact" may seem to speak for themselves (physical harm, a lost job, damaged property, and the like), any viable conception of injury always depends upon a legal context. The existence of a background legal system, including its basic assignment of entitlements and responsibilities, gives any particular assertion of injury its cognizability in the courts. Yet if injuries depend on law, then the legislative branch must have some substantial power to pass laws creating new legal interests—in certain kinds of information, for example[62]—and thus to create new kinds of injuries upon which individuals may sue. And in at least some circumstances, the vindication of those new interests may require a kind of judicial oversight of at least some aspects of the executive function.

Another justiciability constraint implicating the separation of powers is the political question doctrine. As we noted in Chapter 2, the Supreme Court's decision in *Marbury* itself acknowledged that the courts do not involve themselves in "political questions," meaning issues that are constitutional in nature but committed to the political branches. For example, precisely what constitutes impeachable "high Crimes and Misdemeanors" is a constitutional question, but its resolution appears to be committed to the House and Senate.[63] Similarly, the Court has held that by granting the Senate the "sole Power to try all Impeachments," the Constitution also gives the Senate the sole power to determine what form the trial may take.[64] The key insight for separation of powers purposes is that treating a constitutional issue as beyond the purview of the courts is not saying that the Constitution imposes no constraints. Instead, when a court concludes that an issue presents a political question, it simply says that the job of construing and implementing

---

62. *See* FEC v. Akins, 524 U.S. 11, 20–21 (1998).

63. *See* Randall K. Miller, *The Collateral Matter Doctrine: The Justiciability of Cases Regarding the Impeachment Process*, 22 OHIO N.U. L. REV. 777, 784–88 (1996).

64. Nixon v. United States, 506 U.S. 224, 229–38 (1993).

the Constitution lies with the political branches. The political question doctrine, then, recognizes that the constitutional separation of powers entails independent obligations for all three branches to uphold the Constitution.

At the other end of the spectrum are cases in which the courts invoke the separation of powers to preserve an active role for the judiciary. These cases arise when one or both of the political branches try to insulate their actions from judicial review. Although the jurisdiction of the federal courts is clearly subject to substantial regulation by Congress (indeed, the very existence of the lower federal courts is a matter of congressional discretion), courts have taken pains to preserve some ongoing role for themselves in certain critical matters, especially involving individual rights. This has been a trend in the Supreme Court's war-on-terror decisions. In *Hamdi v. Rumsfeld*, for example, Justice Sandra Day O'Connor's plurality opinion invoked the separation of powers to reject the idea that courts should treat as conclusive the executive's determination that a given individual is subject to extraordinary detention as an enemy combatant. As she explained, "the position that the courts must forgo an examination of the individual case and focus exclusively on the legality of the broader detention scheme cannot be mandated by any reasonable view of the separation of powers, as this approach serves only to *condense* power into a single branch of government."[65] The key point here is that, at least in areas where the political branches are prone to infringe individual liberty in the pursuit of security, constitutional checks and balances are best achieved by preserving a role for the third branch. As Justice O'Connor put it, "[w]hatever power the United States Constitution envisions for the Executive in its exchanges with other nations or with enemy organizations in times of conflict, it most assuredly envisions a role for all three branches when individual liberties are at stake."[66]

---

65. Hamdi v. Rumsfeld, 542 U.S. 507, 535–36 (2004).

66. *Id.*

Indeed, at least when core individual freedoms are at stake, joint executive-legislative attempts to exclude the judiciary from the equation may be the most significant exception to Justice Jackson's suggestion that the courts grant maximal deference to cooperation between the political branches. A dramatic case in point is the Supreme Court's decision in *Boumediene v. Bush*, which not only extended the constitutional right to habeas corpus to noncitizens held as enemy combatants at Guantanamo Bay, but also struck down the alternative judicial review mechanism that the Bush Administration and Congress had put in place. Casting habeas corpus as a judicial instrument for checking executive power and thus maintaining the separation of powers, the Court invalidated Congress's and the Administration's joint effort to replace the writ in the enemy combatant context with a more truncated scheme of judicial review.[67] That the executive and legislative branches agreed on that scheme was not decisive. Instead, the Court emphasized the basic three-branch structure of the federal government, and resisted attempts by the other two branches to circumvent that structure.

If there is a single theme that emerges from the diverse components of separation of powers law, it is that the Madisonian vision of each branch protecting its own continues to hold sway. Although the courts will occasionally police executive incursions into the legislative sphere and vice versa, in significant respects the doctrine presumes that the political branches are capable of defending themselves when necessary. And when the political branches combine to limit the role of the judiciary in important matters, the Supreme Court has shown itself willing to defend its own place within the three-branch constitutional structure. In sum, although the idea of institutional ambition checking ambition may not always be practically realistic given the dominance of political parties, a

---

67. Boumediene v. Bush, 128 S.Ct. 2229, 2258–59, 2271–74 (2008).

great deal of separation of powers doctrine continues to embrace
that Madisonian vision.

🏿 Further Reading

David J. Barron & Martin S. Lederman, *The Commander in Chief at the
    Lowest Ebb—Framing the Problem, Doctrine, and Original Understanding*,
    121 HARV. L. REV. 689 (2008).
David J. Barron & Martin S. Lederman, *The Commander in Chief at the
    Lowest Ebb—A Constitutional History*, 121 HARV. L. REV. 941 (2008).
JOHN HART ELY, WAR AND RESPONSIBILITY: CONSTITUTIONAL LESSONS OF
    VIETNAM AND ITS AFTERMATH (1993).
LOUIS HENKIN, FOREIGN AFFAIRS AND THE CONSTITUTION (2d ed. 1996).
Daryl J. Levinson & Richard H. Pildes, *Separation of Parties, Not Powers*,
    119 HARV. L. REV. 2312 (2006).
Trevor W. Morrison, *The Middle Ground in Judicial Review of Enemy
    Combatant Detentions*, 45 WILLAMETTE L. REV. 453 (2009).

SIX

Equal Protection

THE AMERICAN CONSTITUTION was conceived in the original sin of slavery, and much of its subsequent development—from the nullification crisis, through the Civil War and Reconstruction, the Southern "Redemption" and Jim Crow, the civil rights movement of the twentieth century, and even the election of the nation's first African-American President (himself a teacher of constitutional law)—can be characterized as a gradual and halting effort to expiate that sin. The struggle over race has left its mark on nearly every aspect of constitutional law, but on none more directly than on interpretation of the phrase "the equal protection of the laws" in Section 1 of the Fourteenth Amendment.

The Declaration of Independence had, of course, famously declared it "self-evident[] that all men are created equal," but the pre-Civil War Constitution notably omitted any express mention of equality, even as it thinly disguised the fact that it condoned slavery with such euphemisms as "other Persons" (in the Three-Fifths Clause of Article I, Section 2), "migration or importation of such persons" (in the Slave Trade Clause of Article I, Section 9), and "person held to service or labor" (in the Fugitive Slave Clause of Article IV, Section 2). The conflict between egalitarian ideals and hierarchical reality led eventually to the bloodiest conflict in the nation's history, and in its aftermath, to the Thirteenth, Fourteenth, and Fifteenth Amendments.

In this chapter, we examine the Equal Protection Clause of the Fourteenth Amendment and the related equal protection doctrine the Supreme Court has developed under the Due Process Clause of the Fifth Amendment. After a brief survey of the circumstances leading to the adoption and early understanding of the Reconstruction Amendments, we turn to what appears to be common ground—that the Court's unanimous decision in *Brown v. Board of Education*[1] was indubitably correct—but then move quickly to show how the consensus over *Brown*'s correctness masks profound disagreement over *Brown*'s meaning: Did the case establish an "antisubordination" principle, a "color-blindness" principle, or both, and if both, how shall these notions be reconciled? Moving beyond race, we evaluate the elaborate doctrinal structure that the Justices have created to implement the concept of equal protection. We ask how the Court discerns what other grounds of inequality—such as sex, national origin, disability, and sexual orientation—warrant judicial intervention in the political process. We also examine the role of intent in equal protection jurisprudence. We then conclude the chapter by asking whether equality is even a meaningful concept.

✸ Slavery

No issue has ever divided Americans like slavery. Leading Southern slave owners who were embarrassed by the institution included George Washington and Thomas Jefferson. Northerners like John Adams and Benjamin Franklin were willing to swallow their moral disapproval of slavery as the cost of Union. Enlightened leaders in both the South and the North hoped and expected that slavery would prove to be economically unsustainable. They thought that the Constitution's compromises over slavery would thus eventually be rendered moot. They did not anticipate how the cotton gin would revitalize the slave economy.

After the original Constitution, the Missouri Compromise was the next great effort of pro- and anti-slavery forces to coexist. Passed

---

1. 347 U.S. 483 (1954).

by Congress in 1820, it forbade slavery in the territories north of 36°30' (except in the proposed state of Missouri). The Missouri Compromise kept an uneasy peace that was sorely tested after the Kansas-Nebraska Act of 1854 repealed it and the Supreme Court's decision in *Dred Scott v. Sandford* asserted that, in any event, Congress had no power to restrict slavery in the territories or to confer citizenship on African Americans.[2] Any remaining hope for co-existence was shattered by the Confederate attack on Fort Sumter and the ensuing Civil War.

President Abraham Lincoln's Emancipation Proclamation purported to end slavery in the Confederacy, but in both theory and reality, the Proclamation's reach was quite limited. However, less than eight months after Lee's surrender to Grant at Appomattox, the Thirteenth Amendment was ratified, officially abolishing slavery. At the time it was the only provision of the Constitution that expressly applied to private actors. (Section 2 of the Twenty-First Amendment, which repealed Prohibition, also by its terms applies to private actors, though, unlike the Thirteenth Amendment, it is not actively enforced.[3])

In the wake of the Thirteenth Amendment, Southern legislatures enacted "Black Codes." These laws reinstituted slavery in all but name. Among other things, the Black Codes imposed severe restrictions on the rights of African Americans to contract their labor and limited their ability to appear in public except in the company of their "employers." Congress responded with civil rights legislation outlawing the Black Codes, but fearful that the Supreme Court would invalidate this legislation, Reconstruction Republicans also proposed the Fourteenth Amendment, which was ratified in 1868.

---

2. 60 U.S. (19 How.) 393 (1857).

3. *See* Laurence H. Tribe, *How to Violate the Constitution Without Really Trying: Lessons from the Repeal of Prohibition to the Balanced Budget Amendment*, 12 CONST. COMMENT. 217, 219–221 (1995).

In Chapter 9, we examine what authority Section 5 of the Fourteenth Amendment confers on Congress to enact legislation protecting civil rights and civil liberties. In this chapter and the two chapters that follow, we consider the self-executing rights provisions contained in the Fourteenth Amendment's Section 1. We begin with the last clause of that Section, which forbids any State to "deny to any person within its jurisdiction the equal protection of the laws."

▨ From *Plessy* to *Brown*

Much like the election of 2000, the Presidential election of 1876 was too close to call. The Electoral College outcome hinged on contested results in three states (including Florida). The special commission established to adjudicate the outcome produced a result that was part of an unofficial political bargain: Republican Rutherford B. Hayes would become President but in exchange the Democrats (in those days the dominant party in the South) were assured that federal troops would leave the states of the former Confederacy. Within a relatively short period, and notwithstanding the Reconstruction Amendments, African Americans were effectively disenfranchised. The system of segregation that came to be called Jim Crow was also established in the aftermath of the Compromise of 1877.[4]

Nineteenth-century civil rights lawyers attacked Jim Crow on a variety of grounds,[5] most prominently losing in the Supreme Court

---

4. *See* ERIC FONER, RECONSTRUCTION: AMERICA'S UNFINISHED REVOLUTION 1863–1877, at 575–87 (1989).

5. *See* Cheryl I. Harris, *The Story of* Plessy v. Ferguson: *The Death and Resurrection of Racial Formalism, in* CONSTITUTIONAL LAW STORIES 187, 207–16 (Michael C. Dorf, ed., 2d ed. 2009).

in *Plessy v. Ferguson*.[6] Louisiana, like other Southern states, mandated racial segregation among passengers on railway cars. In upholding the law against the charge that it denied African Americans equal protection of the laws, Justice Henry Brown wrote for the Court that separate facilities were not necessarily unequal facilities:

> We consider the underlying fallacy of the plaintiff's argument to consist in the assumption that the enforced separation of the two races stamps the colored race with a badge of inferiority. If this be so, it is not by reason of anything found in the act, but solely because the colored race chooses to put that construction upon it.[7]

The *Plessy* rationale had two crucial components, both of which would be challenged during the next six decades. First, what came to be known as the "separate-but-equal" doctrine offered civil rights lawyers a blueprint to argue that the separate facilities for African Americans were almost never in fact equal.[8] Second, these lawyers attempted to show that the *Plessy* Court was looking in the wrong place for a badge of inferiority. Although the law was formally neutral, the social meaning of Jim Crow was not. As Charles Black would later explain, only a Court suffering from "self-induced blindness" could fail to notice "the fact that the social meaning of segregation is the putting of the Negro in a position of walled-off inferiority."[9] The Supreme Court removed its own blinders in 1954, when it unanimously decided, in *Brown v. Board of Education*, that,

---

6. 163 U.S. 537 (1896).

7. *Id.* at 551.

8. *See* Sweatt v. Painter, 339 U.S. 629, 633–34 (1950).

9. Charles L. Black, Jr., *The Lawfulness of the Segregation Decisions*, 69 YALE L.J. 421, 426–27 (1960).

at least as practiced in the United States, "[s]eparate educational facilities are inherently unequal."[10]

Brown itself did not directly overrule *Plessy*. Insofar as the *Brown* Court based its decision on the meaning and impact of segregated *education*, it left open the possibility that de jure segregation in other contexts might still be constitutional. However, in a series of *per curiam* opinions, the Court soon made clear that state-mandated racial segregation was impermissible in all of its manifestations.

The Justices themselves correctly anticipated that *Brown* would encounter resistance. They attempted to soften the impact by holding, in a follow-up case that came to be called *Brown II*, that Southern legislatures and school districts should go about desegregating "with all deliberate speed."[11] That curious mandate was taken by recalcitrant defenders of Jim Crow as a license for foot dragging, and following a decade and a half of "massive resistance," the Supreme Court finally lost patience. "The burden on a school board today," the Court ruled in 1968, "is to come forward with a plan that promises realistically to work, and promises realistically to work now."[12]

Notwithstanding pockets of resistance, most school boards met that burden. School districts that had once practiced de jure segregation eventually sought to be released from federal court supervision, and the Supreme Court allowed as much.[13] In many parts of the country, public schools remained highly segregated, but the Court attributed such de facto segregation to private choices[14]— "white flight" in common parlance. Federal courts had no authority to impose remedies for such segregation because, under a narrow

---

10. 347 U.S. at 495.

11. Brown v. Board of Education, 349 U.S. 294, 301(1955).

12. Green v. County School Bd. of New Kent County, 391 U.S. 430, 439 (1968).

13. *See, e.g.,* Freeman v. Pitts, 503 U.S. 467 (1992).

14. *See id.* at 495.

definition of "state action," the Court found that they were not viola-tions of the Equal Protection Clause, which does not apply to pri-vate discrimination.[15]

To recognize the persistence of de facto segregation is not to deny that substantial progress was made. Undoubtedly, racial atti-tudes changed, and *Brown*, at least, went from being a highly con-troversial decision to a canonical text. That change, in turn, posed jurisprudential difficulties for judges and scholars who equated the Constitution with its original meaning.

Thus, today no one who contested *Brown*'s correctness could be confirmed to a federal judgeship, much less a seat on the Supreme Court. Former federal appeals court judge Robert Bork learned that lesson the hard way after he was nominated to the Supreme Court by President Reagan in 1987. In 1963, Bork had called a provision of then-pending civil rights legislation forbidding private businesses from refusing to serve African-American customers "a principle of unsurpassed ugliness."[16] Bork's strong preference for libertarian over egalitarian values almost certainly did not reflect personal racism, but by 1987 the comment appeared positively retrograde. Worse, Bork's own avowed originalism made it appear that he would have opposed *Brown* itself, for there is strong evidence that the Reconstruction Congress that proposed and the states that ratified the Fourteenth Amendment did not understand it to forbid de jure racial segregation.

Most tellingly, as the *Plessy* Court had observed, the Congress that proposed and the states that ratified the Fourteenth Amendment simultaneously passed laws requiring racially segre-gated schools.[17] It is possible for an originalist to argue that the

---

15. *See* Milliken v. Bradley, 433 U.S. 267 (1977).

16. Robert H. Bork, *Civil Rights—A Challenge*, NEW REPUBLIC, Aug. 31, 1963, at 22.

17. *See Plessy*, 163 U.S. at 545. Michael McConnell has argued that the framers of the Fourteenth Amendment in fact did intend to outlaw official racial segrega-tion. *See* Michael W. McConnell, *Originalism and the Desegregation Decisions*, 81 VA. L. REV. 947, 984–1078 (1995). We think his evidence is ultimately unpersuasive.

Equal Protection Clause adopted a principle that was inconsistent with the real-world practices of its framers and ratifiers, and Bork gamely made an effort to do just that during his unsuccessful confirmation hearings. However, his arguments rang hollow.

For one thing, a committed originalist must reckon with not only *Brown* but also with *Bolling v. Sharpe*.[18] In that companion case to *Brown*, the Supreme Court ruled that de jure segregation in the District of Columbia public schools was unconstitutional. Yet the Equal Protection Clause only limits the states, not the federal government. Undeterred by this gap, the *Bolling* Court found that segregating African-American schoolchildren amounted to "an arbitrary deprivation of their liberty in violation of the Due Process Clause" of the Fifth Amendment, which does apply to the federal government.[19] Later cases would come to refer to *Bolling* as establishing that there is "an equal protection component of the Fifth Amendment's Due Process Clause,"[20] but even accepting that the framers and ratifiers of the 1791 Bill of Rights meant the Fifth Amendment to include some federal obligation of equal protection, it cannot be seriously maintained that they thereby intended to outlaw de jure racial segregation, even as they clearly meant to permit slavery! Accordingly, there is no good traditional originalist account of *Bolling*.

What Bork and others have tended to say in defense of *Brown* and *Bolling* is that these cases properly reflect the original understanding

---

See Michael J. Klarman, Brown, *Originalism, and Constitutional Theory: A Response to Professor McConnell*, 81 VA. L. REV. 1881, 1884–1914 (1995); Earl M. Maltz, *Originalism and the Desegregation Decisions—A Response to Professor McConnell*, 13 CONST. COMMENT. 223, 228–31 (1996); Herbert Hovenkamp, *The Cultural Crises of the Fuller Court*, 104 YALE L.J. 2309, 2337–43 (1995) (reviewing OWEN M. FISS, TROUBLED BEGINNINGS OF THE MODERN STATE, 1888–1910 (1994)).

18. 347 U.S. 497 (1954).

19. *Id.* at 500.

20. *E.g.*, Edmonson v. Leesville Concrete Co., 500 U.S. 614, 617 (1991).

at a much higher level of generality than the concrete practices of the framers and ratifiers of the Fifth and Fourteenth Amendments. That is a perfectly valid argument, but it comes at a very high price, for it appears to sacrifice the very determinacy that is supposed to make originalism attractive. If the interpretations placed on "due process" and "equal protection" in *Bolling* and *Brown* are consistent with originalism, then at least in terms of outcomes, there is no substantial difference between originalism and living Constitutionalism. And because Judge Bork insisted on the virtues of the narrower, more conventional form of originalism when not being questioned about *Bolling* and *Brown*, his most thoughtful critics took his defense of those cases as insincere, as a kind of confirmation conversion.[21]

The Bork hearings demonstrated that fealty to *Brown* had become a litmus test for anyone purporting to be in the mainstream of American constitutional jurisprudence. Does *Brown* deserve its iconic status? Gerald Rosenberg has argued at length that *Brown* itself did little to end Jim Crow. Real progress did not come until Congress authorized the Justice Department to bring enforcement actions against recalcitrant state and local governments and officials.[22] Others have responded that Rosenberg's view understates the extent to which *Brown* catalyzed the civil rights movement by putting the Court's prestige behind it.[23] We will not attempt to referee this debate, which seems to us to pose an inherently unanswerable question: How would American history since 1954 have unfolded had the plaintiffs in *Brown* lost? Who can say? Such a

21. *See* RONALD DWORKIN, FREEDOM'S LAW: THE MORAL READING OF THE AMERICAN CONSTITUTION 298–303 (1996). More broadly, the malleability of the newfangled version of originalism calls the entire originalist project into question. *See* Thomas B. Colby & Peter J. Smith, *Living Originalism*, 59 DUKE L.J. 239, 282–86 (2009).

22. *See* GERALD N. ROSENBERG, THE HOLLOW HOPE: CAN COURTS BRING ABOUT SOCIAL CHANGE? (1991).

23. *See, e.g.,* Neal Devins, *Judicial Matters*, 80 CAL. L. REV. 1027, 1042 (1992); JACK GREENBERG, CRUSADERS IN THE COURTS: LEGAL BATTLES OF THE CIVIL RIGHTS MOVEMENT (Anniversary ed. 2004).

counterfactual question asks us to set aside the considerable path dependence of the real world and to assume that we can trace the likely course of hypothetical events over more than half a century.

Whatever the influence of *Brown* on the subsequent course of events in the real world, we can say with confidence that it has been enormously important in equal protection jurisprudence. And yet the precise meaning of *Brown* remains hotly contested.

🎗 Anti-Subordination or Color Blindness?

Contemporary battle lines over *Brown*'s legacy and over the meaning of equal protection more broadly trace their respective lineages to two consecutive sentences in the first Justice John Marshall Harlan's dissent in *Plessy*. Harlan stated: "There is no caste here. Our constitution is color-blind, and neither knows nor tolerates classes among citizens."[24] To use the somewhat anachronistic categories of contemporary politics, liberals emphasize the first sentence and its condemnation of caste, in describing equal protection as an anti-subordination principle. Meanwhile conservatives emphasize the second sentence and its invocation of color-blindness. Either the anti-subordination principle or the color-blindness principle would suffice to condemn de jure segregation of the sort the Court faced in both *Plessy* and *Brown*: Jim Crow was a system of subordination of African Americans that relegated them to an inferior caste or class. And the relevant caste distinctions were very much the product of attention, rather than blindness, to color.

But what does equal protection command when we separate the anti-subordination and color-blindness threads? That question most often arises in contemporary debates over the constitutionality of race-based affirmative action in education and employment. If the core meaning of equal protection is color-blindness, then such

---

24. 163 U.S. at 559.

programs—in advantaging racial minorities over non-minorities—
are no less suspect than discrimination *against* minorities.
Accordingly, proponents of color-blindness offer a straightforward
prescription: "The way to stop discrimination on the basis of race,"
they say, "is to stop discriminating on the basis of race."[25] By contrast, an anti-subordination principle would distinguish such laws
and policies on the ground that "to get beyond racism, we must first
take account of race."[26]

The choice between, or at least the question of how to reconcile,
the anti-subordination and color-blindness principles, has both a
historical and a normative dimension. Let us begin with history. If
we go back to the period of the framing and adoption of the
Fourteenth Amendment, we find that the Reconstruction Congress
was not opposed to programs designed to help African Americans
as such. As Eric Schnapper summarizes the evidence:

> From the closing days of the Civil War until the end of civilian
> Reconstruction some five years later, Congress adopted a series
> of social welfare programs whose benefits were expressly limited
> to blacks. These programs were generally open to all blacks, not
> only to recently freed slaves, and were adopted over repeatedly
> expressed objections that such racially exclusive measures were
> unfair to whites. The race-conscious Reconstruction programs
> were enacted concurrently with the fourteenth amendment and
> were supported by the same legislators who favored the consti-
> tutional guarantee of equal protection. This history strongly sug-
> gests that the framers of the amendment could not have intended

25. Parents Involved in Community Schools v. Seattle School Dist. No. 1, 551 U.S.
701, 748 (2007) (plurality opinion).

26. Regents of Univ. of Cal. v. Bakke, 438 U.S. 265 (1978) (statement of
Blackmun, J.).

it generally to prohibit affirmative action for blacks or other disadvantaged groups.[27]

Thus, if fidelity to the original understanding is to be our touchstone, it would appear that contemporary programs of race-based affirmative action are constitutional.

Yet the original understanding does not play a dominant role in equal protection jurisprudence. As noted above, *Plessy* itself probably better reflected the original understanding with respect to segregation than *Brown* does. And modern equal protection doctrine invalidates sex distinctions that the (almost entirely male) framers and ratifiers of the Fourteenth Amendment would almost certainly have deemed valid. Thus Schnapper's evidence, while embarrassing to the conservative Justices who typically espouse originalism when they are not espousing color-blindness, does not really answer the question of whether race-based affirmative action is valid for those of us who are not thoroughgoing originalists.

Indeed, even originalists could distinguish Reconstruction-era programs such as the Freedmen's Bureau from contemporary affirmative action. The principle of color-blindness, as it has been articulated by the modern Supreme Court, is only a very strong presumption. It requires courts to apply "strict scrutiny" to all race-based classifications, whether they burden or benefit a traditionally disadvantaged minority group. Under this exacting standard, racial "classifications are constitutional only if they are narrowly tailored measures that further compelling governmental interests."[28]

One could argue that programs designed to aid African Americans in their transition to freedom would have met this exacting test, whereas by now the taint of slavery and Jim Crow have been attenuated. True, the Reconstruction-era programs also

---

27. Eric Schnapper, *Affirmative Action and the Legislative History of the Fourteenth Amendment*, 71 Va. L. Rev. 753, 754 (1985).

28. Adarand Constructors, Inc. v. Pena, 515 U.S. 200, 227 (1995).

benefited African Americans who had never themselves been enslaved, but in the immediate aftermath of slavery, Congress would still have had a compelling interest in broadly combating racial discrimination. Continuing the admittedly anachronistic exercise of testing Reconstruction by judicial doctrines announced a century later, we might also say that the race-conscious Reconstruction programs were "narrowly tailored." By contrast, today, nearly a century and a half after the Civil War, and more than a half century after *Brown*, race-based affirmative action is much harder to justify. Justice Clarence Thomas made a version of this argument in a concurring opinion in a case involving the Voting Rights Act and the Fifteenth Amendment,[29] and even the more liberal Supreme Court Justices signed onto a majority opinion expressing the expectation that race-based affirmative action will become unnecessary (and by implication, unconstitutional) by the seemingly arbitrary date of 2028.[30]

Yet even if credited, the argument that color-blindness had different implications in the nineteenth and twenty-first centuries does not purport to *derive* the principle of color-blindness from the original understanding. At most, it shows that the race-based programs adopted during Reconstruction do not clearly violate contemporary doctrine implementing the color-blindness principle. Moreover, the idea that race-based classifications are not categorically prohibited but are instead subject to strict judicial scrutiny is itself a doctrinal innovation of the twentieth century. In the late nineteenth century, the Supreme Court seemed simply to ask whether the state law in question entailed the sort of race-based discrimination targeted by the Fourteenth Amendment. If the answer was yes, the law was struck down.[31] But even setting aside

---

29. *See* Northwest Austin Municip. Voting Dist. No. One v. Holder, 129 S.Ct. 2504, 2517–27 (2009) (Thomas, J., concurring in the judgment).

30. *See* Grutter v. Bollinger, 539 U.S. 306, 343 (2003).

31. *See* Strauder v. West Virginia, 100 U.S. 303, 309–10 (1880).

the non-originalist nature of strict scrutiny itself and focusing just on the concept of color-blindness, we need to know whether the Fourteenth Amendment requires a strong presumption of color-blindness in the first place. Where can we turn to decide whether color-blindness, anti-subordination, or some other principle best expresses the meaning of equal protection?

Answering that question requires us to shift from a purely historical to a more normative focus. We must now ask not what our history was but what it teaches. Different people will draw different lessons. Proponents of the color-blindness principle point to the dangers inherent in all racial classifications, whereas supporters of the anti-subordination principle see the core evil as group subordination.

Part of the argument for color-blindness rests on the supposed difficulty of distinguishing truly remedial programs from mere racial politics. Proponents of the anti-subordination principle, by contrast, contend that distinguishing between laws that burden racial minorities and laws that benefit them simply entails attending to "the difference between a 'No Trespassing' sign and a welcome mat."[32] However, those who favor color-blindness counter that "No Trespassing" signs can come disguised as welcome mats. Thus, although a minority nationally, African Americans constitute the political majority in some jurisdictions, and if one of those jurisdictions adopts race-based programs that benefit African Americans, it will not immediately be clear whether those programs are laudable efforts to remedy discrimination against African Americans or ugly efforts to benefit a favored racial group. Accordingly, champions of color-blindness argue that strict scrutiny is needed for all racial classifications in order to "smoke out" impermissible racial favoritism and stereotyping.[33]

---

32. *Adarand*, 515 U.S. at 244 (Stevens, J., dissenting).

33. Richmond v. J.A. Croson Co., 488 U.S. 469, 493 (1989) (plurality opinion).

But if strict scrutiny even for assertedly benign racial classifications can indeed detect racial favoritism, that fact still does not
explain why such favoritism is especially problematic under the
Equal Protection Clause. Proponents of color-blindness would say
that American history teaches the acute dangers that lie in the
"sordid business" of "divvying us up by race."[34] Yet why is that the
appropriate level of generality at which to describe our history?
Surely those on the other side in this debate have a valid point when
they counter that it is not racial *classifications* per se that bedeviled
our past, but a system of racial *subordination*. Whatever else one
thinks of racial politics in a city like Richmond (the site of a leading
Supreme Court case), there was very little indication that the
African-American majority intended to subordinate the white
people of Richmond when their elected officials set aside thirty per-
cent of government contracts for businesses owned by African
Americans and other minorities.

Perhaps the best support for the principle of color-blindness can
be found by looking beyond the United States. Although historical
examples of "reverse discrimination" in the United States typically
do not involve anything like the sort of systematic subordination of
racial minorities that African Americans experienced, in other parts
of the world racial oppression has sometimes been a two-way
street.

Tamils are a minority in Sri Lanka, where many of them believe
they are oppressed by the Sinhalese majority; meanwhile, many
Sinhalese regard themselves as an oppressed minority relative to
the Tamils, whose numbers in the nearby Indian state of Tamil
Nadu are much greater. Traditionally, Han Chinese regarded non-
Chinese as barbarians and today the Chinese government can be
said to oppress non-Han Uighurs in Xinjiang and ethnic Tibetans in

---

34. League of United Latin American Citizens v. Perry, 548 U.S. 399, 511 (2006)
    (Roberts, C.J., concurring in part, concurring in the judgment in part, and dis-
    senting in part).

Tibet; at the same time, however, ethnic Chinese in southeast Asia, not to mention Chinese under Japanese occupation during World War II, have suffered brutal acts of repression based on race or ethnicity. Since ancient times, Jews have been among the most persecuted minorities on the globe, and today Israeli Jews find themselves the victims of profoundly anti-Semitic propaganda in the official media of Israel's Arab neighbors, as well as a campaign of terrorism even targeting civilian Jews outside Israel; at the same time, Palestinian Arabs point to the indignities they suffer under Israeli occupation of the West Bank, and the casualties they incur at the hands of the Israeli military. These and many other examples that could be marshaled are not meant to take sides in any of these conflicts or to suggest moral equivalence. They do, however, illustrate the risk that racial, ethnic, and religious divisions may erupt into some of the worst forms of oppression and violence.[35]

Ironically, the Supreme Court's strongest supporters of the color-blind interpretation of equal protection have tended to disparage efforts to look to laws and practices in other countries as a basis for interpreting the American Constitution.[36] Accordingly, they have not invoked world history as a basis for the principle of color-blindness. Were they not so opposed to the project of comparative law, they might find in world history substantially stronger arguments for the color-blindness principle than those they have in fact offered. Instead, they sometimes write as though they think the literal words of the Fourteenth Amendment command color-blindness because they guarantee "equal protection" to each individual "person."[37] That is at best hyperbole. Color-blindness is certainly a

35. *See* AMY CHUA, WORLD ON FIRE: HOW EXPORTING FREE MARKET DEMOCRACY BREEDS ETHNIC HATRED AND GLOBAL INSTABILITY (2003).

36. *See, e.g.,* Roper v. Simmons, 543 U.S. 551, 624–28 (2005) (Scalia, J., dissenting); Printz v. United States, 521 U.S. 898, 921 n.11 (1997).

37. *See Croson,* 488 U.S. at 493 (plurality opinion).

plausible interpretation of the text of the Equal Protection Clause, but so is the anti-subordination principle.

Nevertheless, at the level of official doctrine, the fight is now over. After years of struggle, the Supreme Court finally ruled in 1995 that all race-based classifications by all levels of government must satisfy the strict scrutiny test.[38] Yet even as it did so, it cautioned that, at least in the context of affirmative action programs, the Court might apply the strict scrutiny standard with a thumb on the scale. The majority rejected as inapplicable Gerald Gunther's earlier characterization of strict scrutiny as "strict in theory, but fatal in fact."[39] Less than a decade later, the Court, in upholding the University of Michigan Law School's affirmative action program, carried through on this promise, explaining that "[a]lthough all governmental uses of race are subject to strict scrutiny, not all are invalidated by it."[40]

Moreover, even the most liberal members of the Supreme Court have stated that they would apply some form of heightened judicial scrutiny to race-based classifications that benefit minorities, just not the strictest scrutiny. Instead of demanding a "compelling" government interest, these Justices would have required only an "important" one; instead of insisting that the challenged racial classification be the "least restrictive means," they would have required that it be "substantially related" to the benign purposes asserted by the government.[41] This "intermediate scrutiny" standard was drawn from the Court's sex discrimination cases. The constitutional law novice may have difficulty discerning the difference between intermediate scrutiny and the somewhat relaxed version of the strict scrutiny standard that the majority applied in the University of

---

38. *See Adarand*, 515 U.S. at 235.

39. *Id.* at 237. *See* Gerald Gunther, *The Supreme Court, 1971 Term—Foreword: In Search of Evolving Doctrine on a Changing Court: A Model for a Newer Equal Protection*, 86 HARV. L. REV. 1, 8 (1972).

40. *See* Grutter v. Bollinger, 539 U.S. 306, 326–27 (2003).

41. *See* Regents of Univ. of Cal. v. Bakke, 438 U.S. 265, 359 (1978) (opinion of Brennan, J.).

Michigan Law School case. Indeed, even seasoned experts may be left scratching their heads over what all the fuss is about.

The answer may be that there is no difference, that the Justices in the majority in the University of Michigan Law School case said they were applying strict scrutiny in accordance with the principle of color-blindness, but were really applying something like the more forgiving intermediate scrutiny test. That was the accusation made by four dissenters who would have struck down the challenged affirmative action program.[42] Accordingly, we might now understand the core disagreement in race cases as no longer posing a choice between anti-subordination and color-blindness, but as a debate over what color-blindness entails.

Alternatively, we might understand the gradual morphing of strict scrutiny—and the pushing back against that morphing—as an illustration of a famous maxim of Justice Oliver Wendell Holmes, Jr.: "General propositions do not decide concrete cases."[43] The real factors in play in cases of alleged race discrimination, in this view, are the facts and the values the Justices find in the Constitution. Formal tests at best imperfectly encapsulate and translate these factors.

We think there is much wisdom in the Holmesian perspective, but it is possible to go too far with it. The different levels of scrutiny in equal protection doctrine do make a difference, especially in lower courts that must try to apply them faithfully. Whether the particular doctrinal edifice that the Supreme Court has created out of the Equal Protection Clause makes sense is a different question.

Tiers of Scrutiny

As we explained in Chapter 3, the post-New Deal Supreme Court has made deference to political actors the default setting of

---

42. *Grutter*, 539 U.S. at 380 (Rehnquist, C.J., dissenting).

43. Lochner v. New York, 198 U.S. 45, 76 (1905) (Holmes, J., dissenting).

American constitutional law. Nearly all laws and policies can be challenged as drawing unfair distinctions or unduly infringing liberty. But if the courts are not to usurp the legislative role, they must be prepared to reject most such challenges. In its interpretation of both equal protection and due process (which we discuss in Chapter 8), the courts grant deference via the "rational basis" test. To prevail in a claim that some law or policy denies her equal protection, a litigant must show that the law or policy is not "rational." Under this standard, the fit between means and ends need not be perfect. Indeed, under the rational basis test, the fit need not even exist: So long as the court can *imagine* a state of facts that would render the challenged law or policy rational, the challenge will fail.

New York City Transit Authority v. Beazer nicely illustrates the rational basis test. A blanket rule forbade drug users from working in the New York City subway and bus system. The rule was challenged by recovering heroin addicts who legally used methadone, a drug that satisfies cravings without producing euphoria. Evidence adduced in the trial court and credited by the Supreme Court showed that recovering heroin addicts who had been successfully maintained on methadone for a year or longer were no less qualified to work for the Transit Authority than persons who used no drugs. Nonetheless, the Supreme Court rejected the challenge as raising only policy questions. The Transit Authority could have made some exceptions to its blanket policy for methadone users without ill effect, but that was not a matter of constitutional obligation. "No matter how unwise it may be for [the Transit Authority] to refuse employment to individual car cleaners, track repairmen, or bus drivers simply because they are receiving methadone treatment," the Court ruled, "the Constitution does not authorize a federal court to interfere in that policy decision."[44]

In *Beazer* and other cases, before the courts apply the deferential rational basis test, they must first conclude that the challenged law

---

44. 440 U.S. 568, 594 (1979).

or policy does not employ an invidious criterion. Laws that discriminate based on "suspect classifications" such as race do not trigger the deferential rational basis test but the demanding strict scrutiny test.

It is not difficult to name the classifications that the Supreme Court has deemed suspect, thus triggering strict scrutiny. Race, ethnicity, national origin (as distinct from nationality), and religion are suspect classifications, as is alienage in some contexts.[45] Sex has been described as "semi-suspect,"[46] and thus a trigger for intermediate rather than strict scrutiny. Federal, state, and local anti-discrimination laws protect against age and disability discrimination, but the Court has found neither category suspect or semi-suspect. As this book goes to press, the Court has not clearly said that sexual orientation discrimination triggers heightened scrutiny, either in its own right or as a form of sex discrimination.

How did the Supreme Court arrive at the foregoing lists of suspect, semi-suspect, and non-suspect criteria? For race, we can give an historical answer. There is general agreement that the central, original purpose of the Equal Protection Clause, indeed of the entire Fourteenth Amendment, was to protect African Americans against the Black Codes. As our discussion of racial discrimination revealed, however, virtually no one thinks the meaning of the Equal Protection Clause can be restricted to its original purpose, narrowly defined. The Clause is majestically inclusive in its language, not confined to burdens on African Americans, inequalities based on race, or even unequal treatment among citizens.

How does the Supreme Court decide which categories, other than race, end up on which lists? The Court has identified relevant criteria for suspectness. Unfortunately, none of these criteria is

---

45. *See* Foley v. Connelie, 435 U.S. 291, 295 (1978).

46. *See* Michael C. Dorf, *Equal Protection Incorporation*, 88 VA. L. REV. 951, 963 & n.36 (2002).

individually satisfactory, nor has the Court articulated any principled means of combining them.

The leading formulation comes from footnote four of *United
States v. Carolene Products Co.* With African Americans clearly his
paradigmatic example, Chief Justice Stone opined there that "discrete and insular minorities" constitute what came to be known as
suspect classes.[47] In the process theory account of *Carolene Products*,
discussed in Chapter 3, heightened judicial scrutiny is justified by
the fact that prejudice prevents a discrete and insular minority from
building coalitions in the manner described by Madison in *Federalist
No. 10*. Yet political science teaches that discrete and insular groups
should be *better* able to organize and thus achieve their political
aims than groups, like women, that are diffused throughout the
general population.[48] There is little doubt that if any group qualifies
for judicial solicitude under equal protection doctrine, African
Americans do. But the fact that they have been discrete and insular
does not obviously account for that fact. Meanwhile, women are
neither insular nor a minority; yet there is something clearly correct
about the judgment that laws containing sex classifications that
reinforce gender stereotypes deny equal protection. Accordingly,
despite its canonical status, the "discrete and insular minority"
principle does not do a very good job of explaining or justifying
equal protection doctrine.

Courts also sometimes ask whether discrimination is based on
an "immutable characteristic,"[49] but immutability is hardly a necessary condition for suspectness. For example, religion is mutable,
but constitutional doctrine, whether under the Equal Protection
Clause or the First Amendment, nonetheless appropriately subjects
religious discrimination to strict scrutiny. Other characteristics,

---

47. 304 U.S. 144, 152 n.4 (1938).

48. *See* Bruce A. Ackerman, *Beyond Carolene Products*, 98 HARV. L. REV. 713, 718–40
    (1985).

49. *See* Frontiero v. Richardson, 411 U.S. 677, 686 (1973).

such as race and sex, are immutable, but so what? Suppose that medical technology made it possible to change one's skin color or sex through a safe, inexpensive, and painless procedure. That would hardly justify race- or sex-based discrimination against those people who opted not to undergo the transformative procedure.

Finally, in deciding which classifications are presumptively invalid, courts sometimes inquire into whether there is a history of discrimination on the basis of a trait. Yet this criterion is also problematic, because it raises the bedeviling question of how to describe the relevant history. For example, under current doctrine, the history of discrimination against African Americans leads the Court to conclude that race is a suspect classification, and that conclusion in turn is used to justify strict scrutiny of laws that disadvantage white men, who have historically fared quite well. If the Court were to hold tomorrow that sexual orientation is suspect based on the history of discrimination against gay men, lesbians, bisexuals, and transgender persons, and if it were also to embrace in this context the symmetrical approach it uses for race-based classifications, its holding would stand as an obstacle to discrimination against straight people, who have not been on the receiving end of any history of discrimination. Historical discrimination clearly should be relevant to equal protection analysis, but it fits poorly with the symmetry on which the Court has frequently insisted.

These and other difficulties led Justices Thurgood Marshall and John Paul Stevens to suggest abandoning the entire project of two or three discrete levels of scrutiny in favor of a more context-specific approach that would evaluate challenged laws more directly against a general norm of equality. That proposal has the advantages that flexible standards typically have over rigid rules; it would allow greater customization and avoid the over- and under-inclusiveness of the rule-like tiers-of-scrutiny approach. However, the Marshall/Stevens sliding scale would also, conversely, bring the vices that standards have relative to rules: lack of predictability and discretion that can be abused.

To some extent, we may currently have the worst of both rules and standards. According to both Justices Marshall and Stevens, the Court's cases *already* employ a context-specific sliding scale, albeit one masked by the tiers-of-scrutiny rhetoric.[50]

It can also be argued that, at least in some areas, the tiers of scrutiny have become less important in recent years. In select cases involving discrimination against "hippies," the developmentally disabled, and gays and lesbians, the Court has invalidated laws that were based on "animus" towards the disfavored groups, even without officially applying heightened scrutiny of any sort.[51] Yet these cases raise their own thorny issues. For example, in *Romer v. Evans*, the Court struck down a Colorado state constitutional provision, adopted by ballot initiative, that forbade the state or any subdivision thereof from adopting laws or policies prohibiting discrimination on the basis of "homosexual, lesbian or bisexual orientation, conduct, practices or relationships. . . ."[52] Without purporting to apply any form of heightened scrutiny, the Court found the challenged provision's "sheer breadth . . . so discontinuous with the reasons offered for it that the amendment seems inexplicable by anything but animus toward the class it affects."[53]

But if the Court were truly applying conventional rational basis scrutiny in *Romer*, it would not have required anything resembling a close fit between ends and means. Surely it is possible to *imagine* that the Coloradans who voted for the ballot initiative struck down in *Romer* simply hoped thereby to conserve the state's limited resources for fighting other forms of discrimination, such as race or sex discrimination. And that act of judicial imagination is all that

---

50. *See* San Antonio Indep. School Dist. v. Rodriguez, 411 U.S. 1, 98 (1973) (Marshall, J., dissenting); Craig v. Boren, 429 U.S. 190, 211–12 (1976) (Stevens, J., concurring).

51. *See* Romer v. Evans, 517 U.S. 620 (1996); City of Cleburne v. Cleburne Living Ctr., Inc., 473 U.S. 432 (1985); U.S. Dep't of Agric. v. Moreno, 413 U.S. 528 (1973).

52. 517 U.S. 620, 624 (1996) (quoting Amendment 2).

53. *Id.* at 632.

conventional rational basis scrutiny would seem to require. For this reason, various commentators have sometimes referred to *Romer* and the cases involving hippies and the developmentally disabled as applying "covert" heightened scrutiny or a rational basis test with "teeth."[54]

🎗 Purpose and Effect

Another way to explain the *Romer* line of cases would be to characterize them as adopting a forbidden purpose test.[55] In general, the rational basis test allows merely rational government means and ends, but some ends are off limits. As the Court first said in the hippie case, "if the constitutional conception of 'equal protection of the laws' means anything, it must at the very least mean that a bare . . . desire to harm a politically unpopular group cannot constitute a legitimate governmental interest. . . ."[56] Yet how, exactly, does the Court determine that such a desire underwrites a challenged law or policy? The Court's cases do not say. Perhaps some form of judicial notice applies in these cases, although we are still left with the puzzle of precisely defining the category to which it applies.

If the *Romer* line of cases remains somewhat mysterious, in one important respect it is continuous with the rest of equal protection doctrine: the focus on government intent. Since the nineteenth century, the Court has not hesitated to strike down facially neutral laws that were either being applied in a discriminatory manner[57] or that were adopted for a discriminatory purpose. Thus, in *Guinn v. United States*, the Court had little difficulty finding that a formally

54. *See* Dorf, *supra* note 46, at 964.

55. *See* Ashutosh Bhagwat, *Purpose Scrutiny in Constitutional Analysis*, 85 CAL. L. REV. 297, 314 (1997).

56. *Moreno*, 413 U.S. at 534.

57. *See* Yick Wo v. Hopkins, 118 U.S. 356 (1886).

race-neutral Oklahoma state constitutional provision violated the Fifteenth Amendment's prohibition on race discrimination in voting. Oklahoma imposed a literacy test for voting but exempted from the test anyone who was a lineal descendant of a person who had voted before 1866. Because African Americans were not entitled to vote in Oklahoma at that time, the provision clearly advantaged white Oklahomans, and seeing that this was the law's obvious purpose, the Court accordingly invalidated it.[58]

Guinn was a case in which the challenged law's purpose and effect were to discriminate based on a suspect classification. What if a law or other government policy merely has a discriminatory impact? Certainly there is nothing oxymoronic in referring to an "unequal effect."

Nonetheless, the Court's cases make clear that a disparate impact, standing alone, does not violate equal protection. Where the challenged law or policy is nominally neutral, a successful equal protection challenge requires a showing that the government decision maker "selected or reaffirmed a particular course of action at least in part 'because of,' not merely 'in spite of,' its adverse effects upon an identifiable group.[59] Discriminatory effect can be adduced as evidence of discriminatory intent, but under the Court's cases, effect alone does not violate equal protection. Indeed, one recent case may call into question the ability of Congress and state legislatures to provide *statutory* rights against disparate impact; insofar as these statutory rights yield race-conscious remedies, it has been argued, they must themselves be measured by strict scrutiny.[60]

58. 238 U.S. 347, 365 (1915).

59. Personnel Adm'r of Mass. v. Feeney, 442 U.S. 256, 279 (1979). *Accord* Washington v. Davis, 426 U.S. 229 (1976).

60. *See* Ricci v. DeStefano, 129 S. Ct. 2658, 2681–83 (2009) (Scalia, J., concurring).

✌ Is Equality an Empty Idea?

Although the Supreme Court may have settled some of the thornier equal protection questions as a matter of official doctrine, debate among academics and the broader public persists. Do abortion laws deny equality to women? Would their repeal deny equality to fetuses? Should discrimination on the basis of sexual orientation count as sex discrimination or as suspect (or semi-suspect) in its own right? What makes an interest "compelling" under the strict scrutiny test? And on and on.

Contestation over such questions may lead one to conclude that the concept of equality does no real work, that it is, as Peter Westen argued, "empty." Equality demands that likes be treated alike, but Westen explained that the concept of equality itself does not tell us what circumstances should count as alike. Only a substantive account of value can do that, and so we should focus our attention on what substantive rights people ought to have.[61]

Although we agree with Westen that the principle "likes should be treated alike" requires an external standard of relevant and irrelevant characteristics that make different people either similarly or dissimilarly situated, we disagree with the conclusion that equality is therefore empty.[62] Purely as a conceptual matter, the notion of "equality" does not strike us as substantially more indeterminate than other legal concepts invoked by the Constitution, such as "liberty" (in the Due Process Clauses) or "unreasonable" (in the Fourth Amendment). More importantly, whether we like it or not, the Fourteenth Amendment does indeed use the term "equal protection," and that fact alone requires courts and other government actors to grapple with its meaning. Such grappling will no doubt be

---

61. *See* Peter Westen, *The Empty Idea of Equality*, 95 HARV. L. REV. 537 (1982).

62. *See* Patrick S. Shin, *The Substantive Principle of Equal Treatment*, 15 LEG. THEORY 149 (2009).

value-laden, but that is true of cases arising under many other constitutional provisions as well.

%% Further Reading

Bruce A. Ackerman, *Beyond Carolene Products*, 98 HARV. L. REV. 713 (1985).

Michael C. Dorf, *Equal Protection Incorporation*, 88 VA. L. REV. 951 (2002).

JACK GREENBERG, CRUSADERS IN THE COURTS: LEGAL BATTLES OF THE CIVIL RIGHTS MOVEMENT (Anniversary ed. 2004).

Cheryl I. Harris, *The Story of* Plessy v. Ferguson: *The Death and Resurrection of Racial Formalism, in* CONSTITUTIONAL LAW STORIES 187 (Michael C. Dorf ed., 2d ed. 2009).

GERALD N. ROSENBERG, THE HOLLOW HOPE: CAN COURTS BRING ABOUT SOCIAL CHANGE? (1991).

Joseph Tussman & Jacobus ten Broek, *The Equal Protection of the Laws*, 37 CAL. L. REV. 341 (1949).

SEVEN

Enumerated Rights
The First Amendment

THE ORIGINAL CONSTITUTION contained no bill of rights as such. To be sure, Sections 9 and 10 of Article I set forth a small number of limitations on the federal and state governments, respectively. For example, both are forbidden from enacting ex post facto laws (laws criminalizing conduct after it has occurred) or bills of attainder (legislative acts finding particular individuals guilty of crime). Yet other rights that both we and the founding generation thought vital were completely omitted. The original Constitution forbids religious tests for federal office, but does not guarantee a right of free exercise of religion. It provides for jury trials in federal criminal cases but not in civil cases. It contains no protection for free speech or the press. The list of prohibitions in Sections 9 and 10 is short and its omissions curious. Accordingly, many of the opponents of the Constitution's ratification pointed to the lack of a comprehensive bill of rights as a fatal defect.[1]

Proponents of the Constitution had three chief responses. First, they argued that (notwithstanding Sections 9 and 10 of Article I) a bill of rights was unnecessary. A bill of rights has no place in a republican government in which power derives from the People, they said, because the government has only the powers bestowed upon it. As Alexander Hamilton put the point in *Federalist No. 84*, "bills of rights are, in their origin, stipulations between kings and

---

1. *See, e.g.,* Essays of Brutus II (Nov. 1, 1787), *reprinted in* 2 THE COMPLETE ANTI-FEDERALIST 373–77 (Herbert Storing ed., 1981).

their subjects, abridgments of prerogative in favour of privilege. . . ."[2]
Thus, the Federalists pointed to the enumeration of powers in
Article I, Section 8, as the main safeguard. Likewise, James Madison
succinctly stated in a letter to Thomas Jefferson (who was then
Ambassador to France): "the rights in question are reserved by the
manner in which the federal powers are granted."[3]

Second, as Hamilton further explained in *Federalist No. 84*, a bill
of rights could be dangerous because it would "contain various
exceptions to powers which are not granted; and, on this very
account, would afford a colorable pretext to claim more than were
granted."[4] Hamilton gave the example of a hypothetical freedom of
the press, which, if included in a bill of rights, would suggest that
the government had the power to infringe other rights, not so
included. Madison likewise worried that an attempt to spell out
rights in detail would end up limiting rights which, if left unenumerated, could be assumed to exist, though he ultimately found the
Ninth Amendment (and political necessity) sufficient to overcome
those concerns.[5]

Third, Madison (in his letter to Jefferson) termed declarations of
rights mere "parchment barriers" that would provide no real protection when most needed.[6] Structural protections that check the
power of majorities to oppress minorities—in other words, checks
and balances—Madison argued, were likely to be much more effica-
cious than bills of rights. (At the time, Madison apparently did not
consider judicial review to be such a structural mechanism.)

---

2. THE FEDERALIST NO. 84, at 512 (Alexander Hamilton) (Clinton Rossiter ed., 1961).

3. Letter from James Madison to Thomas Jefferson (Oct. 17, 1788), *in* 5 THE
   WRITINGS OF JAMES MADISON, (Gaillard Hunt ed., 1904) at 269, 271.

4. THE FEDERALIST NO. 84 (Alexander Hamilton), *supra* note 2, at 513.

5. 1 ANNALS OF CONG. 439 (Joseph Gales ed., 1834).

6. Letter from James Madison to Thomas Jefferson (Oct. 17, 1788), *in* Madison,
   WRITINGS, *supra* note 3, at 272.

Whatever the merits of these and other arguments against the inclusion of a bill of rights in the Constitution, they failed in the court of public opinion. Ratifying conventions in key states insisted on the promise of a bill of rights as the price of ratification.[7] When Congress met for the first time in 1789, it quickly made good on the promise, asking Madison to compose an initial draft.

Madison looked to the numerous proposals that had come out of the ratifying conventions, as well as to the rights provisions of recently adopted state constitutions. He then proposed a collection of amendments that were, after substantial stylistic changes, largely accepted by Congress. In one fateful move, however, the Senate rejected a proposed amendment that would have forbidden any state to "violate the equal rights of conscience, or the freedom of the press, or the trial by jury in criminal cases."[8] In both *Federalist No. 10* and *Federalist No. 51*, Madison had expounded the view that the risk of tyranny of the majority is greater in a smaller polity than a larger polity,[9] and for just that reason, he had argued at the 1787 Convention that the federal government ought to be given the power to nullify oppressive state laws.[10] He lost that battle in 1787 and lost again in 1789. Congress did not include his proposed amendment limiting state power in the package of amendments it sent to the states for ratification. Years later, in 1833, the Supreme

---

7. *See, e.g.,* Michael Allen Gillespie, *Massachusetts: Creating Consensus, in* RATIFYING THE CONSTITUTION 138, 153–58 (Michael Allen Gillespie & Michael Lienesch eds., 1989); John P. Kaminski, *The Constitution Without a Bill of Rights, in* THE BILL OF RIGHTS AND THE STATES 16, 33–39 (Patrick T. Conley & John P. Kaminski eds., 1992); Jean Yarbrough, *New Hampshire: Puritanism and the Moral Foundations of America, in* RATIFYING THE CONSTITUTION, *supra,* at 235, 250–51.

8. *See* CREATING THE BILL OF RIGHTS: THE DOCUMENTARY RECORD OF THE FIRST FEDERAL CONGRESS 13, 41 (Helen E. Veit et al. eds., 1991); LEONARD W. LEVY, ORIGINAL INTENT AND THE FRAMERS' CONSTITUTION 166–70 (1988).

9. THE FEDERALIST NOS. 10, 51 at 80–84, 323–35 (James Madison), *supra* note 2.

10. *See, e.g.,* James Madison, Notes on the Constitutional Convention (June 8, 1787), *in* 1 THE RECORDS OF THE FEDERAL CONVENTION OF 1787 (Max Farrand ed., 1937), at 164–65.

Court punctuated Madison's defeat on this point. The Justices held that the Bill of Rights only limited the federal government, not the states.[11] Not until the adoption of the Reconstruction Amendments following the Civil War were additional limits placed on the ability of states to infringe constitutional rights, and not until the middle of the twentieth century was the Fourteenth Amendment held to apply most of the provisions of the Bill of Rights to the states.

We consider that process—known as the "incorporation" of the Bill of Rights—in the next chapter. That chapter also considers how the Bill of Rights addressed the danger, noted by both Hamilton and Madison, that by enumerating specific rights, the Constitution would imply that the federal government may override other unenumerated rights: The Ninth Amendment specifically cautions constitutional interpreters not to draw this inference. Nonetheless, as we shall see, judges and legal scholars have repeatedly downplayed or outright ignored that warning.

In this chapter, however, we turn our attention to the topic of enumerated rights. Rather than survey all provisions of the Bill of Rights, we focus our attention on the rights set forth in the First Amendment. Nonetheless, our core point would apply with equal force to other enumerated rights. We contend that enumeration by itself only goes so far, for the rights enumerated do little more than identify constitutional values. The implementation of enumerated rights instead depends on the generation of doctrines not easily deducible from the constitutional text or its original understanding. In that respect, the constitutional law of enumerated rights is not different in kind from the constitutional law of unenumerated rights.

First Amendment cases also nicely illustrate the artificiality of dividing the Constitution into structural provisions and rights provisions. Freedom of speech and the press can be understood as playing an important function in the mechanics of government. Without open political debate and electoral campaigns, the constitutional

---

11. Barron v. Baltimore, 32 U.S. (7 Pet.) 243, 250–51 (1833).

mechanisms for democratically choosing and empowering representatives would be a sham. Likewise, the religion clauses can be understood not only as protecting individual conscience, but also as slicing up sovereignty. Just as the federal government may not legislate on matters reserved to the states, so too must it leave spiritual matters to the regulation of individual conscience and voluntary communities of faith.

The balance of this chapter considers the four main provisions of the First Amendment: freedom of the press, freedom of speech, free exercise of religion, and the prohibition on an establishment of religion. (We do not discuss the right to assemble and petition for redress of grievances.)

Freedom of the Press

Despite the specific protection that freedom of the press receives in the text of the First Amendment, the Supreme Court has generally not afforded any special protection to the institutional media.[12] For example, in *Branzburg v. Hayes*, the Justices rejected the claim that the First Amendment entitles reporters to protect the anonymity of their sources.[13] Nearly all states provide some degree of protection for reporters' sources,[14] but the federal Constitution, according to the Court, does not require the government to treat reporters differently from any other person with knowledge relevant to the

---

12. *But see* C. Edwin Baker, *The Independent Significance of the Press Clause Under Existing Law*, 35 Hofstra L. Rev. 955 (2007).

13. 408 U.S. 665, 679–708 (1972).

14. Forty-nine states and the District of Columbia afford journalists some form of statutory, common law, or constitutional privilege, and the fiftieth (Wyoming) has neither rejected nor confirmed such a privilege. *See* David Abramowicz, Note, *Calculating the Public Interest in Protecting Journalists' Confidential Sources*, 108 Colum. L. Rev. 1949, 1956 n.46 (2008).

government's official business (including the business of adjudicating a lawsuit between private parties).

The Court's refusal to afford the media any special rights can be seen as a betrayal of the First Amendment's text, but it can also be seen as vindicating a First Amendment principle: that the government should not favor some speakers over others. Any attempt to give special rights to the press—such as the ability to shield sources or receive special access to government documents—requires a definition of "the press." Because their actions typically involve compromise, legislatures can be given some leeway to define the relevant distinguishing criteria. A decision by the Supreme Court drawing such distinctions as a matter of the First Amendment itself, however, would be potentially problematic. (Of course, a legislature could grant protections to "the press" while leaving that term to judicial elaboration over time, but court decisions in that context would be interpretations of the governing statute, not the First Amendment itself.)

To an important extent, the First Amendment is designed to protect dissent,[15] that is, the sort of view not likely to be found in the largest media outlets. Yet once one acknowledges that the universe of actors potentially qualifying as "the press" includes anyone with a leaflet—or these days, a blog—one is hardly making a meaningful distinction between the press and other speakers, who would enjoy less protection. Thus, First Amendment doctrine does not generally distinguish between freedom of the press and freedom of speech, treating the former as simply an example of the latter. Let us therefore turn to freedom of speech.

15. See STEVEN H. SHIFFRIN, THE FIRST AMENDMENT, DEMOCRACY, AND ROMANCE 5–6, 86–109 (1990); Steven Shiffrin, *The Politics of the Mass Media and the Free Speech Principle*, 69 IND. L.J. 689, 719 (1994).

Freedom of Speech

The doctrinal landscape of free speech is littered with categorical distinctions. To name a few of the most prominent, case law distinguishes between content-based and content-neutral regulations of speech; between speech and action; and among high-value, low-value, and nominally unprotected speech. Behind these and other classificatory schema surely lies an anxiety: At its core, the freedom of speech protects individuals and groups against censorship, whereby government officials decide what views can and cannot be expressed. Yet in sitting in judgment over laws and policies challenged as infringing free speech, judges worry that they themselves may become censors; resorting to categorical rules accordingly enables judges to constrain (or at least to appear to constrain) their own discretion. A set of free speech doctrines shot through with sorting criteria aims to limit both the ability of judges to decide, case by case, whether particular statements advance the public good, as well as the perception that judges do so according to their own subjective beliefs.

Before coming to some of the doctrinal categories, we consider a very basic question: What values does freedom of speech serve? Concurring in the 1927 case of *Whitney v. California*, Justice Louis Brandeis wrote that the framers of the First Amendment "valued liberty both as an end and as a means."[16] Brandeis and Justice Oliver Wendell Holmes, Jr. are typically credited as the prophets of modern free speech law. In a series of separate opinions around the time of the first "Red Scare" (coinciding roughly with the end of World War I), they took issue with the then-dominant view on the Court, which was quite deferential to legislative interference with freedom of speech and association. Thus, although Brandeis's *Whitney* concurrence attributed his espoused version of the free speech principle to the founding generation, it only became law in the middle of the

16. 274 U.S. 357, 375 (1927).

twentieth century, when the Court began to adopt the Brandeisian and Holmesian formulations.

When Brandeis invoked the value of free speech as both an end and a means, he may have had in mind something like what Isaiah Berlin would later famously call two concepts of liberty, one negative and one positive.[17] Constitutional doctrines concerned with "negative freedom," or "freedom from" government interference, typically place a value on liberty as an end.[18] In such a conception, the individual, acting alone or in concert with others, has the right to decide what to think, read, write, and say. Free speech as an end reflects a strongly anti-totalitarian view of the role of government in people's lives. It typically rests on the assumption that the aggregate social good will likely be impeded by restrictions on speech (an assumption largely vindicated by the misfortunes of those who have lived under totalitarian governments) and the further assumption that even if aggregate welfare were somehow enhanced by restrictions on speech, those restrictions would remain unjustifiable.

To describe free speech as a means is to emphasize what Berlin called positive liberty—the freedom of the political community to come together to govern itself.[19] In order to hold government accountable, the People must have the ability to know and criticize what the government is doing. Freedom of speech and of the press play such a vital role that we sometimes refer to the press as an unofficial "fourth branch" of government—even as we understand that to do its job effectively, the press must be independent of government.

The distinction between free speech as an end and as a means manifests itself in two oddly contradictory ways in constitutional doctrine and theory. On one hand, speech as a means to

---

17. Isaiah Berlin, *Two Concepts of Liberty, in* FOUR ESSAYS ON LIBERTY 118, 121–22 (1969).

18. *Id.* at 122–23, 131.

19. *Id.* at 131.

self-government—what the Court sometimes calls "core political speech"—lies at the center of what the First Amendment protects. Thus, other kinds of speech—such as commercial speech (which is a means to a different end), or sexual speech (which is typically an end in itself), or artistic speech without any discernible political message—may be regarded as less central to the First Amendment, and thus entitled to somewhat less protection. On the other hand, insofar as free speech exists as a means to the end of self-government, government regulation of political speech that undermines rather than serves self-government may be justified as consistent with the core purposes of the First Amendment.

Debates over campaign finance regulation exemplify the tension between the speech-protective and the speech-restrictive consequences of classifying particular communications as core political speech. In *Buckley v. Valeo* the Supreme Court held that federal statutory limits on campaign expenditures by candidates, their campaigns, and independent groups and individuals violated the rights of these actors to free speech;[20] at the same time, the *Buckley* Court sustained limits on how much money one could contribute to candidates and others.[21] Since then, interest groups, scholars, and Justices have divided over whether the distinction between expenditures and contributions makes sense, and if not, whether the tension ought to be resolved by permitting greater regulation of expenditures or less regulation of contributions.

The pro-regulatory conception of the First Amendment treats the influence of money on electoral campaigns as problematic in at least two ways. First, even without an express quid pro quo, campaign contributors often expect access and responsiveness from candidates whom they have supported. Thus, campaign finance regulation has been justified as combating the reality and the

---

20. 424 U.S. 1, 39–59 (1976) (per curiam).

21. *Id.* at 23–38.

appearance of corruption.[22] Second, some academics (though for the most part, not courts) have emphasized an equality rationale.[23] In this view, inequalities of wealth are tolerable as the price we as a society pay for sharing in the benefits that a generally free-market economy generates; however, economic inequality should not be permitted to create political inequality by undermining the principle of one-person/one-vote. At least with respect to elections, the argument goes, the inevitable inequalities that arise in a market economy should not spill over into the marketplace of ideas.

On the opposite side, some opponents of campaign finance restrictions stress their supposed inefficacy. People who seek to influence politics inevitably will find a way to do so, and campaign finance restrictions merely channel money away from politicians who can be held responsible for their political speech, and towards independent speakers who cannot be. The rise of independent advocacy groups like the "Swift Boat Veterans for Truth," which in the 2004 presidential election attacked Democratic candidate John Kerry, could be seen as an unintended—but foreseeable—side effect of campaign finance limits.

Opponents of campaign finance restrictions also make arguments of principle. Can the government really forbid people from using their money on speech, when it permits them to spend it on all manner of other goods and services? In this view, the marketplace of ideas is the one marketplace that should be most immune from regulation.

We will not attempt to resolve these questions here. We do note that the campaign finance debate also highlights another pervasive

---

22. *See, e.g., id.* at 26.

23. *See, e.g.,* CASS SUNSTEIN, DEMOCRACY AND THE PROBLEM OF FREE SPEECH 94–98 (1998); David A. Strauss, *Corruption, Equality, and Campaign Finance Reform,* 94 COLUM. L. REV. 1369, 1382–85 (1994). *But see* Buckley v. Valeo, 424 U.S. 1, 48–49 (1976).

problem in fashioning free speech doctrine: What is speech? Some critics of the decisions limiting campaign finance regulation point out that money is not speech; therefore, they argue, limiting the contribution or expenditure of funds is not the same thing as limiting speech itself.

If taken literally, this criticism is surely overbroad, for many activities that are not literally speech must nonetheless be protected in order to protect speech. Imagine a law forbidding the purchase of pen and paper, or a typewriter, or, to make the example current, a computer that is capable of connecting to the Internet. The purchase of the computer is not itself an expressive act, but undoubtedly such a law would violate the freedom of speech because, in the twenty-first century, government efforts to restrict access to the Internet amount to censorship.

But if taken to the extreme, of course, nearly any government action can be construed as restricting some activity or item that is needed to facilitate speech. Payment of the income tax leaves people with less money to buy books and newspapers, a government decision to convert a public park into a parking lot deprives the public of a gathering place to hold rallies, protection for property owners against vandalism deprives would-be graffiti artists of valuable canvas, and so forth. It is intuitively obvious that none of these cases should properly be seen as even raising First Amendment concerns. Constitutional doctrine largely instantiates that intuition by focusing attention less on whether any person means to express a particular message than on whether disfavored messages are the predicate for government regulation.

Thus, there is no First Amendment right, as such, to burn an American flag. If a state law forbade the lighting of a fire in a state park, a person charged under that law for burning an American flag in a public park would have no First Amendment defense—unless she could show that the law had been invoked selectively against burners of American flags while burners of other flags or other flammable objects were unmolested. However, prosecution under a law that singles out the anti-government message of burning an American flag as such, has been held to violate the First Amendment.[24]

More generally, the cases distinguish between laws and policies that target expression for its message, and laws and policies that target legitimate problems having nothing to do with expression. For example, the Supreme Court upheld a prohibition on sound trucks on the plausible ground that it aimed not to shield people from any particular message, but to protect their eardrums.[25] To be sure, we are glossing over some fine doctrinal distinctions between time, place, and manner regulations; restrictions of speech in so-called "public fora;" and regulation of speech mixed with conduct. It is nonetheless only a small oversimplification to say that laws and policies that target speech for its message—laws and policies that are "content-based"—are presumptively invalid (unless they fit into one of a relatively small number of categorical exceptions, such as "fighting words" or "incitement"), while "content-neutral" laws will be subject either to very deferential First Amendment scrutiny or none at all.[26]

Free speech doctrine also distinguishes among categories of speech. The Supreme Court has sometimes inaccurately described some forms of expression as "not within the area of constitutionally protected speech. . . ."[27] These nominally unprotected areas include

---

24. United States v. Eichman, 496 U.S. 310, 312 (1990); Texas v. Johnson, 491 U.S. 397, 399 (1989).

25. Kovacs v. Cooper, 336 U.S. 77, 86–89 (1949).

26. It can be argued that the Court invariably invalidates speech regulations it deems content-based, but that the Court also sometimes labels what appear to be content-based laws as content-neutral. *See* Barry P. McDonald, *Speech and Distrust: Rethinking the Content Approach to Freedom of Expression*, 81 NOTRE DAME L. REV. 1352, 1355–1412 (2006).

27. *See, e.g.,* Roth v. United States, 354 U.S. 476, 483 (1957).

defamation,[28] obscenity,[29] and "fighting words,"[30] a technical term that usually refers to the profanity-laced equivalent of "care to step outside?". Yet such categorical claims are clearly overstatements.[31]

For example, in the landmark decision of *New York Times v. Sullivan*, the Court held that libelous speech is in fact partly protected: Public officials (and by extension in later cases, so-called "public figures") can only recover for libel by showing that a defendant acted with reckless disregard for the truth; the First Amendment prevents state law from treating as defamatory the mere publication of a false statement.[32]

Likewise, in *R.A.V. v. City of St. Paul*, a 1992 case widely viewed at the time as having implications for "political correctness," a narrow majority of the Court held that even within a properly bounded proscribable category—in that case, fighting words—laws may not single out disfavored messages based on their content.[33] Whether or not the result in *R.A.V.* itself is correct, the broad principle seems clearly right: A law banning defamation of Republicans but not Democrats (or vice versa) would surely violate the First Amendment (or the Equal Protection Clause as informed by First Amendment principles) even if defamation itself were defined in accordance with the *New York Times* rule.

The *R.A.V.* case also stands for the proposition that so-called "hate speech" is not a proscribable category, because the government may not censor even hateful messages.[34] (The facts of *R.A.V.* itself involved the burning of a cross.) That same principle was employed in an influential federal appeals court decision to

---

28. *See* Beauharnais v. Illinois, 343 U.S. 250, 266 (1952).

29. *See* Miller v. California, 413 U.S. 15, 23–30 (1973); *Roth*, 354 U.S. at 484–85.

30. *See* Chaplinsky v. New Hampshire, 315 U.S. 568, 573–74 (1942).

31. *See* R.A.V. v. City of St. Paul, 505 U.S. 377, 383–84 (1992).

32. 376 U.S. 254, 279–83 (1974).

33. *R.A.V.*, 505 U.S. at 391–92.

34. *Id.* at 395–96.

invalidate an Indianapolis ordinance that proscribed "pornography," defined as "the graphic sexually explicit subordination of women, [men, or children] whether in pictures or in words. . . ."[35] The ruling, which was summarily affirmed by the Supreme Court, anticipated the decision in *R.A.V.* by protecting degrading sexual materials precisely because they communicate a message of degradation.[36]

Government may proscribe some sexual expression, if it qualifies as "obscenity," another term of art in the Court's cases, but one that does not depend on distinguishing between degrading and uplifting sexually explicit material. (The Court's doctrine does, however, distinguish erotica that appeals to the "prurient" interest from that which appeals to "normal, healthy sexual desires."[37]) Much could be, and has been, written about how to define obscenity, but here we pause only to ask why the government should have any power to proscribe it. One possible answer is the protection of children, but a separate line of cases already permits substantial regulation—including regulation of material that is not obscene for adults—to prevent children from gaining access to sexual material beyond their maturity level.[38]

Another possibility is that sexually explicit pictures and words have more in common with sex toys than with non-erotic art and literature. In this view, obscenity appeals to the groin rather than to the brain. Yet the appeals court rejected this argument in the Indianapolis case because it is both inaccurate and over-inclusive.[39] People may view or read sexual expression for the purpose of arousal, but the brain clearly mediates the experience (as it

---

35. Am. Booksellers Ass'n v. Hudnut, 771 F.2d 323, 324 (7th Cir. 1985), aff'd, 475 U.S. 1001 (1986) (quoting Indianapolis Code § 16-3(q)).

36. *Id.* at 325, 327–32.

37. Brockett v. Spokane Arcades, Inc., 472 U.S. 491, 498 (1985).

38. *See, e.g.,* FCC v. Pacifica Found., 438 U.S. 726, 748–51 (1978); Ginsberg v. New York, 390 U.S. 629, 635–43 (1968).

39. *Hudnut,* 771 F.2d at 329–30.

mediates more direct physical stimulation for that matter). The real argument here is not that obscenity (or pornography) bypasses the brain entirely but that, in Freudian terms, it bypasses the ego and goes straight to the id. But so what? Much of the most powerful expression—including cherished works of art and music—functions at a non-rational or sub-rational level. The First Amendment has appropriately been interpreted to protect broader emotional appeals,[40] and thus any effort to censor sexual material on the grounds of its inarticulateness would be overbroad.

There may be no good rationale for interpreting the First Amendment to permit prohibitions on the dissemination to consenting adults of sexually explicit material that was produced by consenting adults. Justice William O. Douglas, a persistent dissenter from the Court's obscenity cases, noted that the text of the First Amendment contains no exception for obscene or otherwise sexual material.[41] The Court, meanwhile, has never articulated a persuasive rationale for banning obscenity. The Indianapolis pornography case rejected a feminist argument, and obscenity doctrine as developed by the courts does not map well onto equal protection. Perhaps the best that can be said for the doctrine as it stands is that by long tradition obscenity has been regulated in the interest of public morality. But that only raises the question of why other traditional regulations of speech—including defamation lawsuits against public officials that do not satisfy the *New York Times* rule—are not likewise exempt from First Amendment scrutiny.

If government authority to proscribe sexually explicit expression is dubious, few doubt that government may sometimes suppress speech to prevent violence or other grave harm. The question is when. Early twentieth-century cases resolved this question under the "clear and present danger" test, which in both its origin and

---

40. *See, e.g.,* Cohen v. California, 403 U.S. 15, 26 (1971).

41. Miller v. California, 413 U.S. 15, 40 (1973) (Douglas, J., dissenting).

application was quite deferential to government claims of danger.[42] In a notorious but hardly atypical case, Justice Holmes wrote an opinion for a unanimous Supreme Court upholding the conviction and ten-year sentence under the 1917 Espionage Act of socialist and five-time Presidential candidate Eugene Debs.[43] Debs had given a speech in Canton, Ohio, cagily expressing the view that American workers ought to resist the draft. Although he did not urge any immediate violence and none occurred, that was nonetheless sufficient for the Court to find the clear and present danger test satisfied.[44]

Holmes sometimes joined or led the Court in sustaining convictions for what would now be regarded as protected speech, but he also authored powerful dissents from Red Scare era decisions. Most famously, dissenting in another Espionage Act case, Holmes (joined by Brandeis) associated constitutional protection for free speech with his own skepticism of absolute truths. After acknowledging the logic of censorship, he went on to write that

when men have realized that time has upset many fighting faiths, they may come to believe even more than they believe the very foundations of their own conduct that the ultimate good desired is better reached by free trade in ideas—that the best test of truth is the power of the thought to get itself accepted in the competition of the market, and that truth is the only ground upon which their wishes safely can be carried out. That at any rate is the theory of our Constitution.[45]

Despite those stirring words, the clear and present danger test was so closely associated with deference to government that by the

<hr />

42. *See, e.g.,* Schenck v. United States, 249 U.S. 47, 52 (1919).

43. Debs v. United States, 249 U.S. 211 (1919).

44. *Id.* at 214–17.

45. Abrams v. United States, 250 U.S. 616, 630 (1919).

time the Supreme Court came around to the views of Brandeis and
Holmes, it appeared to discard that formula for another: the incitement test. As expressed in *Brandenburg v. Ohio*, the operative rule
now provides that government may not "forbid or proscribe advocacy of the use of force or of law violation except where such advocacy is directed to inciting or producing imminent lawless action
and is likely to incite or produce such action."[46] The crucial shift
from the clear and present danger test was not a matter of verbal
formulae. It would be child's play to interpret "clear and present" to
mean "imminent." The main shift was more one of attitude. By dis-
placing the clear and present danger test, the Court largely dis-
avowed the cases that used it to permit government to justify
censorship in the present based on feared adverse consequences—
such as draft resistance—in the hypothetical future.

But why should government have to wait for a danger to become
imminent? If a speaker today advocates horrific acts in the future,
is it not better to nip the danger in the bud? Supporters of robust
free speech protections traditionally give two main answers. First,
they point to the unintended consequences that often flow from
censorship. In this view, free speech functions as a safety valve:
Silencing speakers with dangerous ideas will often lead them to
make their point through violence rather than words. Or as Brandeis
put the point in *Whitney*, the framers

> knew that order cannot be secured merely through fear of pun-
> ishment for its infraction; that it is hazardous to discourage
> thought, hope and imagination; that fear breeds repression; that
> repression breeds hate; that hate menaces stable government;
> that the path of safety lies in the opportunity to discuss freely
> supposed grievances and proposed remedies; and that the
> fitting remedy for evil counsels is good ones.[47]

---

46. 395 U.S. 444, 447 (1969).

47. Whitney v. California, 274 U.S. 357, 375 (1927) (Brandeis, J., concurring).

The foregoing passage ends with the second basic reason why government should not be allowed to silence dangerous speech: Censorship is unnecessary if the same end—averting violence—can be accomplished through less restrictive means. As Brandeis put the point more fully (again in his *Whitney* concurrence), "[i]f there be time to expose through discussion the falsehood and fallacies, to avert the evil by the processes of education, the remedy to be applied is more speech, not enforced silence."[48]

Neither Brandeis nor Holmes cited empirical evidence for these propositions. Instead, they simply assumed them to be true or attributed them to the framers of the First Amendment and thus to that provision's meaning. But there are other, considerably narrower, interpretations of the text available. For example, Robert Bork, who admired the eloquence though not the content of the *Whitney* concurrence,[49] thought that the First Amendment ought to protect only political speech in the narrow sense, because any broader notion of free speech would not be logically subject to cabining.[50]

Bork thought that his narrow interpretation of free speech better accorded with the First Amendment's purposes even on the assumption that Brandeis and Holmes were right about the benefits of broader protection. But that assumption is itself open to question: Are human societies better off with freedom of speech than without it? Empirical measures of political rights and civil liberties do show a clear correlation between freedom and economic well-being.[51] Most of the countries with substantial freedom, like those in North America and most of Europe, also enjoy high standards of

---

48. *Id.* at 377.

49. *See* Robert H. Bork, *Neutral Principles and Some First Amendment Problems*, 47 IND. L.J. 1, 24 (1971).

50. *Id.* at 27–29.

51. *See* Freedom House, Map of Freedom 2008, http://www.freedomhouse.org/template.cfm?page=363&year=2008.

living, but it is not clear in which direction causation runs. Some free countries, such as Mali in western Africa, are among the world's poorest. Ultimately, the conviction that a broad understanding of free speech benefits the American people may be simply an article of faith. But if so, it is a widely shared article of faith. As Judge Learned Hand once put it, the First Amendment "presupposes that right conclusions are more likely to be gathered out of a multitude of tongues, than through any kind of authoritative selection. To many this is, and always will be, folly; but we have staked upon it our all."[52] Or if that explanation is too doctrinaire, we might say—following Holmes—that protecting dangerous ideas under the First Amendment "is an experiment, as all life is an experiment."[53]

🏵 Free Exercise of Religion

Free speech doctrine confronts a welter of questions—including many that we have not even discussed, such as those involving government funding of speech, commercial speech, and expressive association. By contrast, the case law governing free exercise of religion is now quite simple. It is barely an overstatement to say that the doctrine can be encapsulated in a single question: Does some law or government program single out a particular religion, or religion in general, for disadvantageous treatment? If so, that law or program will almost certainly be found invalid.

For example, in 1993, the Supreme Court invalidated ordinances in Hialeah, Florida, that forbade ritual animal sacrifice.[54] The Court found that the ordinances had been adopted with the purpose of targeting practitioners of Santeria, a Cuban blend of Catholicism

---

52. United States v. Associated Press, 52 F. Supp. 362, 372 (S.D.N.Y. 1943).

53. Abrams v. United States, 250 U.S. 616, 630 (1919) (Holmes, J., dissenting).

54. Church of the Lukumi Babalu Aye, Inc. v. City of Hialeah, 508 U.S. 520, 524 (1993).

and animist beliefs that had been brought to the island by enslaved Africans.[55] The Justices unanimously held that government may not single out for prohibition the methods of animal slaughter of a particular religion, at least where the basis for the special adverse treatment was the nature of the religion rather than, say, the method of killing.[56] A concurrence by Justice Blackmun, joined by Justice O'Connor, observed that a harder case would be presented by the application to a sect like Santeria of a general law forbidding cruelty to animals.[57]

However, under current precedent, Justice Blackmun's hypothetical case would not be at all difficult. In the 1990 ruling in *Employment Division v. Smith*, a five-Justice majority established a nearly blanket rule that general laws—that is, laws that do not target religion or any particular religion as such—do not infringe free exercise rights.[58] In *Smith* itself the question (as perceived by the Court after some procedural wrangling) was whether Oregon could apply a general criminal law forbidding use of the hallucinogenic drug peyote to members of the Native American Church using the drug sacramentally.[59] Writing for the majority, Justice Scalia essentially overruled earlier decisions holding that persons of faith are constitutionally entitled to exemptions from laws substantially burdening their religious practices, unless the laws satisfy strict scrutiny—that is, unless the laws are narrowly tailored to advance a compelling government interest.[60] (We say "essentially" because Justice Scalia purported to distinguish rather than overrule the earlier cases, characterizing those that had upheld free exercise claims as involving a "hybrid" of

---

55. *Id.* at 534–42.
56. *Id.* at 539.
57. *Id.* at 580 (Blackmun, J., concurring).
58. 494 U.S. 872, 878–82 (1990).
59. *Id.* at 874.
60. *Id.* at 882–89.

free exercise and other rights.[61]) Thus, the *Smith* Court imposed no burden of justification on the state to explain why it could not exempt ritual peyote use from the ban. Under *Smith*, so long as a challenged law does not target religion, the fact that it has the effect of burdening religion, no matter how severely, is irrelevant.

The *Smith* ruling was highly controversial both inside and outside the Court. Beyond the vociferous dissents in *Smith*[62] and later cases,[63] Congress reacted with rare bipartisan near-unanimity. In 1993, Congress passed and President Clinton signed the Religious Freedom Restoration Act (RFRA), which purported to overrule *Smith* and "restore" the prior law, under which strict scrutiny would apply to any law that substantially burdened religious practice, whether or not the law targeted religion.[64] Congress claimed power to enact the law under Section 5 of the Fourteenth Amendment, which authorizes Congress to "to enforce, by appropriate legislation, the provisions of" the Amendment. In *City of Boerne v. Flores*, a case we discuss at greater length in Chapter 9, the Supreme Court held that RFRA itself was unconstitutional, at least as applied to states and their subdivisions.[65] The Court later applied RFRA as a valid limit on the federal government,[66] and Congress fought back against the *Boerne* decision itself by enacting new legislation making RFRA's standard applicable in particular settings where it has greater constitutional power.[67] Moreover, many states—either

---

61. *Id.* at 882.

62. *Id.* at 891 (O'Connor, J., concurring only in the judgment); *id.* at 907 (Blackmun, J., dissenting).

63. *See, e.g.,* City of Boerne v. Flores, 521 U.S. 507, 565–66 (1997) (Souter, J., dissenting).

64. 42 U.S.C. § 2000bb et seq. (2006).

65. *Boerne*, 521 U.S. at 533–36.

66. Gonzales v. O Centro Espirita Beneficente Uniao do Vegetal, 546 U.S. 418, 430–32 (2006).

67. *See* Religious Land Use and Institutionalized Persons Act of 2000, 42 U.S.C. § 2000cc.

as a matter of state constitutional law[68] or as a result of state-level RFRAs[69]—have rejected the *Smith* rule. Nonetheless, so far as the Supreme Court's interpretation of the First Amendment is concerned, *Smith* remains good law.

Does the *Smith* rule make sense? As with so many other areas of contested constitutional meaning, historical arguments about the original understanding are inconclusive.[70] However, at least two powerful functional arguments can be made in favor of the *Smith* rule.

First, as Justice Scalia contended in *Smith* itself, judges are not well positioned to make the sorts of judgments that the RFRA test requires of them.[71] All laws potentially impose some burden on religious exercise, and thus one needs to distinguish among minor and "substantial" burdens on religion, or between peripheral and "central" elements of religious practice. The spirit if not the letter of the Establishment Clause (to which we turn below) makes such judgments problematic.

Second, the RFRA rule appears to favor religion over non-religion. Suppose that, in violation of local zoning laws, Ms. Green and Ms. Brown would each like to open a soup kitchen in her

---

68. *See, e.g.*, Christine M. Durham, *What Goes Around Comes Around: The New Relevancy of State Constitution Religion Clauses*, 38 VAL. U. L. REV. 353, 366–68 (2004).

69. *See generally* Alan E. Brownstein, *State RFRA Statutes and Freedom of Speech*, 32 U.C. DAVIS L. REV. 605, 607–08 & 607 n.4 (1999).

70. *Compare* Church of the Lukumi Babalu Aye, Inc. v. City of Hialeah, 508 U.S. 520, 574–77 (Souter, J., concurring); Michael W. McConnell, *Free Exercise Revisionism and the* Smith *Decision*, 57 U. CHI. L. REV. 1109, 1116–19 (1990); *and* Michael W. McConnell, *The Origins and Historical Understanding of Free Exercise of Religion*, 103 HARV. L. REV. 1409 (1990), *with Boerne*, 521 U.S. at 537–44 (Scalia, J., concurring); Philip A. Hamburger, *A Constitutional Right of Religious Exemption: An Historical Perspective*, 60 GEO. WASH. L. REV. 915, 932–48 (1992); *and* Ronald J. Krotoszynski, Jr., *If Judges Were Angels: Religious Equality, Free Exercise, and the (Underappreciated) Merits of* Smith, 102 Nw. U. L. REV 1189, 1248–59 (2008).

71. 494 U.S. 872, 886–87 (1990).

respective home. Green has a religious motive while Brown simply wants to help her fellow human beings.[72] Under the RFRA test, Green but not Brown would be eligible for an exemption from the zoning laws. That approach appears quite unfair to people moved by conscience unconnected to religion, and one Supreme Court Justice has even argued that it violates the Establishment Clause,[73] although he later appeared to change his mind.[74]

These are thus strong reasons to support the *Smith* rule, but there are also strong reasons to question it. Insofar as *Smith*'s opponents would sometimes give special treatment to religious motives they deny to secular reasons of conscience, the fault may lie not with *Smith*'s opponents but with the Free Exercise Clause itself. Perhaps an unenumerated right of conscience can be inferred from the First Amendment or the Bill of Rights as a whole, but the text protects free exercise of *religion*; it is not surprising to think that this enumeration might result in some special constitutional protection for religion that other sorts of felt moral obligations do not receive.

Moreover, Justice Scalia's fears about the inappropriateness of judicial consideration of the importance or centrality of religious practices would seem to prove too much. The *Smith* Court itself said that legislatures are permitted to craft specific exemptions from generally applicable laws;[75] since then, the Court has unanimously accepted that when acting within the scope of its enumerated powers, Congress can even mandate that the courts grant religious exemptions.[76] To the extent that the *Smith* majority worried that

---

72. *See* CHRISTOPHER L. EISGRUBER & LAWRENCE G. SAGER, RELIGIOUS FREEDOM AND THE CONSTITUTION 11 (2007).

73. *Boerne*, 521 U.S. at 536–37 (Stevens, J., concurring).

74. *See* Cutter v. Wilkinson, 544 U.S. 709, 720–24 (2005).

75. *Smith*, 494 U.S. at 890.

76. *See* Gonzales v. O Centro Espirita Beneficente Uniao do Vegetal, 546 U.S. 418, 439 (2006); *Cutter*, 544 U.S. at 714–17, 726.

judges, as secular officials, should not weigh such matters as the centrality of religious practices, that worry would also seem to apply to legislatures. And to the extent that the *Smith* concern was specific to judicial competence, it is hard to understand how judges could be incompetent to apply a test proferred as an interpretation of the First Amendment but competent to apply the same exact test when embodied in a statute.

Perhaps most fundamentally, *Smith's* critics charge that the Court misunderstood the very nature of religious obligation. The *Smith* Court relied on an analogy to other constitutional rights for the proposition that only *targeted* burdens should trigger strict scrutiny, pointing in particular to equal protection and free speech cases.[77] Yet neither analogy is entirely apt.

As we saw in the last chapter, the Court's equal protection jurisprudence does indeed draw a sharp distinction between targeted discrimination and disparate impact. Thus, if we conceptualize free exercise as nothing more than an equal protection provision, we might have good reason to adopt the *Smith* rule. But why should we conceptualize free exercise in that limited way? If understood as simply an equality principle, the Free Exercise Clause would appear to be redundant with the Establishment Clause if not (at least for the states) the Equal Protection Clause. Indeed, the whole notion of free *exercise* of religion would seem to suggest that people have a right actually to engage in religious practices, and not merely to avoid being singled out based on religion.

To be sure, one might say the same thing about speech; yet, as the *Smith* Court rightly notes, free speech doctrine applies heightened scrutiny only to content-based restrictions on speech, not to all generally applicable laws that may incidentally burden speech in particular cases. However, free speech and free exercise differ in a crucial respect. When a general law infringes free speech, it will nearly always leave open alternative avenues of communication;

---

77. *See Smith*, 494 U.S. at 886 n.3.

indeed, for one category of content-neutral regulations of speech—time, place, and manner restrictions—the First Amendment has been construed to require that alternative means of communication must be left available.[78] For example, if the government denies a permit to the organizers of a protest march because of traffic issues raised by the proposed route, it generally must offer an alternative route. By contrast, for persons of faith, often there are no alternatives; even though acting through a law of general applicability, when the state forbids a person to engage in a ritual he believes is commanded by God (or obligates him to perform an act he believes forbidden by God), the possibility of obeying *other* commandments is cold comfort.

To be sure, there are secular policies of such importance that the majority may insist on their adherence regardless of the cost to religious exercise. No one could successfully claim a right to an exemption from the murder laws in order to perform ritual human sacrifice. But of course, laws forbidding extreme behavior of this sort would readily be upheld even under strict scrutiny. The *Smith* rule lumps together such cases of compelling government interest with cases like *Smith* itself, in which we could well imagine a religious exemption that would not seriously undermine any compelling government interest.

In relegating free exercise to the status of an equal protection principle, Justice Scalia in *Smith* acknowledged "that leaving accommodation to the political process will place at a relative disadvantage those religious practices that are not widely engaged in. . . ."[79] Nevertheless, he noted that some states afforded substantial protection to minority religions, and still more states did so in response to *Smith* itself.

---

78. *See, e.g.,* Ward v. Rock Against Racism, 491 U.S. 781, 791 (1989) (quoting Clark v. Cmty. for Creative Non-Violence, 468 U.S. 288, 293 (1984)).

79. *Smith*, 494 U.S. at 890.

Still, we would have greater confidence in the *Smith* rule if the Court were willing to apply a broader notion of neutrality. Consider *Smith* itself. As the Court there noted, even during Prohibition, the law permitted sacramental use of wine, and today we cannot imagine a state or subdivision thereof forbidding alcohol consumption without granting an exemption for sacramental wine use. The groups that use wine sacramentally—Catholics and Jews, among others—are substantial. Given the availability in Oregon of sacramental wine to members of mainstream religions, why was Oregon's prohibition on peyote use deemed neutral in the first place?

With neutrality playing an ever greater role in the Court's understanding of the First Amendment and constitutional rights more broadly, much of the real action has shifted to debates about how to understand neutrality itself. Nowhere is that point more clearly illustrated than in Establishment Clause cases.

ℳ No Establishment of Religion

There is general consensus that the First Amendment's prohibition on any law "respecting an establishment of religion" forbids the creation of an official national church, but a great many other questions about the Establishment Clause generate intense disagreement. In recent years, Supreme Court doctrine has moved towards (though not entirely to the point of) addressing all Establishment Clause issues under the single legal principle of neutrality: Government may not favor or disfavor any particular religion, or religion versus non-religion. Here we briefly consider three contexts in which Establishment Clause controversies have arisen: religious displays on government property; group religious activities under government auspices; and government payments in aid of religious institutions. As we shall see, it is hardly clear that the notion of neutrality is sufficiently determinate to resolve the relevant controversies, and attempts to make it substantially more determinate may produce unattractive results.

Religious display cases fall into two broad categories. In some circumstances, the government opens its property to private speech. Such cases of truly private speech do not typically present Establishment Clause issues. Although the doctrine might conceivably have evolved differently, it is by now reasonably well settled that, as a matter of freedom of speech, government may not exclude religious viewpoints from a public forum for the expression of private viewpoints.[80]

Harder cases arise when government itself is the speaker or when government plays an active role in selecting speakers. During the winter holiday season, for example, many communities decorate their public buildings and grounds with displays commemorating Christmas (and sometimes the Jewish holiday of Hanukkah). The relevant Supreme Court cases hold that such displays are permissible to the extent that they recognize the secular elements of the holiday or to the extent that expressly religious elements (such as a crèche scene depicting the birth of the baby Jesus) are surrounded by secular elements (such as Santa Claus, elves, and plastic reindeer) and symbols of the holidays of other religions (such as Hanukkah).[81]

The "plastic reindeer rule" is easy to ridicule. The notion that there even are secular elements to Christmas may be offensive to some devout Christians, as well as to non-Christians. Moreover, it is not at all clear that Santa and the reindeer neutralize the primary message of the crèche, namely the divinity of Christ.

That said, these cases are legitimately difficult. A rule that completely forbade official religious displays on public property would seem to disadvantage religion and would inaccurately project the message that religion is not an important institution in the lives of

---

80. *See, e.g.*, Lamb's Chapel v. Center Moriches Union Free Sch. Dist., 508 U.S. 384 (1993); Widmar v. Vincent, 454 U.S. 263 (1981).

81. *See* County of Allegheny v. ACLU, 492 U.S. 573, 601–02, 616–21 (opinion of Blackmun, J.); *id.* at 626–27, 632–37 (1989) (O'Connor, J., concurring).

Americans. At the other extreme, a rule that permitted any religious display whatsoever—including, say, a crèche display expressly proclaiming the divinity of Christ or the falsity of alternative beliefs—would send an unmistakable message that some faiths are preferred by the state over other faiths. The existing doctrine attempts, however imperfectly, to balance the government's legitimate ability to recognize the role that religion has played and continues to play in Americans' lives against the concern that government endorsement of particular creeds will marginalize those who subscribe to other faiths (or to none at all).

Justice Sandra Day O'Connor sought to instantiate that balance with a legal test that asked whether a reasonable observer would infer from a government display a message that the government was "endorsing" (rather than merely recognizing) religion.[82] A somewhat more permissive test, favored by Justices generally regarded as ideologically to the right of Justice O'Connor, would only forbid official religious messages when they appear to coerce participation of non-believers.[83] Yet that test (which the Court has not consistently applied or even formulated) raises the question of what constitutes coercion. A majority of the Supreme Court has ruled that peer pressure among minors is sufficient to make prayers at a high school graduation ceremony[84] or a football game coercive,[85] even though students were given the formal option of not participating in the prayer.

Moreover, the Court's landmark case in this area, which invalidated organized prayer in public schools, is hard to explain entirely in terms of coercion. In the 1962 decision in *Engel v. Vitale*, the Court

82. *See Allegheny*, 492 U.S. at 625–37 (O'Connor, J., concurring); Lynch v. Donnelly, 465 U.S. 668, 690–95 (1984) (O'Connor, J., concurring).

83. *See* Santa Fe Ind. Sch. Dist. v. Doe, 530 U.S. 290, 310–13 (2000); Lee v. Weisman, 505 U.S. 577, 587 (1992) (opinion of Kennedy, J.); *id.* at 642 (Scalia, J., dissenting).

84. *Lee*, 505 U.S. at 599.

85. *Santa Fe*, 530 U.S. at 317.

invalidated an official public school prayer, notwithstanding the fact that students were given the formal right to opt out.[86] Social pressure, we might say, made that formal right less than fully effective, but then we must reconcile the rule of *Engel* with the free speech rule of *West Virginia State Board of Educ. v. Barnette*.[87] In that 1943 case, the Court held that the state may not compel schoolchildren to recite the Pledge of Allegiance at the beginning of each school day,[88] but the ruling meant only that schoolchildren could individually opt out of the Pledge.

The difference between the Establishment Clause rule of *Engel* and the free speech rule of *Barnette* is well illustrated by a case the Supreme Court almost decided in 2004. A federal appeals court in California had found that, even with an opt-out possibility, having the Pledge of Allegiance at the beginning of the school day violated the Establishment Clause because it contained the phrase "under God."[89] (These words were added in 1954, after *Barnette* was decided.) The Supreme Court ordered the lawsuit dismissed on jurisdictional grounds,[90] but it is quite clear that a victory on the merits for the plaintiff would have resulted in completely banning public school recitation of the "under God" Pledge, as students already had the right to opt out, per *Barnette*.

Setting aside the question of whether the appeals court was right to find that the "under God" version of the Pledge violates the Establishment Clause, we think the difference in remedy is instructive. It seems unlikely that pressure from peers and teachers to participate in the Pledge would depend on whether it contains "under God." Yet a free speech violation triggers only an opt-out right, whereas an Establishment Clause violation (whether via the Pledge

---

86. 370 U.S. 421, 430–33 (1962).

87. 319 U.S. 624 (1943).

88. *Id.* at 642.

89. Newdow v. U.S. Congress, 292 F.3d 597, 612 (9th Cir. 2002).

90. Elk Grove Unified Sch. Dist. v. Newdow, 542 U.S. 1, 11–18 (2004).

or in a more obvious case involving, say, a prayer to "Jesus Christ, our Lord and Savior") forbids the exercise even for willing students. The difference in the two results cannot be captured by the degree of "coercion" exerted over minors or others. Rather, we think that if *Engel* and *Barnette* are both rightly decided, the difference derives from a principle that limits the ability of the government to promote religious messages but leaves government largely free to "speak" on other subjects.

In general, when the government is the speaker, it need not act in a content-neutral way.[91] Government may urge children to "say no to drugs" without thereby constitutionally obligating itself also to urge children to "give drugs a try." Smokey, the Forest Service spokesbear, may advise visitors to our National Parks to prevent forest fires, without thereby obligating the government to create a different character who urges them to "torch the trees." By contrast, expressly religious government speech is highly problematic. A government campaign urging citizens to "attend worship services weekly" would, in our view, violate at least the spirit of the Establishment Clause.

We say the spirit rather than the letter of the Establishment Clause because religious speech by the government in fact occurs with some frequency. Some instances of government religious speech can be easily rationalized. For example, prison and military chaplains fill a need that incarceration and military service respectively prevent from being filled by the nongovernmental sector. Likewise, when Presidents routinely close speeches by invoking God's blessing, they can be understood to be speaking on their own behalf. Other cases, to be sure, are more difficult. Thus, the Supreme Court made an exception to its formal doctrine for legislative prayer based on longstanding tradition and the original understanding that the tradition presumably reflects.[92] Likewise, the inclusion of

---

91. *See* Nat'l Endowment for the Arts v. Finley, 524 U.S. 569, 587–88 (1998).

92. Marsh v. Chambers, 463 U.S. 783, 786–92 (1983).

the motto "In God We Trust" on our money has been dismissed as essentially de minimis.[93]

Whether such explanations are persuasive is not our concern here. We certainly do not contend that *all* religious speech by the government violates the Establishment Clause (in letter or spirit). Our point is simply that government speech on religious matters can be more problematic than government speech on other matters. Thus, it is an overstatement to say that government must be strictly neutral between religion and non-religion. Government has some greater constitutional freedom to express secular messages than to express religious ones. A rule of complete neutrality would allow government to speak in favor of (or against) religion whenever it would be permitted to advance positions on analogous non-religious topics.

Neutrality is nonetheless an attractive principle in resolving the sorts of Establishment Clause cases in which more than symbols are at stake—namely, cases of government funding of religion. Both extremes here are untenable. Direct government funding for the erection and operation of a church, synagogue, or mosque would violate the core prohibition of the Establishment Clause. Yet a rule that absolutely forbade any government funding for religion would be equally harsh. Must publicly-funded fire departments abstain from putting out fires in churches? Are religious institutions constitutionally barred from attaching their pipes to city water and sewer lines? A strict no-subsidy rule truly would disadvantage religion.

It is tempting to draw a line that distinguishes between the religious and the secular activities of religious institutions, and the Supreme Court has often succumbed to this temptation. Thus, the Court has held that it is permissible for the government to fund bus

---

93. *See, e.g.,* O'Hair v. Murray, 588 F.2d 1144, 1144 (5th Cir. 1979) (per curiam); Aronow v. United States, 432 F.2d 242, 243 (9th Cir. 1970); *cf.* McCreary County v. ACLU, 545 U.S. 844, 888–89 (2005) (Scalia, J., dissenting); Van Orden v. Perry, 545 U.S. 677, 716 (2005) (Stevens, J., dissenting); County of Allegheny v. ACLU, 492 U.S. 573, 602–03 (1989) (opinion of Blackmun, J.).

transportation to religious schools,[94] though not school materials used to teach religious subjects.[95] But complicating such line-drawing exercises is the fact that money is fungible. If the government funds school buses, a religious school can use the money it otherwise would have spent on buses for something else, such as purchasing Bibles.

The neutrality principle goes a long way towards resolving this conundrum. It posits that the government does not violate the Establishment Clause if it permits religious institutions to participate in government programs on the same basis as non-religious institutions. Thus, subject to some further constraints that we gloss over here, a system of government vouchers for children to attend private school does not violate the Establishment Clause merely because some of the private schools at which parents use the vouchers are religious.[96] (Indeed, in the actual case before the Supreme Court, the overwhelming majority of vouchers were used at Catholic schools.) Likewise, state assistance to a blind student was found to be permissible notwithstanding the fact that the student attended a religious college and trained for the ministry, because the student, not the government, made that selection.[97] In these and other cases, the courts permit the expenditure of government funds for religious purposes, so long as private choices rather than the government itself is directing funds towards religion.

If neutrality has thus proved to be a useful concept, it is nonetheless hardly self-applying. Often there will be no obvious secular comparator. Consider, for example, state laws that either define "kosher" or designate rabbinical authorities empowered to certify food as kosher. Are such laws neutral in that they simply apply the more general principle of truth-in-advertising to claims about the compliance of food with Jewish dietary laws, or, in their specificity,

---

94. Everson v. Bd. of Educ., 330 U.S. 1, 17–18 (1947).

95. Mitchell v. Helms, 530 U.S. 793, 857, 867 (2000) (O'Connor, J., concurring).

96. Zelman v. Simmons-Harris, 536 U.S. 639, 643–44, 652–53 (2002).

97. Witters v. Wash. Dept. of Svcs. for the Blind, 474 U. S. 481, 488–90 (1986).

do they violate the Establishment Clause?[98] Or consider the provisions of the Internal Revenue Code that exempt churches and most other religious institutions from taxation[99] and grant a tax deduction to people who provide donations.[100] Are these provisions neutral with respect to religion because other charitable organizations receive the same favorable tax treatment? The concept of "neutrality" cannot by itself answer this question. Some activities in which religions engage—such as running soup kitchens—are uncontroversially the same as activities in which secular organizations engage. But others—such as holding worship services—are at least arguably different. As we saw with respect to the broader principle of equal protection in Chapter 6, so too with respect to the principle of neutrality between religion and non-religion, we still need to make substantive value judgments to decide when the objects of treatment are similarly situated. Neutrality may be a useful framework for employing those value judgments, but it cannot supply them.

Further Reading

Vincent Blasi, *The First Amendment and the Ideal of Civic Courage: The Brandeis Opinion in* Whitney v. California, 29 WM. & MARY L. REV. 653 (1988).

CHRISTOPHER L. EISGRUBER & LAWRENCE G. SAGER, RELIGIOUS FREEDOM AND THE CONSTITUTION (2007).

Michael W. McConnell, *The Origins and Historical Understanding of Free Exercise of Religion*, 103 HARV. L. REV. 1409 (1990).

STEVEN H. SHIFFRIN, DISSENT, INJUSTICE, AND THE MEANINGS OF AMERICA (1999).

Geoffrey R. Stone, PERILOUS TIMES: FREE SPEECH IN WARTIME FROM THE SEDITION ACT OF 1798 TO THE WAR ON TERRORISM (2004).

---

98. Ran-Dav's County Kosher, Inc. v. State, 608 A.2d 1353, 1355 (N.J. 1992).

99. 26 U.S.C. § 501(c)(3) (2006).

100. 26 U.S.C. § 170(a), (c) (2006).

EIGHT

Unenumerated Rights

IN THE LAST CHAPTER we noted that the Ninth Amendment was the framers' chief response to the problem of enumeration: how to prevent readers from inferring from the enumeration of some rights that unenumerated rights receive no constitutional protection? The Ninth Amendment addresses the problem by simply instructing readers not to draw that inference. It states: "The enumeration in the Constitution, of certain rights, shall not be construed to deny or disparage others retained by the people." Although that express rule of construction appears to settle the matter, in fact, unenumerated rights have been controversial from the early days of the Republic. The exchange over natural justice in *Calder v. Bull*[1] (discussed above in Chapter 3) pre-figures much of the subsequent debate. The Constitution acknowledges the existence of unenumerated rights, but offers courts and other actors little guidance in figuring out just what those rights are.

During his ultimately unsuccessful Senate confirmation hearing for a Supreme Court seat, former federal judge Robert Bork analogized the Ninth Amendment to an ink blot. He asked the Senators to imagine that the only authoritative copy of the Constitution contained what appeared to be a textual right covered by an ink blot. Judges, Bork said, would not then be justified in ascribing whatever rights they thought best to the ink blot. Likewise, he argued that judges have no way of knowing what rights the Ninth Amendment

---

1. 3 U.S. (3 Dall.) 386 (1798).

protects, and in a basically democratic system of government, they may not simply use the Ninth Amendment as an excuse for selecting for enforcement those rights that they happen to prefer.[2]

Yet Judge Bork's argument appears to contradict the Ninth Amendment, as it employs the very method of construction—construing non-enumeration to mean non-existence—that the Ninth Amendment expressly forbids. A better analogy than an ink blot might be a constitutional provision that said: "Judges should figure out, using whatever methods they conclude are best suited to such a task, what other, unenumerated rights the people retain, so long as they find some such rights." Could Judge Bork or anyone else honestly claim fidelity to the constitutional text by saying that even this provision should be ignored? And is this hypothetical provision really any different in its import from the actual Ninth Amendment?

Aware of this difficulty, some skeptics of unenumerated rights have suggested that the Ninth Amendment does not mean what it pretty clearly says. On one reading, "the people" who retain unenumerated rights are in fact the people of the several states, who are left free to recognize whatever rights they deem appropriate in their state constitutions and other legal provisions.[3] But this reading of the Ninth Amendment would render it redundant with the Tenth Amendment—which already reserves to the states the powers not delegated to the federal government, including the power to recognize rights. Moreover, as the Supreme Court observed in the 2008 Second Amendment decision in *District of Columbia v. Heller*, whenever the Bill of Rights uses the term "right of the people," as it does in the First, Second, Fourth, and Ninth Amendments, it "unambiguously refer[s] to individual rights, not 'collective' rights, or rights

2. *Nomination of Robert H. Bork to Be Associate Justice of the Supreme Court of the United States: Hearing Before S. Comm. on the Judiciary*, 100th Cong. 249 (1987) (testimony of Judge Bork).

3. *See* Raoul Berger, *The Ninth Amendment: The Beckoning Mirage*, 42 RUTGERS L. REV. 951, 953–56 (1990); Kurt T. Lash, *Three Myths of the Ninth Amendment*, 56 DRAKE L. REV. 875 *passim* (2008).

that may be exercised only through participation in some corporate body," such as a state.[4]

Another means of evading the duty that the Ninth Amendment appears to impose, would be to read the individual rights that it protects to be common law or statutory rights.[5] Yet this gambit also renders the Ninth Amendment pointless. Why would anyone think that the enumeration of *constitutional* rights could in any way support an inference that governments lack the power to recognize statutory or common law rights? The risk against which the Ninth Amendment guards—and the risk of a bill of rights about which Hamilton and Madison worried (as discussed in Chapter 7)—was that readers of the Constitution would think the enumerated *constitutional* rights were the only *constitutional* rights. The rather obvious logic and the history of the Bill of Rights rule out reading the Ninth Amendment as involving statutory or common law rights.

A somewhat more promising way of limiting the impact of the Ninth Amendment would be to say that it refers to individual constitutional rights, but not to judicially enforceable ones.[6] In this view, courts are empowered to enforce the enumerated constitutional rights, but elected officials have an obligation to go further, and recognize constitutional rights—such as, say, a right to health care, or a right to education—that the courts are poorly situated to identify, define, and enforce. Indeed, as we explain in Chapter 9, Congress and various legal academics—especially Lawrence Sager—have championed a related notion that the courts "under-enforce" the Constitution.[7]

---

4. 128 S.Ct. 2783, 2790 (2008).

5. *See, e.g.,* Russell L. Caplan, *The History and Meaning of the Ninth Amendment,* 69 VA. L. REV. 223, 259–65 (1983).

6. For a critique of this approach, see Lawrence G. Sager, *You Can Raise the First, Hide Behind the Fourth, and Plead the Fifth. But What on Earth Can You Do with the Ninth Amendment?,* 64 CHI.-KENT L. REV. 239, 250–51 (1988).

7. *See* LAWRENCE G. SAGER, JUSTICE IN PLAINCLOTHES 86–95 (2004).

However, the under-enforcement thesis is a poor vehicle for judges hoping to avoid the apparent Ninth Amendment obligation of recognizing unenumerated constitutional rights. The under-enforcement thesis is not restricted to unenumerated rights but applies to the whole of the Constitution. It is a thesis about judicial competence to make judgments about matters such as how to allocate funds and other policy issues better left to political judgments. Thus, Sager and others would treat many of the constitutional obligations imposed by the Fourteenth Amendment's Equal Protection Clause, which is an enumerated right, as under-enforced by the courts. Moreover, whatever one might think of the under-enforcement thesis as an academic matter, the Supreme Court has squarely rejected it in one narrow context (which we describe in Chapter 9[8]), and its status in other contexts is uncertain.

Thus, there appears no escape route for judges fearful of recognizing unenumerated constitutional rights, and the courts have long recognized an obligation to do so. However, precisely *which* unenumerated constitutional rights merit protection, and precisely *how* courts should enforce them, have always been matters of considerable controversy. In the remainder of this chapter, we examine the efforts of the Supreme Court to identify unenumerated rights during four post-Civil War periods. We show how the *Slaughterhouse Cases*[9] diverted the doctrine away from perhaps the most natural textual basis for unenumerated rights against the states, the Fourteenth Amendment's Privileges or Immunities Clause. Partly as a result of that move, the Court in a series of late nineteenth- and early twentieth-century cases including *Lochner v. New York*[10] turned to the Due Process Clause as the basis for protecting the freedom of contract as a substantive economic liberty substantially immune to

---

8. *See* Bd. of Trs. of the Univ. of Ala. v. Garrett, 531 U.S. 356, 365 (2001); Kimel v. Fla. Bd. of Regents, 528 U.S. 62, 88 (2000).

9. 83 U.S. (16 Wall.) 36 (1873).

10. 198 U.S. 45 (1905).

state regulation. From there we trace the Court's abandonment of the *Lochner* doctrine in the 1930s and then its gradual embrace, in the decades following the Second World War, of two further grounds for unenumerated rights: first, the notion that the Fourteenth Amendment incorporates most of the specific provisions of the Bill of Rights against the states; and second, a new substantive due process jurisprudence focusing on certain personal freedoms and intimate relationships—including a woman's right to abort her pregnancy and the right of adult consensual sex. In our discussion of the contemporary era, we pay particular attention to the question of whether the modern conception of substantive due process can be distinguished from *Lochner*-era substantive due process.

The Privileges or Immunities Clause

Most highly contentious cases involving claims of constitutional right pit individuals against states rather than against the federal government.[11] Yet as we discussed in Chapter 7, with the exception of a small number of provisions set forth in Article I, Section 10, the original Constitution placed few rights-based limits on the states. The Reconstruction Amendments imposed further restrictions on

---

11. Historically the Court has held federal statutes to be unconstitutional much less often than it has state statutes. *See* CHARLES L. BLACK, JR., STRUCTURE AND RELATIONSHIP IN CONSTITUTIONAL LAW 75–76 (1969) (noting only twelve Supreme Court cases invalidated federal statutes between 1937 and 1967). Recent years have seen greater balance in the rate of federal and state invalidations, due in large part to the Rehnquist Court's assertiveness in First Amendment and federalism cases, though state laws are still overturned much more frequently. *See* Lori A. Ringhand, *The Rehnquist Court: A "By the Numbers" Retrospective*, 9 U. PA. J. CONST. L. 1033, 1037–38, 1044 (2007). The Rehnquist Court invalidated 1.79 federal statutes per Term, compared to 1.24 and 1.18 annual invalidations for the Burger and Warren Courts, respectively. *Id.* at 1035–36. It overturned 4.47 state laws per Term, while the Burger and Warren Courts overturned 10.76 and 6.31 state laws each Term, respectively. *Id.* at 1044.

the states. The Thirteenth Amendment forbade slavery and the Fifteenth Amendment barred race discrimination with respect to voting, although once Reconstruction ended, African Americans were effectively disenfranchised throughout the states of the former Confederacy, and would remain so until the 1960s.

The Fourteenth Amendment contains four principal substantive rights provisions: It overrules the *Dred Scott* decision by conferring U.S. citizenship on persons born in the United States and provides a residence criterion for state citizenship; it forbids the denial of equal protection; it forbids deprivations of life, liberty, or property without due process of law; and it forbids state enforcement of "any law which shall abridge the privileges or immunities of citizens of the United States."

The citizenship provision mostly speaks for itself, although it has sometimes been invoked in controversial cases involving rights of interstate migration.[12] We discussed the Equal Protection Clause in Chapter 6. Here we turn our attention first to the Privileges or Immunities Clause and then to the Due Process Clause.

The Fourteenth Amendment did not invent the terms "privileges" and "immunities." Article IV of the original Constitution entitles "Citizens of each State . . . to all Privileges and Immunities of Citizens in the several States." The landmark decision interpreting that Privileges and Immunities Clause was issued by Justice Bushrod Washington, a nephew of the first President, in his capacity as Circuit Judge. (For much of the early history of the Republic, Supreme Court Justices worked overtime as intermediate appellate judges.) In *Corfield v. Coryell*, Washington construed the Privileges and Immunities as consisting of the fundamental rights of "citizens of all free governments."[13] Contending that "it would perhaps be more tedious than difficult to enumerate" these fundamental

---

12. *See* Saenz v. Roe, 526 U.S. 489, 502–04, 510–11 (1999).

13. 6 F. Cas. 546, 551 (C.C.E.D. Pa. 1823).

rights,[14] Washington went on to name general categories of rights. These were: "[p]rotection by the government; the enjoyment of life and liberty, with the right to acquire and possess property of every kind, and to pursue and obtain happiness and safety; subject nevertheless to such restraints as the government may justly prescribe for the general good of the whole."[15] Washington then followed these categories with a list of particular examples that included a right to travel, a right to practice a trade or profession, a right to habeas corpus, a right to bring suit in court, a right to property, a right against unequal taxation, and a right to vote.[16]

The *Corfield* case was a challenge to a New Jersey law that forbade out-of-staters from gathering oysters under circumstances in which New Jersey citizens were permitted that privilege. After his exposition of the meaning of "privileges and immunities," Justice Washington held for the state on the ground that the oysters were essentially state property that could be reserved to state citizens.[17] Although the opinion is not entirely clear on this point, it appears that Washington therefore thought that harvesting oysters from the commons managed by the state was not a fundamental right protected by Article IV. Modern cases interpret *Corfield* and the Article IV Privileges and Immunities Clause more broadly to presumptively forbid states from discriminating against non-citizens, but only with respect to fundamental rights.[18]

Leading congressional proponents of the Fourteenth Amendment frequently invoked *Corfield* in explaining what they intended by the Privileges or Immunities Clause.[19] Undoubtedly, the rest of

---

14. *Id.*

15. *Id.* at 551–52.

16. *Id.* at 552.

17. *Id.*

18. *See* United Bldg. & Const. Trades v. Camden, 465 U.S. 208 (1984).

19. See AKHIL REED AMAR, THE BILL OF RIGHTS: CREATION AND RECONSTRUCTION 177–78 & 367 n. 59 (1998).

the Reconstruction Congress and ratifiers of the Reconstruction Amendments also would have associated the new Privileges *or* Immunities Clause with the existing Privileges *and* Immunities Clause. Indeed, when the Supreme Court first had occasion to construe the former in the *Slaughterhouse Cases,* it expressly acknowledged both Article IV and *Corfield* as the backdrop against which the new provision operated.[20] Nonetheless, the *Slaughterhouse* Court took a very narrow view of both the old and the new rights.

According to the *Slaughterhouse* Court, the "sole purpose" of the Article IV Privileges and Immunities Clause

> was to declare to the several States, that whatever those rights, as you grant or establish them to your own citizens, or as you limit or qualify, or impose restrictions on their exercise, the same, neither more nor less, shall be the measure of the rights of citizens of other States within your jurisdiction.[21]

Yet this understanding glosses over two very different ideas traceable to *Corfield* and Article IV. In *Corfield,* Justice Washington acknowledged that the Privileges and Immunities Clause proclaims an equality principle: It entitles out-of-staters to the same treatment as state citizens.[22] But Justice Washington also read in the Clause an additional limitation: The non-discrimination principle only applies with respect to fundamental rights.[23] Precisely because oyster gathering was not, in Washington's view, such a fundamental right, unequal treatment of out-of-staters with regard to oyster gathering was not problematic. Note, crucially, that for Washington, the question of whether a right is fundamental for these purposes is not to be decided solely by reference to state law but also by reference

---

20. 83 U.S. (16 Wall.) 36, 75–77 (1873).

21. *Id.* at 77.

22. 6 F. Cas. 546, 552 (C.C.E.D. Pa. 1823).

23. *Id.* at 551–52.

to external principles, presumably something like natural law. Washington takes for granted that there exist certain fundamental rights with respect to which state law cannot treat state citizens and non-citizens unequally.

In the *Slaughterhouse Cases*, the Court says that the content of fundamental rights turns entirely on the state's own decision of what rights to recognize.[24] Even if a confused reading of *Corfield*, that move makes considerable sense given the equality-focused phrasing of the Article IV provision: "The Citizens of each State shall be entitled to all Privileges and Immunities of Citizens in the several States." In other words, out-of-staters receive the same protections—but only those protections—that state citizens receive, and then only in matters of fundamental rights, however defined.

Notice, however, that the phrasing of the Privileges or Immunities Clause of the Fourteenth Amendment differs from the older provision of Article IV in a subtle but important way. The Fourteenth Amendment version provides substantive protection, not just equality, declaring: "No State shall make or enforce any law which shall abridge the privileges or immunities of citizens of the United States." Moreover, what are the privileges and immunities of U.S.—as opposed to state—citizens? Given the backdrop of *Corfield*, one might think that they are roughly the same fundamental rights of which Justice Washington spoke. Or perhaps they are the rights that obtain against federal action, such as those contained in the Bill of Rights.

The *Slaughterhouse Cases* rejected such expansive readings in favor of an extraordinarily narrow reading. Reasoning that it could not have been the purpose of the Fourteenth Amendment to transfer primary responsibility for defining and respecting basic civil rights from the states to the federal government,[25] the Court concluded that the Fourteenth Amendment's Privileges or Immunities

---

24. 83 U.S. (16 Wall.) at 77.
25. *Id.* at 77–78.

Clause only forbids states from abridging distinctively national rights. Citing prior case law, the Court gave the following examples: the right to travel to the national capital; the right of access to seaports and state courts; the right to demand protection from the federal government when on the high seas or traveling abroad; the right to petition and assemble; the right to habeas corpus; and the other rights protected by the Constitution, including the Reconstruction Amendments themselves.[26] Yet the list consists mostly of federal rights that are protected against state action, either expressly or by structural implication, in other parts of the Constitution, or rights—such as to demand protection from the *federal* government—that, by their nature, do not readily admit of infringement by *states*. In its zeal to ensure that the Privileges or Immunities Clause would not become the vehicle by which federal power completely displaced state law (in virtue of congressional enforcement power under the Fourteenth Amendment's Section Five, discussed in Chapter 9), the *Slaughterhouse* Court construed the Clause as doing almost nothing.

Consequently, to this day, the Privileges or Immunities Clause is a virtual dead letter, despite recent efforts to breathe new life into it. For example, in a 2010 case, lawyers challenging a Chicago ordinance urged the Court to find that the right to possess a handgun for personal protection was among the privileges and immunities of national citizenship. Although a majority agreed that the Chicago handgun ban was unconstitutional, the Court declined to overrule *Slaughterhouse*.[27]

𝍦 The *Lochner* Era

Despite its sweeping implications for the future of the Privileges or Immunities Clause, the actual holding of the *Slaughterhouse Cases*

---

26. *Id.* at 78–80.

27. *See* McDonald v. City of Chicago, 78 U.S.L.W. 4844 (2010).

was narrower. At issue was a Louisiana law that created a state
monopoly on the operation of slaughterhouses. Independent businesses engaged in slaughtering livestock were required to close,
although butchers could use the state facilities for a fee.[28] The
owners of the displaced businesses sued, alleging a variety of claims
under the Thirteenth and Fourteenth Amendments. In rejecting all
of these claims, the Supreme Court expressed an attitude of deference to elected officials. "The wisdom of the monopoly granted by
the legislature may be open to question," the Court explained, but
given the legitimate health and safety concerns that slaughtering
livestock raises, the Court was not willing to second-guess the legislative judgment that a state monopoly was best suited to protecting the public.[29]

The Slaughterhouse Cases were decided in 1873. In the two and a
half decades that followed, the Court continued to uphold state legislation challenged on Fourteenth Amendment grounds, but
dropped ever-more-pointed hints that deference to legislative
action had its limits.[30] Then, in another Louisiana case, the Justices
dropped the other shoe. *Allgeyer v. Louisiana* struck down a state
law forbidding out-of-state insurance companies from contracting
with Louisiana residents for marine insurance.[31] Although there was
a plausible argument that the Louisiana law violated the
dormant Commerce Clause (in those days before the federal
McCarran-Ferguson Act[32] authorized state insurance laws to discriminate against interstate commerce), the *Allgeyer* Court rested its
holding on the Due Process Clause.[33] Explaining that the ability of
Louisiana residents to form contracts with out-of-state corporations

---

28. 83 U.S. (16 Wall.) at 111–12 (Bradley, J., dissenting).

29. *Id.* at 61–63 (opinion of Miller, J.).

30. *See* LAURENCE H. TRIBE, AMERICAN CONSTITUTIONAL LAW 565–67 (2d ed.
    1988).

31. 165 U.S. 578, 592–93 (1897).

32. 15 U.S.C. § 1011 *et seq.*

33. 165 U.S. at 589.

was part of the "liberty" protected by the Fourteenth Amendment, Justice Peckham, writing for the Court, waxed poetic:

> The "liberty" mentioned in that amendment means, not only the right of the citizen to be free from the mere physical restraint of his person, as by incarceration, but the term is deemed to embrace the right of the citizen to be free in the enjoyment of all his faculties; to be free to use them in all lawful ways; to live and work where he will; to earn his livelihood by any lawful calling; to pursue any livelihood or avocation; and for that purpose to enter into all contracts which may be proper, necessary, and essential to his carrying out to a successful conclusion the purposes above mentioned.[34]

We can grant that freedom of contract is indeed a form of "liberty," yet still puzzle over why that entails protection against the *substance* of laws limiting contractual freedom, rather than just requiring fair procedures for adjudicating disputes involving whatever contracts state law deems enforceable. After all, the Fourteenth Amendment does not protect liberty as such. It forbids deprivations of liberty (and life and property) *without due process of law.*

The answer given by the Court—and the one that still underpins much constitutional doctrine—goes roughly like this: The Due Process Clauses of the Fifth and Fourteenth Amendments, which are traceable to the Magna Carta, forbid arbitrary exercises of power; laws that unreasonably deny persons the ability to exercise their rights to life, liberty, or property have the form of law but not its substance; thus, they deprive persons of liberty without due process of law.[35] Hence we have the doctrine that has come to be known as "substantive due process."

---

34. *Id.*

35. *See* Planned Parenthood of Southeastern Pennsylvania v. Casey, 505 U.S. 833, 847 (1992) (plurality opinion) (citing Poe v. Ullman, 367 U.S. 497, 541 (1961)

For the four decades following the *Allgeyer* decision, the Supreme
Court repeatedly invoked the doctrine of substantive due process
to invalidate state and federal legislation that, in the Justices' view,
unduly interfered with freedom of contract. The most notorious
case in this period—and the one that gave its name to the era—was
Lochner v. New York.[36] There, the Court invalidated a New York law
establishing a maximum work week for bakers of sixty hours.
Notwithstanding evidence that bakers who labored longer hours
put their own health and the health of the public at risk, the Court
concluded that "[t]here must be more than the mere fact of the possible existence of some small amount of unhealthiness to warrant
legislative interference with liberty."[37] Sounding a strongly libertarian note, the majority deemed laws "limiting the hours in which
grown and intelligent men may labor to earn their living . . . mere
meddlesome interferences with the rights of the individual."[38]

The *Lochner* decision inspired an even more well-known dissent.
Justice Oliver Wendell Holmes, Jr. wrote that "a Constitution is not
intended to embody a particular economic theory, whether of
paternalism and the organic relation of the citizen to the state or of
laissez faire."[39] Although his championship of free speech has made
Holmes something of a hero to liberals, he held policy views that
could be fairly described as social Darwinist.[40] Nonetheless, Holmes
warned in his *Lochner* dissent against the dangers of judges conflat-
ing their policy preferences with the Constitution's command,[41] a

---

(Harlan, J., dissenting from dismissal on justiciability grounds)); Wilson v. New,
243 U.S. 332, 365–68 (1917) (Day, J., dissenting) (citing Hurtado v. California,
110 U.S. 516, 531 (1884)).

36. 198 U.S. 45 (1905).

37. *Id.* at 59.

38. *Id.* at 61.

39. *Id.* at 75 (Holmes, J., dissenting).

40. *See* Buck v. Bell, 274 U.S. 200, 207 (1927); ALBERT W. ALSCHULER, LAW WITHOUT
VALUES *passim* (2000).

41. *Lochner*, 198 U.S. at 75–76 (Holmes, J., dissenting).

risk that seems particularly acute when dealing with a text as open-ended as "liberty."

During the *Lochner* era, the Court invalidated maximum-hour laws,[42] minimum-wage laws,[43] laws banning "yellow dog" contracts (that is, contracts waiving the worker's right to join a labor union),[44] and numerous other forms of progressive legislation. Nonetheless, it is something of an exaggeration to say, as Justice Holmes implied, that the Court in this period simply equated the Due Process Clause (or the Constitution more broadly) with laissez-faire capitalism. After all, the Justices upheld even more laws than they struck down.[45]

The touchstone of judicial review in the *Lochner* era was the reasonableness of legislation. In principle, a court could apply such a test deferentially. The familiar notion that reasonable minds can differ suggests the possibility that judges might, under the rubric of reasonableness review, uphold legislation that they thought quite unwise. In practice, however, *Lochner*-era reasonableness review amounted to nearly de novo consideration of the necessity of laws restricting freedom of contract.

The abandonment of *Lochner*-era jurisprudence in 1937 eventually resulted in the substitution of a new formal test and, more importantly, a new attitude towards economic regulations challenged on substantive due process grounds. Modern doctrine ordinarily asks only whether such regulations are supported by a "rational basis."[46] As we saw in Chapter 6, that test—which is essentially the same in the equal protection and the substantive due process contexts[47]—is extraordinarily deferential. It requires only that

---

42. *Id.* at 64.

43. Adkins v. Children's Hospital, 261 U.S. 525, 558–62 (1923).

44. Coppage v. Kansas, 236 U.S. 1, 14, 26 (1915).

45. *See* TRIBE, *supra* note 30, at 567 n.2.

46. *See, e.g.,* Williamson v. Lee Optical Co., 348 U.S. 483, 487–88 (1955).

47. *See id.* at 488–49; *see also* Railway Express Agency v. New York, 336 U.S. 106, 109–10 (1949).

a reviewing court be able to imagine circumstances under which the challenged law would be sensible.

✿ Incorporation of the Bill of Rights

Even as the Court abandoned substantive due process in liberty-of-contract cases, it retained substantive due process itself. As we saw in Chapters 3 and 6, the roadmap was laid out in 1938 in the *Carolene Products* footnote. Among the categories of laws the Court exempted from the general post-*Lochner* rule of deference to elected officials were those burdening "discrete and insular minorities" and those that restricted the very democratic processes themselves.[48] In addition, the *Carolene Products* Court questioned "the presumption of constitutionality when legislation appears on its face to be within a specific prohibition of the Constitution, such as those of the first ten Amendments, which are deemed equally specific when held to be embraced within the Fourteenth."[49] In other words, and as we saw in Chapter 7, even after the overruling of *Lochner*, the Court would apply non-deferential review of government action challenged under the specific provisions of the Bill of Rights.

The Bill of Rights, however, only applies to the federal government. In referring to Bill of Rights provisions "embraced within the Fourteenth" Amendment, the *Carolene Products* Court adverted to what has come to be known as the doctrine of incorporation—the notion that the Fourteenth Amendment takes rights that people have against federal action, and turns them into shields against the state governments as well. How does the Fourteenth Amendment accomplish that task? The literal language of the Privileges or Immunities Clause would seem to be a natural vehicle. It protects against state infringement just those privileges and immunities of

---

48. United States v. Carolene Products Co., 304 U.S. 144, 152 n.4 (1938).

49. *Id.*

citizens of the United States—on this reading, the protections guaranteed under the Bill of Rights. Yet as we have seen, the *Slaughterhouse Cases* ruled out this interpretation. Accordingly, the Privileges or Immunities Clause was unavailable as a text for incorporation of the Bill of Rights. Instead, the Supreme Court turned to the Due Process Clause.

Many of the provisions of the Bill of Rights are procedural, and thus *substantive* due process was unnecessary to incorporate them; such provisions simply give meaning to the "process" each citizen is "due" by the states under the Fourteenth Amendment. For example, incorporation of the Sixth Amendment right to counsel in criminal cases can be readily understood as an essential element of the fair trial that the state must afford if it is to deprive someone of his life or liberty upon conviction. Likewise, the Fourth Amendment requirements of probable cause and a warrant (where they apply) can be readily understood as the procedural guarantees necessary to depriving people of their security—no doubt an aspect of liberty— "in their persons, houses, papers, and effects."

Yet if these and other provisions of the Bill of Rights can be incorporated without resort to *substantive* due process, still other rights cannot. Most prominently, the First Amendment rights to free speech, freedom of the press, and free exercise of religion—all of which have been incorporated against the states[50]—do more than prescribe procedural fairness. The most careful proof that a defendant "sold a copy of Huckleberry Finn" would not validate a conviction for distributing banned books. First Amendment rights, if incorporated via the Due Process Clause, necessarily invoke *substantive* due process. Thus, for those linguistic purists who think that substantive due process is an oxymoron—akin, in John Hart

50. *See, e.g.*, Cantwell v. Connecticut, 310 U.S. 296, 303 (1940); Gitlow v. New York, 268 U.S. 652, 666 (1925).

Ely's famous phrase, to "green pastel redness"[51]—even incorporation of the First Amendment is, or should be, problematic.

Moreover, the Due Process Clause is a curious provision by which to incorporate even procedural protections such as the right to counsel and the right against unreasonable searches and seizures. After all, the Fifth Amendment contains its own Due Process Clause, which is essentially identical in its wording to the Due Process Clause of the Fourteenth Amendment. Yet if the Fourteenth Amendment is a shorthand for the provisions of the Bill of Rights, then, one wonders, why does the original Bill of Rights itself contain anything other than the Fifth Amendment's Due Process Clause?

Although it may be good sport to identify such textual anomalies, this exercise misses the larger issues in play. If the Court wanted to clean up its incorporation doctrine it could simply overrule the *Slaughterhouse Cases* and place the burden of incorporation on the Privileges or Immunities Clause. In fact, the chief champion of incorporation, Justice Hugo Black, proposed just such a course, arguing that the first Section of the Fourteenth Amendment, "taken as a whole,"—that is, including the Privileges or Immunities Clause—incorporates the Bill of Rights.[52]

Thus, we have a textually straightforward basis for inferring that unenumerated rights limit the states: The Fourteenth Amendment, either taken as a whole or just through the Privileges or Immunities Clause, makes the Bill of Rights applicable to the states; and the Bill of Rights includes the Ninth Amendment, which forbids the denial or even the disparagement of unenumerated rights.

---

51. JOHN HART ELY, DEMOCRACY AND DISTRUST 18 (1980).

52. Adamson v. California, 332 U.S. 46, 74–75 (1947) (Black, J., dissenting). The "taken as a whole" approach may be superior to reliance on the Privileges or Immunities Clause alone, because that Clause applies only to "citizens" rather than the "persons" to which the Due Process and Equal Protection Clauses refer. A version of incorporation that relied solely on the Privileges or Immunities Clause might therefore leave resident aliens and lawful visitors without full protection against state violations of the Bill of Rights.

That straightforward route has not been taken by the Supreme Court, however. Justice Black himself favored what came to be known as "jot-for-jot" incorporation, the notion that the Fourteenth Amendment incorporates each and every provision of the first eight amendments. Why eight rather than nine? Although he made historical arguments about the original understanding of the Fourteenth Amendment,[53] Justice Black chiefly saw incorporation as a means of cabining judicial discretion. If judges got to pick and choose which rights to incorporate, he worried, they would repeat the mistake of the *Lochner* era, substituting their policy preferences for those of elected officials. Black believed that the first eight provisions of the Bill of Rights, while hardly fully determinate in their content, were sufficiently specific to give rise to judicially manageable rules and standards.[54] Although his textual and historical analysis might better have led to the conclusion that the Fourteenth Amendment incorporated the first *nine* amendments, his disdain for natural law led him to stop at eight.

As a formal matter, Black lost the incorporation debate. The Supreme Court never adopted the view that the Fourteenth Amendment incorporates either the first eight or the first nine amendments. Instead, as an official matter, the Court "looks to the Bill of Rights for guidance" in determining which rights are so fundamental that they are protected by the Due Process Clause.[55] In practice, this procedure has led to incorporation of most of the provisions of the first eight amendments.[56] The Supreme Court has not incorporated the grand jury requirement of the Fifth Amendment[57] or the civil jury requirement of the Seventh Amendment,[58] but for

---

53. *Id.* at 92–123 (appendix of Black, J.).

54. *Id.* at 91–92.

55. Duncan v. Louisiana, 391 U.S. 145, 147–48 (1968).

56. *See id.*

57. *See* Hurtado v. California, 110 U.S. 516 (1884).

58. *See* Walker v. Sauvinet, 92 U.S. 90 (1875).

the most part, Justice Black's positive goals were largely accomplished indirectly.

Yet Black clearly lost on the issue that was perhaps of greatest importance to him: unenumerated rights. There was a flip side to the Court's conclusion that the Bill of Rights is not the measure of the Due Process Clause: It also meant that there could be rights that, though not expressly enumerated in the first eight amendments, were nonetheless so fundamental that they limited state action. In different contexts, the Court has used a variety of verbal formulas to convey this idea. It has sometimes asked what rights are "implicit in the concept of ordered liberty."[59] It has at other times asked whether a putative right is "deeply rooted in this Nation's history and tradition."[60] And it has also from time to time indicated that the relevant "tradition is a living thing."[61] However the general test is formulated, two facts stand out: First, the Justices remain in the business of recognizing and enforcing unenumerated rights against the states and the federal government; and second, they do so uneasily.

ⅶ The Right of "Privacy"

The line between unenumerated and enumerated rights is not always clear. For example, the First Amendment expressly enumerates both a right to "freedom of speech" and a "right of the people peaceably to assemble, and to petition the government for a redress of grievances," but contains no express right of association as such.

---

59. *See, e.g.,* Palko v. Connecticut, 302 U.S. 319, 325 (1937).

60. *See, e.g.,* Washington v. Glucksberg, 521 U.S. 702, 720–21 (1997); Moore v. City of East Cleveland, 431 U.S. 494, 503 (1977) (plurality opinion).

61. *E.g.,* Planned Parenthood of Southeastern Pennsylvania v. Casey, 505 U.S. 833, 850 (1992) (citing Poe v. Ullman, 367 U.S. 497, 542 (1961) (Harlan, J., dissenting from dismissal on justiciability grounds)); *Moore,* 431 U.S. at 501 (plurality opinion) (same).

Nonetheless, the Supreme Court has inferred a right of expressive association, even when the people who associate to express themselves are holding a St. Patrick's Day parade rather than formally petitioning for a redress of grievances.[62] Should we characterize the right to expressive association as a protected unenumerated right or as an interpretation of the First Amendment? Likewise, the Constitution contains no express right to interstate travel, but one can be inferred from the Privileges and Immunities Clause of Article IV: The very possibility of claiming the protections of another state must presume a right to travel from one's home state.[63] Should we deem the right to travel a protected unenumerated right or part of the right protected by the Privileges and Immunities Clause? The recognition that the Constitution protects unenumerated as well as enumerated rights renders unnecessary such fine parsing of rights into these two categories.

Nonetheless, to avoid the appearance (and perhaps the reality) of unguided judicial discretion in determining what unenumerated rights exist, the Court has been guided—but not strictly limited— by the enumerated rights. The now-canonical statement of this process was set forth by the second Justice John Marshall Harlan in a dissent on procedural grounds that presaged a later Supreme Court decision finding a constitutional right of married couples to use contraceptives. Harlan wrote in *Poe v. Ullman* that

> the full scope of the liberty guaranteed by the Due Process Clause cannot be found in or limited by the precise terms of the specific guarantees elsewhere provided in the Constitution. This "liberty" is not a series of isolated points pricked out in terms of the taking of property; the freedom of speech, press, and religion; the right to keep and bear arms; the freedom from unreasonable

---

62. *See* Hurley v. Irish American Gay, Lesbian, and Bisexual Group of Boston, 515 U.S. 557 (1995).

63. *Cf.* Saenz v. Roe, 526 U.S. 489 (1999); Shapiro v. Thompson, 394 U.S. 618 (1969).

searches and seizures; and so on. It is a rational continuum which, broadly speaking, includes a freedom from all substantial arbitrary impositions and purposeless restraints . . . and which also recognizes, what a reasonable and sensitive judgment must, that certain interests require particularly careful scrutiny of the state needs asserted to justify their abridgment.[64]

Early twentieth-century cases upholding the rights of parents to direct the upbringing and education of their children,[65] combined with a mid-twentieth-century case invalidating a criminal penalty of sterilization (nominally on equal protection grounds),[66] became the basis for the modern doctrine that sometimes goes under the heading of a right to "privacy."

The lead opinion in the landmark case, *Griswold v. Connecticut,* somewhat strangely suggests that the right of married couples to use contraception is a right protected by the Bill of Rights itself, or through the "penumbras" and "emanations" to which those rights give rise.[67] Justice William O. Douglas, the author of *Griswold,* had joined Justice Black's earlier statements articulating the view that the Fourteenth Amendment incorporated all of the first eight provisions of the Bill of Rights and nothing else;[68] thus, when it came time to write for the Court in *Griswold,* Douglas attempted to argue that various provisions of the Bill of Rights themselves gave rise to a right of privacy,[69] disavowing freestanding substantive due process. The argument was at best awkward, however, and subsequent decisions have treated the Harlan position as more substantial.

---

64. *Poe,* 367 U.S. at 543.

65. *See* Pierce v. Society of Sisters, 268 U.S. 510 (1925); Meyer v. Nebraska, 262 U.S. 390 (1923).

66. *See* Skinner v. Oklahoma, 316 U.S. 535 (1942).

67. 381 U.S. 479, 484 (1965).

68. *See, e.g.,* Adamson v. California, 332 U.S. 46, 68 (1947) (Black, J., dissenting).

69. *Griswold,* 381 U.S. at 484–86.

According to Harlan, the enumerated rights instruct readers of the Constitution about the sorts of interests that receive protection, leaving readers to interpolate and extrapolate the specific protected unenumerated rights. As with incorporation itself, the Bill of Rights serves only as a guide.[70]

Following *Griswold*, the Court has found substantive due process protection for: contraceptive use by *unmarried* couples;[71] refusal, by a competent adult, of medical treatment (in dicta);[72] co-habitation by relatives who are not a conventional nuclear family;[73] same-sex sexual intimacy;[74] and, most controversially, abortion.[75] In the same period, the Court rejected a putative right of terminally ill patients to physician-assisted suicide.[76]

During the time since *Griswold*, the Court's verbal formula for substantive due process rights evolved. The earlier cases described a general right of "privacy" that was "fundamental," and therefore could only be infringed by laws that satisfied strict scrutiny.[77] Later cases eschewed the vocabulary of privacy and fundamental rights, rather confusingly substituting the term "liberty interest," a phrase that had previously been used to describe the sort of interest to which only the procedural protections of the Due Process Clause applied. Indeed, the use of the term "liberty interest" in Chief Justice Rehnquist's plurality opinion in a 1989 abortion case may well have

---

70. *Id.* at 499–500 (Harlan, J., concurring).

71. Eisenstadt v. Baird, 405 U.S. 438 (1972).

72. *See* Cruzan v. Dir., Mo. Dept. of Health, 497 U.S. 261, 279 (1990); *id.* at 287 (O'Connor, J., concurring); *id.* at 302 (Brennan, J., dissenting); *see also* Washington v. Glucksberg, 521 U.S. 702, 720 (1997); Washington v. Harper, 494 U.S. 210, 221–22 (1990).

73. Moore v. City of East Cleveland, 431 U.S. 494 (1977) (plurality opinion).

74. Lawrence v. Texas, 539 U.S. 558 (2003).

75. Planned Parenthood of Southeastern Pennsylvania v. Casey, 505 U.S. 833 (1992); Roe v. Wade, 410 U.S. 113 (1973).

76. *Glucksberg*, 521 U.S. 702.

77. *See, e.g., Roe*, 410 U.S. at 155.

reflected an effort on his part to undermine the abortion right itself.[78] Since then, however, the Court has sometimes used the term "liberty interest" to mean more or less what it formerly meant by the term "fundamental right."[79] In addition, in reaffirming what it termed the "central holding" of *Roe v. Wade*, in 1992 the Court replaced "strict scrutiny" for abortion regulations with a somewhat less restrictive "undue burden" test,[80] and the three authors of the lead opinion in that case later disagreed among themselves over what exactly that test entailed in the context of so-called "partial-birth" abortion bans.[81] Finally, and perhaps most confusingly of all, in its 2003 decision invalidating a Texas law that banned same-sex sodomy, the Court never clearly indicated what standard of review it was applying.[82]

As a consequence of these doctrinal meanderings, constitutional lawyers and lower court judges—not to mention new law school graduates studying for the bar examination!—may have difficulty saying exactly what constitutional tests apply to laws challenged as infringing various unenumerated rights. Nonetheless, taking a bird's eye, rather than a worm's eye, view of the topic, we can see that the Court will apply some form of heightened scrutiny to laws that infringe the freedom of competent adults to make important decisions about family formation, child-rearing, and bodily autonomy.

The Court's decisions in this area are vulnerable to the criticism that in deciding what counts as a sufficiently important or sufficiently

---

78. Webster v. Reproductive Health Servs., 492 U.S. 490, 520 (1989).

79. *See, e.g.,* Cruzan v. Dir., Mo. Dept. of Health, 497 U.S. 261, 278 (1990).

80. *Casey,* 505 U.S. at 871, 874 (joint opinion of O'Connor, Kennedy, and Souter, JJ.).

81. *Compare* Gonzales v. Carhart, 550 U.S. 124, 127 S.Ct. 1610, 1626–27 (2007) (opinion of Kennedy, J.), *and* Stenberg v. Carhart 530 U.S. 914, 977–78 (2000) (Kennedy, J., dissenting), *with Gonzales,* 127 S.Ct. at 1640–41 (Ginsburg, J., dissenting, joined by Souter, J.), *and Stenberg,* 530 U.S. at 948 (O'Connor, J., concurring).

82. Lawrence v. Texas, 539 U.S. 558, 578 (2003).

private decision to warrant substantive due process protection, the Justices simply choose the values they hold. In an opinion rejecting a right to same-sex sodomy (later overruled), Justice White expressed the concern this way: "The Court is most vulnerable and comes nearest to illegitimacy when it deals with judge-made constitutional law having little or no cognizable roots in the language or design of the Constitution."[83] Justice White then specifically invoked the specter of *Lochner*,[84] as other Justices have in dissenting from modern-era cases recognizing substantive due process rights.[85]

It would thus appear that the question that has haunted the modern cases is, not to put too fine a point on it, whether *Roe v. Wade* can be distinguished from *Lochner v. New York*. The Justices themselves attempted to answer this question in explaining why *Roe* ought not to be overruled. They averred that *Lochner* rested on a view of the world that, by 1937, had been shown to be false: "[T]he Depression had come and, with it, the lesson that . . . the interpretation of contractual freedom protected in [the *Lochner* line of cases] rested on fundamentally false factual assumptions about the capacity of a relatively unregulated market to satisfy minimal levels of human welfare."[86]

No doubt there is much to this explanation, but it is worth noting three cautions. First, objections to *Lochner* were in its day and remain now at least as much normative as factual. Second, many people in the pro-life movement would likely counter with the objection that *Roe* too is based on false factual assumptions, in this context, factual assumptions about fetal development. And third, recent years have seen a wave of revisionist scholarship aimed at

83. Bowers v. Hardwick, 478 U.S. 186, 194 (1986).

84. *Id.* at 194–95.

85. *See, e.g., Casey,* 505 U.S. at 998 (Scalia, J., dissenting).

86. *Id.* at 861–62 (opinion of the Court).

showing that *Lochner* was in fact correctly decided.[87] Of course, to the extent that this scholarship argues for a libertarian interpretation of the Constitution across the board, it may actually support the result in *Roe*, for then it would not be important to distinguish *Lochner*.

Whereas most efforts to distinguish *Roe* and substantive due process more broadly from *Lochner* develop categories of good and bad judicial activism, an influential 1987 law review article by Cass Sunstein sought instead to characterize the *Lochner* era as fundamentally about privileging

> government inaction, the existing distribution of wealth and entitlements, and the baseline set by the common law. Governmental intervention was constitutionally troublesome, whereas inaction was not; and both neutrality and inaction were defined as respect for the behavior of private actors pursuant to the common law, in light of the existing distribution of wealth and entitlements.[88]

Working in the legal realist tradition, Sunstein argued that contractual freedom is not pre-legal but depends entirely on a web of regulation and ultimately the state's willingness to use force to back up legal judgments. Thus, the mistake of *Lochner* was to treat progressive legislation as any more an "intervention" into the prepolitical world than the existing baseline already reflected.[89]

---

87. *See, e.g.*, Randy E. Barnett, *Justice Kennedy's Libertarian Revolution*: Lawrence v. Texas, 2003 CATO SUP. CT. REV. 21, 22–23; David E. Bernstein, Lochner *Era Revisionism, Revised:* Lochner *and the Origins of Fundamental Rights Constitutionalism*, 92 GEO. L.J. 1 (2003); Richard A. Epstein, *Liberty, Equality, and Privacy: Choosing a Legal Foundation for Gay Rights*, 2002 U. CHI. LEGAL F. 73, 84–90.

88. Cass R. Sunstein, *Lochner's Legacy*, 87 COLUM. L. REV. 873, 874 (1987).

89. *Id.* at 885.

There is much power in this approach too, but Sunstein's diagnosis of *Lochner* threatens to do away with not only substantive due process protection for freedom of contract but all constitutional rights. Indeed, that implication seems not to have been lost on Sunstein. In his book *Democracy and the Problem of Free Speech*, he made much the same point about freedom of speech: There is no neutral pre-political baseline because laws concerning such matters as private property, monopolies, and use of the electromagnetic spectrum construct the space in which speech occurs.[90] Thus, in Sunstein's view, it is a mistake—indeed, the Lochnerian mistake— to treat laws that target the content of speech as somehow distinctively interventionist. The upshot for Sunstein would be to permit much more government regulation of the content of speech than conventional doctrine allows. Sunstein's re-imagining of *Lochner's* mistake ends up providing no good ground for distinguishing *Roe* (and to be fair to Sunstein, he never claimed that it did).

So, is there a persuasive ground for distinguishing *Roe* from *Lochner?* Although the matter is much debated, we nonetheless think this is the wrong question. The *Lochner* era ultimately came to an end less because *Lochner* was "wrong" in some metaphysical sense than because the Court's jurisprudence in this period was wildly unpopular.[91] Likewise, in the current era, there may be legitimate concerns about the soundness of the doctrine of substantive due process, but those concerns do not explain the continued controversy over the abortion right.

What should we make of the fact that even conservative Supreme Court nominees typically state during their confirmation hearings

---

90. CASS SUNSTEIN, DEMOCRACY AND THE PROBLEM OF FREE SPEECH 28–51 (1993).

91. Barry Friedman, *The History of the Countermajoritarian Difficulty, Part Three: The Lesson of* Lochner, 76 N.Y.U. L. REV. 1383, 1452–55 (2001).

that they accept *Griswold* as settled law?[92] The one nominee who squarely challenged *Griswold*—Judge Bork—was rejected. Yet there is nothing in the constitutional text that provides a stronger grounding for a right to contraception than for a right to abortion. The reason that *Roe* but not *Griswold* is controversial today is that the vast majority of Americans now believe that government has no business forbidding contraception, while substantial numbers of Americans consider abortion to be immoral or even murder.

In the end, then, the continued controversy surrounding unenumerated rights may have less to do with questions of judicial legitimacy than with the fact that the hottest of the hot-button social issues of our era has been decided under the rubric of substantive due process. Consider a thought experiment. Suppose that the Supreme Court in 1973 had decided *Roe* not as a substantive due process case but under the Equal Protection Clause, finding that the burden of abortion laws unfairly falls on women rather than men.[93] Is it likely that the different textual ground—the *enumerated* right to Equal Protection—would have much altered the subsequent controversy over the decision?

Or suppose that at some point in the near future, the Supreme Court invalidates laws barring same-sex marriage. Existing doctrine might be argued to support such a ruling either on the ground that marriage is a fundamental right under substantive due process or on the alternative ground that same-sex marriage bans discriminate either on the basis of sex or sexual orientation. Is it likely that the particular doctrinal basis the Court chose—equal protection

92. *Nomination of John G. Roberts, Jr., to Be Chief Justice of the United States: Hearing Before S. Comm. on the Judiciary,* 109th Cong. 259 (2005); *Nomination of Samuel Alito to Be Associate Justice of the Supreme Court of the United States: Hearing Before S. Comm. on the Judiciary,* 109th Cong. 318, 452–54 (2006).

93. *See* Ruth Bader Ginsburg, *Speaking in a Judicial Voice,* 67 N.Y.U. L. REV. 1185, 1200 (1992); Ruth Bader Ginsburg, *Some Thoughts on Autonomy and Equality in Relation to* Roe v. Wade, 63 N.C. L. REV. 375, 382–83 (1985).

versus substantive due process—would make any real difference in the reaction of the American people and the political branches?

To be clear, we are not saying that the Supreme Court should do and say whatever it pleases. There are better and worse arguments for rooting any given holding in any given constitutional text. In the case of abortion and same-sex marriage, we do think that concerns about equality are important, and for that reason, those who would emphasize equality either instead of, or in addition to, liberty, have a valid point—though whether the equality argument should actually prevail in the same-sex marriage context is not something we address here. But critics of unenumerated rights who see continued deep opposition to *Roe* by a large minority of the population as a repudiation of unenumerated rights as such are, in our view, naive.

To put the point somewhat more charitably, the issues of judicial legitimacy raised in unenumerated rights cases are not different in kind from the issues of judicial legitimacy that arise in other contexts. Whenever the Supreme Court moves from relatively abstract constitutional text to concrete holding, it is vulnerable to the charge that the Justices are simply making value judgments. Thus, the most controversial decision of the last quarter century— *Bush v. Gore*[94]—purported to interpret the enumerated right to equal protection, and some of the fiercest charges of judicial activism have been leveled against the Court for recent decisions involving the Second[95] and Eighth Amendments.[96] Indeed, dissenters from the Rehnquist Court's federalism decisions likened the

---

94. 531 U.S. 98 (2000).

95. *See, e.g.,* Richard A. Posner, *In Defense of Looseness: The Supreme Court and Gun Control,* NEW REPUBLIC, Aug. 27, 2008, at 32; J. Harvie Wilkinson III, *Of Guns, Abortions, and the Unraveling Rule of Law,* 95 VA. L. REV. 253 (2009).

96. *See, e.g.,* Tom Parker, *Alabama Justices Surrender to Judicial Activism,* BIRMINGHAM NEWS, Jan. 1, 2005, at 4B, *available at* http://www.alliancealert.org/2006/20060106.htm; Jeffrey Rosen, *Juvenile Logic,* THE NEW REPUBLIC, March 21, 2005, at 11.

rulings to *Lochner*.[97] The core disputes in constitutional law are both more general—concerning the proper role of unelected judges—and more specific—concerning particular contested issues such as abortion and federalism—than the heated debate about unenumerated rights would suggest.

🎞 Further Reading

RANDY E. BARNETT, RESTORING THE LOST CONSTITUTION: THE PRESUMPTION OF LIBERTY (2004).

John Hart Ely, *The Wages of Crying Wolf: A Comment on* Roe v. Wade, 82 YALE L.J. 920 (1973).

Lucinda M. Finley, *Contested Ground: The Story of* Roe v. Wade *and its Impact on American Society, in* CONSTITUTIONAL LAW STORIES 333 (Michael C. Dorf ed., 2d ed. 2009).

Trevor W. Morrison, *Lamenting* Lochner's *Loss: Randy Barnett's Case for a Libertarian Constitution*, 90 CORNELL L. REV. 839 (2005).

Laurence H. Tribe & Michael C. Dorf, *Levels of Generality in the Definition of Rights*, 57 U. CHI. L. REV. 1057 (1990).

---

97. *See, e.g.,* United States v. Lopez, 514 U.S. 549, 605–08 (1995) (Souter, J., dissenting).

NINE

Congressional Enforcement of Constitutional Rights

AS WE HAVE SEEN at various points in this book, constitutional structure and rights are often intertwined. Nowhere is that more clear
than in the enforcement sections of the Reconstruction
Amendments—Section 2 of the Thirteenth Amendment, Section 5
of the Fourteenth Amendment, and Section 2 of the Fifteenth
Amendment.

Drafted and ratified in the aftermath of the Civil War, the
Reconstruction Amendments dramatically altered the structure
and substance of the Constitution. After setting forth self-executing
guarantees, the enforcement sections of each of the Reconstruction
Amendments then grant Congress "power to enforce" the
Amendments "by appropriate legislation." We will focus here on the
Fourteenth Amendment's enforcement provision, but the discussion generally applies to the virtually identical text of the other two
provisions as well.

As we saw in Chapter 8, the Supreme Court's Reconstruction-era
decision in the *Slaughterhouse Cases* rendered the Privileges or
Immunities Clause of Section 1 of the Fourteenth Amendment
nearly a dead letter.[1] Ever since, Section 1's most important provisions have been the Due Process and Equal Protection Clauses,
the former of which incorporates many provisions of the Bill of
Rights and makes them enforceable against the states. The core of

---

1. 83 U.S. (16 Wall.) 36 (1873).

Congress's power under Section 5 of the Fourteenth Amendment, then, is to enforce the Due Process and Equal Protection Clauses.

The plain text of Section 5 leaves a number of questions unanswered. Here we will focus on three. First, what are the permissible targets of Section 5 legislation—only state actors, or private actors as well? Second, when Congress undertakes to enforce the Amendment's provisions, whose understanding of the provisions' scope governs—the Court's or Congress's? Third, is the power to "enforce" the Fourteenth Amendment's provisions limited to invalidating those state laws and actions that themselves violate the Amendment, or does it include the authority to deter or otherwise protect against such violations? We will address these questions in turn.

※ The State Action Requirement

By its terms, Section 1 of the Fourteenth Amendment applies to the states. Yet the history of racism in America—both the formal institution of slavery and the myriad other practices of exclusion and subordination of African Americans that remained so prevalent after slavery's formal abolition—was not confined to state government. Racial bigotry and subordination were the product of private as well as state action. In undertaking to enforce the provisions of the Fourteenth Amendment, could Congress target both sources of interference with the rights secured by the Amendment?

At least some in the Reconstruction Congress evidently thought the answer was yes. Within a decade of the Fourteenth Amendment's ratification, Congress passed the Civil Rights Act of 1875, part of which secured to all persons in the United States, without regard to race, the right to "full and equal enjoyment of the accommodations, advantages, facilities, and privileges of inns, public conveyances on land or water, theatres, and other places of public amusement."[2]

---

2. 18 Stat. 335 (1875).

By 1883, a set of cases arising out of the exclusion of African Americans from hotels, railroads, and theatres arrived at the Supreme Court. In what have become known as the *Civil Rights Cases*, the Court held that Congress lacked the power under Section 5 to pass the law in question.[3] Observing that it "is State action of a particular character that is prohibited" by Section 1 of the Fourteenth Amendment, the Court reasoned that the Amendment "cannot be impaired by the wrongful acts of individuals. . . ."[4] From there, the Court treated it as obvious that the provision of the Civil Rights Act in question "cannot be sustained by any grant of legislative power made to congress by the fourteenth amendment."[5] In the Court's view, the fact that Section 1 of the Fourteenth Amendment targets only state action made it self-evident that a law targeting private conduct—there, race-based discrimination by the proprietors of public accommodations—could not be sustained on Section 5 grounds.

But is that really so self-evident? Although the rights created by Section 1 of the Fourteenth Amendment are held against the states, private actors might take action that interferes with those rights. Over eighty years after the *Civil Rights Cases*, a majority of the Court seemed to think Section 5 empowered Congress to reach at least some such cases. *United States v. Guest* involved the proper construction of a federal law prohibiting private conspiracies to interfere with constitutional rights.[6] Although the Court decided the case on statutory grounds (concluding that the indictment alleged a conspiracy between private and public actors, thus satisfying whatever requirement of state action the Constitution imposed), two separate opinions commanding the support of six Justices expressed the view that Section 5 "empowers Congress to enact

---

3. 109 U.S. 3 (1883).

4. *Id.* at 11, 17.

5. *Id.* at 18.

6. 383 U.S. 745 (1966).

laws punishing *all* conspiracies to interfere with the exercise of Fourteenth Amendment rights, whether or not state officers or others acting under the color of state law are implicated in the conspiracy.[7] As Justice Brennan wrote in one of those opinions, Section 5 "authorizes Congress to make laws that it concludes are reasonably necessary to protect a right created by and arising under that Amendment; and Congress is thus fully empowered to determine that punishment of private conspiracies interfering with the exercise of such a right is necessary to its full protection."[8] To the extent the *Civil Rights Cases* were to the contrary, Justice Brennan suggested they were wrongly decided.

How far could such a theory go? All agree that Fourteenth Amendment rights themselves are held against the states, not private actors. What sort of connection must there be between the state and any private conduct Congress might try to reach under Section 5? One class of cases might be those where private actors intimidate state officials into violating the state's obligations under the Fourteenth Amendment—by, for example, threatening the officials with violence if they desegregate a school. Insofar as the consequence of such private conduct is an equal protection violation, Congress's power to enforce equal protection rights arguably ought to include the power to reach private conduct that is a but-for cause of the violation.

More ambitiously, Congress might try to reach private violence or intimidation aimed at the rights holders themselves. The Supreme Court faced such legislation in *United States v. Morrison.*[9] At issue was a provision of the 1994 Violence Against Women Act (VAWA) that granted victims of gender-motivated violence a private right of action against their attackers.[10] After concluding that

---

7. *Id.* at 782 (Brennan, J., concurring in part and dissenting in part).

8. *Id.*

9. 529 U.S. 598 (2000).

10. Pub. L. No. 103-322, § 40302 (1994) (codified at 42 U.S.C. § 13981).

the provision could not be sustained as an exercise of Congress's power under the Commerce Clause, a divided Court held that the provision similarly failed under Section 5. The reason, it said, was simple: The Fourteenth Amendment prohibits state action, yet Congress had passed a law directed only at private individuals who have committed crimes motivated by gender bias.

To be sure, the Congress that passed VAWA amassed voluminous evidence showing that gender-motivated violence was not purely a matter of private criminality. It found that this kind of violence was an ongoing problem in part because state and local law enforcement departments, prosecutors, juries, and judges often viewed the issue through lenses colored by discriminatory and erroneous gender stereotypes. Those attitudes produced a pattern of inadequate investigation and prosecution of gender-motivated crime and disproportionately light punishments for those actually convicted. That state neglect and inaction, Congress concluded, deprived the victims of the equal protection of the laws. In an effort "to both remedy the States' bias and deter future instances of discrimination in the state courts," Congress provided the victims with a civil remedy in a federal forum.[11] Thus, although technically the remedy would be sought against the private wrongdoer, VAWA was plausibly understood as Congress's response to the failings of state actors.

Nevertheless, *Morrison* held that those failings did not warrant a private remedy in federal court. Building on the *Civil Rights Cases* and rejecting the contrary views of the two *Guest* opinions, the Court stated that the Reconstruction Congress had also sought to overcome a pattern of state neglect of individual rights in the 1875 Civil Rights Act. And just as state neglect was inadequate to support those prohibitions on private discrimination, so too was it insufficient to sustain VAWA's civil remedy. At a minimum, then,

---

11. *Morrison*, 529 U.S. at 620.

Morrison casts substantial doubt on any attempt by Congress to use Section 5 to target private conduct.

Hovering in the background of the Court's insistence on state action in this area is the same structural theme discussed in Chapter 4: federalism. As the *Morrison* Court put it, "the language and purpose of the Fourteenth Amendment place certain limitations on the manner in which Congress may attack discriminatory conduct" under Section 5.[12] Chief among those limits is the requirement of state action, which is "necessary to prevent the Fourteenth Amendment from obliterating the framers' carefully crafted balance of power between the States and the National Government."[13] Of course, there is some irony in casting a requirement that Congress focus its regulatory attention on the states themselves rather than private actors as a means of crediting the *state* side of the federalism ledger. But at least with regard to the regulation of private parties, the state action requirement clearly does protect broad areas of state regulatory primacy.

Other aspects of Section 5 doctrine reflect the Constitution's other great structural theme, the horizontal separation of powers. We now turn to those issues.

Defining the Rights to be Enforced

At the heart of Congress's Section 5 power is a "who decides" question: Who determines the content of the rights Congress is empowered to enforce?

The answer might seem obvious. *Marbury* confirms the judiciary's power to "say what the law is;"[14] hence the courts retain the power to define the substance of the Fourteenth Amendment.

---

12. *Id.*

13. *Id.*

14. Marbury v. Madison, 5 U.S. (1 Cranch) 137, 177 (1803).

Congress, in turn, has the power to enforce those judicially expounded rights, but not to redefine them. That is the view expressed by the Supreme Court in *City of Boerne v. Flores*.[15] At issue in the case was a provision of the Religious Freedom Restoration Act (RFRA) that prohibited state and local governments from substantially burdening anyone's free exercise of religion, even through generally applicable laws, unless the burden could withstand strict scrutiny.[16] As we discussed in Chapter 7, RFRA was a direct response to an earlier decision of the Supreme Court holding that a "neutral law of general applicability" may be applied to (and thus burden) religious practices despite the lack of a compelling government interest or narrowly tailored means of accomplishing that interest.[17] In *Boerne*, the Court held that RFRA went beyond Congress's power to enforce the First Amendment's Free Exercise Clause (incorporated and made applicable against the states by the Fourteenth Amendment's Due Process Clause[18]) and entailed a congressional redefinition of the substance of the right itself. Both "[t]he design of the [Fourteenth] Amendment and the text of § 5 are inconsistent with the suggestion that Congress has the power to decree the substance of the Fourteenth Amendment's restrictions on the States," the Court said.[19] RFRA was a direct repudiation of the Court's interpretation of the free exercise right in *Smith*. It was a legislative alteration of the right itself and thus went beyond enforcing the right. Put simply, "Congress does not enforce a constitutional right by changing what the right is."[20]

---

15. 521 U.S. 507 (1997).

16. Pub. L. No. 103-141, 1993 U.S.C.C.A.N. (107 Stat.) 1488.

17. *See* Employment Division v. Smith, 494 U.S. 872, 879 (1990) (quoting United States v. Lee, 455 U.S. 252, 263 n.3 (1982) (Stevens, J., concurring)).

18. Cantwell v. Connecticut, 310 U.S. 296 (1940).

19. *Boerne*, 521 U.S. at 519.

20. *Id.*

According to the *Boerne* Court, at stake in that case was not only the courts' power to authoritatively interpret the Constitution, but the supremacy of the Constitution itself: "If Congress could define its own powers by altering the Fourteenth Amendment's meaning, no longer would the Constitution be 'superior paramount law, unchangeable by ordinary means.' It would be 'on a level with ordinary legislative acts, and, like other acts, . . . alterable when the legislature shall please to alter it.'"[21] On this view, laws that usurp the judiciary's power to interpret the Constitution entail a kind of congressional self-dealing and threaten to put the Constitution under Congress, rather than vice versa.

It is understandable that the *Boerne* Court would chafe at a law that so directly targeted and countermanded one of the Court's own constitutional precedents. But does Section 5 truly leave *no* room for independent congressional interpretation of the Constitution? After all, as we saw in Chapter 2, the power of judicial review need not—and, in practice, does not—entail judicial exclusivity in either constitutional interpretation (i.e., identifying constitutional meaning) or constitutional implementation (i.e., deciding how to apply that meaning to discrete cases). Congress has an independent duty of fidelity to the Constitution. Sometimes, as in areas implicating nonjusticiable political questions, Congress, acting on its independent obligation to the Constitution, essentially defines the content of the constitutional provision.[22] More importantly, even when the issue is justiciable, concerns about institutional competence might suggest that Congress is better able than the courts to fully enforce a given constitutional norm.

Consider, for example, the "rational basis" test that courts use to review most government action under the Equal Protection Clause. This test is an instrument of judicial restraint, designed to limit the

---

21. *Id.* at 529 (alteration in original) (quoting Marbury v. Madison, 5 U.S. (1 Cranch) 137, 177 (1803)).

22. *See, e.g.,* Nixon v. United States, 506 U.S. 224 (1993).

unelected judiciary's intrusions into the operation of democratically accountable branches of government. It effectively gives those other branches the benefit of the doubt in many cases, presuming that they have acted consistently with the demands of equal protection unless the courts cannot even hypothesize a legitimate state interest to which the law in question might be rationally related.[23] But to say that a law survives rational basis review is not necessarily to say that it is conclusively constitutional in any comprehensive sense. For example, it is generally accepted that it is unconstitutional for a state to pass a law out of sheer animus towards the group burdened by the law.[24] Yet if the group in question is not a suspect class, courts applying the rational basis test may uphold such laws unless presented with fairly direct evidence of animus. Such a decision, we think, is best viewed not as a conclusive determination of the law's constitutionality but as a statement that, given the various institutional considerations that go into judicially crafted doctrine, *the courts* are simply not prepared to declare the law unconstitutional.

The government pressed this very argument in defense of a number of federal laws challenged in the wake of *Boerne*. In *Kimel v. Florida Board of Regents*, the Court examined whether Congress had the Section 5 authority to subject state employers to the Age Discrimination in Employment Act (ADEA).[25] And in *Board of Trustees of the University of Alabama v. Garrett*, the Court heard a similar challenge to Congress's Section 5 power to subject state employers to Title I of the Americans with Disabilities Act (ADA).[26]

---

23. *See* F.C.C. v. Beach Communications, Inc., 508 U.S. 307, 313 (1993).

24. *See* Romer v. Evans, 517 U.S. 620, 632 (1996).

25. 528 U.S. 62 (2000).

26. 531 U.S. 356 (2001). Insofar as they govern employment, both the ADEA and Title I of the ADA are valid under the Commerce Clause, including as applied to state actors. In a separate series of decisions, however, the Supreme Court has held that the Commerce Clause does not empower Congress to abrogate the states' sovereign immunity from private suits for money damages.

Neither age[27] nor disability[28] is a suspect classification under the Court's equal protection doctrine. Thus, state action that discriminates on either basis is subject to only rational basis review in the courts. The government argued, however, that Congress, with its superior fact-finding capacity, ought not be constrained by the rational basis test. On this view, if Congress amassed evidence supporting the conclusion that states had been making employment-related decisions on the basis of arbitrary, animus-based, or otherwise illegitimate hostility to people on the basis of their age or disabilities, it should have the authority under Section 5 to pass laws addressing such discrimination without regard to how that discrimination would fare under the rational basis test.[29] The same four Justices embraced this position in both *Kimel* and *Garrett*. As Justice Breyer put it in a dissenting opinion in *Garrett*, "Unlike courts, Congress can readily gather facts from across the Nation, assess the magnitude of a problem, and . . . find an appropriate remedy."[30] Accordingly, "[t]here is simply no reason to require Congress, seeking to determine facts relevant to the exercise of its § 5 authority, to adopt rules or presumptions that reflect a court's institutional limitations. . . . To apply a rule designed to restrict

---

See Seminole Tribe of Fla. v. Florida, 517 U.S. 44 (1996). Thus, if supported only by the Commerce Clause, and in the absence of a waiver of state sovereign immunity, those laws would be enforceable against state employers only by the federal government directly. Section 5, in contrast, does grant Congress the power to abrogate sovereign immunity. Because both *Kimel* and *Garrett* arose out of private suits for damages against state employers, and because the employers defended on sovereign immunity grounds, the cases turned on whether the statutes in question could be justified under Section 5, irrespective of their status under the Commerce Clause.

27. Mass. Bd. of Retirement v. Murgia, 427 U.S. 307 (1976).

28. City of Cleburne v. Cleburne Living Center, 473 U.S. 432 (1985).

29. Brief for the United States as Amicus Curiae Supporting Respondents at 35–40, Bd. of Trs. of the Univ. of Ala. v. Garrett, 531 U.S. 356 (2001) (No. 99-1240); Brief for the United States of America as Petitioner at 22–28, Kimel v. Fla. Bd. of Regents, 528 U.S. 62 (2000) (No. 02-516).

30. *Garrett*, 531 U.S. at 384.

courts as if it restricted Congress' legislative power is to stand the underlying principle—a principle of judicial restraint—on its head."[31] Numerous commentators have expressed a similar view.[32]

A majority of the Court, however, has rejected this view. Writing for the *Kimel* majority, Justice Sandra Day O'Connor described the ADEA as "effectively elevat[ing] the standard for analyzing age discrimination to heightened scrutiny,"[33] and, in so doing, crossing the line from definition to enforcement emphasized by the *Boerne* Court. Similarly in *Garrett*, Chief Justice Rehnquist's majority opinion depicted the ADA as violating the principle that "it is the responsibility of this Court, not Congress, to define the substance of constitutional guarantees."[34] In both cases, the Court seems to have denied the existence of any space between the tests and rules that courts use to implement the Constitution and the Constitution itself. This equation of judge-made constitutional doctrine (even obviously under-enforcing doctrine) and the underlying constitutional norm is reminiscent of *Cooper v. Aaron*'s most aggressive account of judicial supremacy[35] (discussed in Chapter 2), and is subject to the same criticisms. The Court, though, appears unmoved. Indeed, it lately seems to have cemented its view, albeit in a non-Section 5 context. In a footnote to its decision declaring an individual right under the Second Amendment to keep and bear arms, the Court declared that in cases subject to rational basis review, "'rational basis' is not just the standard of scrutiny, but the very substance

31. *Id.* at 384–85.

32. *See, e.g.*, Michael W. McConnell, *Institutions and Interpretation: A Critique of* City of Boerne v. Flores, 111 HARV. L. REV. 153 (1997); Robert Post & Reva Siegel, *Legislative Constitutionalism and Section Five Power: Policentric Interpretation of the Family and Medical Leave Act*, 112 YALE L.J. 1943 (2003); Robert Post & Reva Siegel, *Equal Protection by Law: Federal Antidiscrimination Legislation After* Morrison *and* Kimel, 110 YALE L.J. 441 (2000).

33. 528 U.S. at 88.

34. 531 U.S. at 365.

35. 358 U.S. 1, 18 (1958).

of the constitutional guarantee.'"[36] Whatever the status of that statement with respect to equal protection doctrine and due process
generally, it does seem to capture the supremacy and virtual exclusivity of judicial interpretation in the Section 5 context.

※ Enforcement as Deterrence and Prevention, within Limits

To say that Congress's Section 5 power is subject to the judiciary's
definition of the underlying rights is not necessarily to say that
Congress can only reach those state actions that the courts would
themselves deem unconstitutional. The judicial supremacy point
discussed in the previous section goes to how the underlying right
is defined and the institution responsible for defining it. It is a separate question whether, in enforcing the right, Congress may guard
against violations by regulating conduct that is close to unconstitutional but may not actually cross the line. In short, does the power
to enforce a right include any power to legislate prophylactically?

The Supreme Court has long answered yes. In *Katzenbach v.
Morgan*,[37] a 1966 constitutional challenge to a provision of the Civil
Rights Act of 1965, the Court rejected a reading of Section 5 that
"would confine the legislative power in this context to the insignifi-
cant role of abrogating only those state laws that the judicial branch
was prepared to adjudge unconstitutional."[38] That case involved a
provision stating that no person who had completed at least the
sixth grade in Puerto Rico, in a language other than English (typically, Spanish), could be denied the right to vote on account of
inability to read or write English.[39] A group of New York voters

---

36. District of Columbia v. Heller, 128 S.Ct. 2783, 2817 n.27 (2008).

37. 384 U.S. 641 (1966).

38. *Id.* at 648–49.

39. Civil Rights Act of 1965 § 4(e), 42 U.S.C. § 1973(b)(e) (2000).

challenged the federal provision insofar as it effectively prohibited enforcement of a New York law conditioning the right to vote on an ability to read and write English. The Court emphasized that to uphold the federal law, it need not determine that the New York voting requirement itself violated the Equal Protection Clause. Section 5, the Court explained, is "a positive grant of legislative power authorizing Congress to exercise its discretion in determining whether and what legislation is needed to secure the guarantees of the Fourteenth Amendment."[40] That could well include legislation targeting state action that, while not obviously unconstitutional itself, threatened constitutional rights and made full enjoyment of those rights more difficult. In that sense, the *Katzenbach v. Morgan* Court saw Section 5 as authorizing some measure of over-enforcement of Fourteenth Amendment rights.

One question this raises is whether the opposite point holds as well: If Section 5 grants Congress some discretion with respect to over-enforcement of Fourteenth Amendment rights, does it also empower Congress to pass laws affirmatively authorizing state conduct that would otherwise be unconstitutional? Is Section 5, in other words, a two-way ratchet? The *Katzenbach v. Morgan* Court addressed this question directly, and answered no:

> We emphasize that Congress' power under § 5 is limited to adopting measures to enforce the guarantees of the Amendment; § 5 grants Congress no power to restrict, abrogate, or dilute these guarantees. Thus, for example, an enactment authorizing the States to establish racially segregated systems of education would not be—as required by § 5—a measure "to enforce" the Equal Protection Clause since that clause of its own force prohibits such state laws.[41]

---

40. *Katzenbach v. Morgan*, 384 U.S. at 651.

41. *Id.* at 651 n.10.

Section 5, in short, is a one-way ratchet, authorizing some measure of congressional over-enforcement of Fourteenth Amendment rights while countenancing no legislative dilution of those rights. For this reason, Section 5 is not analogous to provisions in other countries' constitutions, including Canada's, authorizing the limited legislative override of certain constitutional rights. The question remains just how far Congress may go in over-enforcing Fourteenth Amendment rights. As we discussed earlier in this chapter, such over-enforcement is subject both to the state action requirement and to the injunction that congressional enforcement not cross over into congressional redefinition of the right itself. But by what metric should Congress and the courts assess any particular piece of enforcement legislation? The modern Court's answer to that question derives from its decision in *Boerne*.

Citing *Katzenbach v. Morgan*, the *Boerne* Court confirmed that "[l]egislation which deters or remedies constitutional violations can fall within the sweep of Congress' enforcement power even if in the process it prohibits conduct which is not itself unconstitutional."[42] The Court acknowledged that it can be difficult to distinguish between measures that remedy or deter unconstitutional actions and those that redefine the substance of the right, but it insisted on the importance of maintaining the distinction. The Court's solution was to require "a congruence and proportionality between the injury to be prevented or remedied and the means adopted to that end."[43]

As elaborated in post-*Boerne* cases like *Kimel* and *Garrett*, this "congruence and proportionality" test has a number of elements. First, the Court begins by determining "the metes and bounds of the constitutional right" that the Section 5 legislation at issue is said to be enforcing.[44] As discussed above, that determination relies

---

42. City of Boerne v. Flores, 521 U.S. 507, 518 (1997).

43. *Id.* at 520.

44. Bd. of Trs. of the Univ. of Ala. v. Garrett, 531 U.S. 356, 368 (2001).

on judicial doctrine; the right in question is the right as defined and implemented by the courts. Next, the Court asks whether Congress has "identified a history and pattern" of state action violating the right.[45] Congress, in other words, is responsible for taking evidence and assembling a legislative record establishing that the problem it is undertaking to address is, in fact, of constitutional dimensions. Among other things, this means that Congress must identify a pattern of unconstitutional state conduct, not private conduct that would be unconstitutional if undertaken by a state. Thus in *Garrett*, the Court found the legislative record inadequate in part because, although it included many instances of disability-based discrimination in employment, the "great majority" of the documented incidents involved private employers.[46]

If the legislative record does establish a pattern of unconstitutional state behavior, the Court then looks at the precise contours of the Section 5 legislation in question to determine whether any statutory overprotection of the right stays within the bounds of congruence and proportionality. As noted above, prophylactic rules are permissible here, provided "there is reason to believe that many of the [state] laws affected by the congressional enactment have a significant likelihood of being unconstitutional."[47] In *Garrett*, for example, the Court explained that above and beyond the inadequacy of the legislative record, the ADA went too far by prohibiting actions involving no possible constitutional violation: "[W]hereas it would be entirely rational (and therefore constitutional) for a state employer to conserve scarce financial resources by hiring employees who are able to use existing facilities, the ADA requires employers to 'mak[e] existing facilities used by employees readily accessible to and usable by individuals with disabilities.'"[48] Because that

---

45. *Id.*

46. *Id.* at 369.

47. *Boerne*, 521 U.S. at 532.

48. *Garrett*, 531 U.S. at 372 (alteration in original).

accommodation requirement "far exceed[ed] what is constitutionally required," the Court held that it exceeded the bounds of congruence and proportionality.[49]

The Court has identified a number of other considerations that can be part of the congruence and proportionality calculus. Because remedial Section 5 legislation ought to be tailored to the constitutional wrong at issue, the Court has suggested that legislation with temporal or geographic limits may be more likely to pass muster. If, for example, the legislative record establishes a pattern of unconstitutional conduct only in certain parts of the country, Congress is more likely to remain within the bounds of congruence and proportionality if its legislation targets those particular areas rather than imposing nationwide mandates.[50] Similarly, a federal law designed to sunset on some future date can help to ensure that its rules remain in effect only as long as necessary to remedy the constitutional problem at hand.[51]

Finally, the Court's most recent Section 5 decisions highlight another, cross-cutting consequence of its judicial supremacist stance in this area. Whereas the Court's rational basis test limits Congress's ability to use Section 5 to protect non-suspect classes and non-fundamental rights, Congress has greater leeway, including with respect to its remedial choices, when enacting laws for the benefit of a group or interest that the courts protect with some measure of heightened judicial scrutiny. As the Court has explained: "The appropriateness of remedial measures must be considered in light of the evil presented."[52] Thus in *Nevada Department of Human Resources v. Hibbs*, the Court upheld under Section 5 a provision of the Family and Medical Leave Act (FMLA) that gave

49. *Id.*

50. *See Boerne*, 521 U.S. at 533 (citing City of Rome v. United States, 446 U.S. 156 (1980); South Carolina v. Katzenbach, 383 U.S. 301 (1966)).

51. *Id.*

52. *Boerne*, 521 U.S. at 530.

eligible employees, men and women, the right to take up to 12 weeks of unpaid annual leave in order to care for children or other family members.[53] The Court understood the legislation as a response to the problem of gender discrimination in employment, a problem that would typically trigger intermediate scrutiny in the courts. Viewing the case through that lens, the Court (in a somewhat surprising opinion by Chief Justice Rehnquist) seemed to grant Congress substantially more leeway than in cases like *Kimel* and *Garrett*.

First, although the Court pointed to evidence in the legislative record documenting pervasive sex stereotyping in the employment context, including in decisions whether to grant employees leave, it stopped short of identifying in the record a pattern of conduct that the courts would hold is actually unconstitutional. Second, the remedy imposed by Congress was anything but a direct targeting of unconstitutional conduct. As the Court explained: "By setting a minimum standard for family leave for *all* eligible employees, irrespective of gender, the FMLA attacks the formerly state-sanctioned stereotype that only women are responsible for family caregiving, thereby reducing employers' incentives to engage in discrimination by basing hiring and promotion decisions on stereotypes."[54] In other words, to the extent state employers viewed women workers as more costly and less productive out of an assumption that they would someday take parental or other family leave, the FMLA's guarantee of leave to all eligible workers sought to eliminate the perceived difference between men and women by enabling men to take leave too. To be sure, this was a perfectly rational and potentially effective regulatory decision. But as Justice Kennedy said in dissent, the connection to unconstitutional gender discrimination

---

53. 538 U.S. 721 (2003). Like the ADEA and Title I of the ADA, the FMLA is obviously valid Commerce Clause legislation. But as with those laws, the FMLA's abrogation of state sovereign immunity from private suits for damages could be upheld only under Section 5. *See supra* note 26.

54. *Id.* at 737.

was rather attenuated.[55] Only by granting Congress substantial remedial discretion could the Court uphold a provision guaranteeing male workers 12 weeks of family leave on the ground that it enforced women's equal protection rights. That leeway was nowhere to be found in earlier cases like *Kimel* and *Garrett.* The difference is that the Court's constitutional doctrine regards gender discrimination as more problematic than age or disability discrimination. In that respect, *Hibbs* may be as much a triumph of judicial supremacy as *Boerne, Kimel,* or *Garrett.*

The lessons here are clear. If Congress takes its cues from the Court and addresses state conduct that the courts would view as constitutionally suspicious, it apparently has considerable discretion in its choice of remedial and preventative measures. If, on the other hand, Congress identifies an area of constitutional concern that may have persisted precisely because the judiciary has not adequately addressed it, Congress must nevertheless play by the Court's rules. Thus, although Section 5 is clearly a substantial and important source of legislative power, under current doctrine it cannot be said to make Congress anything like an equal partner in the implementation of the Constitution. At least for now, Section 5 gives Congress the power to enforce only the Court's Constitution.

🖋 Further Reading

Larry Alexander & Frederick Schauer, *On Extrajudicial Constitutional Interpretation,* 110 HARV. L. REV. 1359 (1997).

Michael C. Dorf & Barry Friedman, *Shared Constitutional Interpretation,* 2000 SUP. CT. REV. 61.

Robert Post & Reva Siegel, *Legislative Constitutionalism and Section Five Power: Policentric Interpretation of the Family and Medical Leave Act,* 112 YALE L.J. 1943 (2003).

Lawrence Gene Sager, *Fair Measure: The Legal Status of Underenforced Constitutional Norms,* 91 HARV. L. REV. 1212 (1978).

---

55. *Id.* at 753.

TEN

Beyond the Courts

ALTHOUGH THIS BOOK has focused chiefly on judicially developed doctrines, constitutional interpretation has never been the exclusive province of the courts. The President, other executive officials, and members of Congress each take an oath to uphold the Constitution, and state executive and legislative officials typically take similar oaths. Nothing in those oaths equates the Constitution with what the courts say about it. Indeed, as we discussed in Chapters 2 and 9, only the most aggressive version of a "judicial exclusivity" approach would grant the judiciary a monopoly on interpreting and construing the Constitution. Yet neither that approach nor its polar opposite—thoroughgoing departmentalism, which grants each branch completely independent authority to interpret the Constitution according to its own lights, and which denies any special status to the Supreme Court's statements of constitutional meaning beyond the particular cases before it— accurately describes American constitutional law in practice.

In fact, on issues that are likely to come before the courts at some point, the political branches of government (both state and federal) usually endeavor to comply with judicial—especially Supreme Court—precedent, lest their actions be invalidated when later challenged in the courts. Whether or not Supreme Court precedent is properly viewed as binding in principle, the political branches generally find it prudent to treat that precedent as authoritative. At the same time, however, there are a whole host of constitutional issues that either lie entirely beyond judicial cognizance or trigger substantial judicial deference to the actions of the political branches. In these areas, constitutional interpretation and implementation by non-judicial actors are critically important.

The clearest examples of extra-judicial constitutional interpretation lie in the realm of political questions. When the Supreme Court concludes that a particular constitutional provision cannot yield "judicially discoverable and manageable standards," or when it finds a "textually demonstrable constitutional commitment of the issue to a coordinate political department" of the government, it will treat the provision as presenting a nonjusticiable political question.[1] But to say that a provision is nonjusticiable is not to say that the political branches are free to do whatever they want in the area, unconstrained by the Constitution.[2] Rather, it means that the political branches must bind themselves to their own best understanding, however derived, of the constitutional provision in question.

A similar point can be made about constitutional norms that the courts enforce only weakly or deferentially. For example, we suggested in Chapter 9 that the "rational basis" test is best viewed as an instrument of judicial restraint, designed to limit the judiciary's intrusions into the workings of the democratically accountable branches of government. And although the Supreme Court has used that test—and its conception of tiered scrutiny more generally—to limit Congressional power to *enforce* the guarantees of due process and equal protection, that does not necessarily mean that the rational basis test provides the definitive measure of the political branches' *compliance* with the constitutional norms of due process and equal protection in their own actions.

For example, even though the Supreme Court has said that age-based discrimination by government employers triggers only rational basis review, a government employer that imposed a mandatory retirement age of 65 out of sheer (but not openly articulated) hostility

1. Baker v. Carr, 369 U.S. 186, 217 (1962).

2. *See* United States Dep't of Commerce v. Montana, 503 U.S. 442, 458 (1992).

to persons above that age would have violated the constitutional norm of equal protection. True, in the absence of direct evidence of such hostility, the government's policy would likely survive the judiciary's scrutiny unless the plaintiff could show that the policy was not rationally related to any hypothetical legitimate state interest, like ensuring the employees' physical or mental capacity to perform the job—a very difficult showing to make. But that does not establish the conclusive constitutionality of the policy. It merely reflects that the courts, using the tools they have developed for adjudicating constitutional challenges, are not prepared to set it aside as unconstitutional. This is an instance, in other words, of a judicially under-enforced constitutional norm. The conscientious legislator who knows that the bill imposing the mandatory retirement policy is being driven by animus against older workers has an independent obligation to vote against the bill on constitutional grounds, even though the courts would likely uphold it.[3] Indeed, a major premise of the judicial deference entailed in doctrines like rational basis review is that the political branches take their independent obligations of constitutional fidelity seriously. Taking that obligation seriously can at times mean constitutional self-constraint that goes beyond the limits of judicial enforcement.

What all of this suggests is that there are many circumstances in which judicially-crafted doctrine is only the tip of the constitutional iceberg. Other government officials play a critical role in forging constitutional meaning. As Akhil Amar observed, "the Constitution is not merely what judges say it is, and well-trained lawyers outside the judiciary, such as Barack Obama, should not feel shy about participating in the constitutional conversation."[4]

---

3. *See* Lawrence Gene Sager, *Fair Measure: The Legal Status of Underenforced Constitutional Norms*, 91 Harv. L. Rev. 1212, 1227 (1978); Richard H. Fallon, Jr., Implementing the Constitution 40–41 (2001).

4. Akhil Reed Amar, Heller, *HLR, and Holistic Legal Reasoning*, 122 Harv. L. Rev. 145, 190 (2008).

Who else should likewise feel free to participate in that conversation? Other government officials, certainly, but not only government officials. We also have a broader "constitutional culture" that arises out of popular participation in constitutional interpretation.[5] When the Supreme Court held in 2003 that a Texas law banning same-sex sodomy violated the Fourteenth Amendment,[6] and when it held in 2008 that the Second Amendment protects an individual right to possess firearms for self-defense,[7] it was reacting to changes that began in social and political movements of ordinary people.

But constitutional politics occurs even when the courts do not ratify it. As this book goes to press, the nation is engaged in debates over the wisdom of recently enacted health care legislation, how to respond to global warming and other environmental issues, and a host of other questions. We strongly doubt that even one member of the Supreme Court will soon opine that there is a constitutional right to health care or an unpolluted environment (as constitutional courts in other countries have sometimes said). Yet that does not by itself delegitimate arguments before the court of public opinion seeking to couch the case for universal health care or a livable environment in constitutional language.

Nor would we even go so far as to say that the People are "wrong" when they make constitutional claims belied by the constitutional text itself. Consider voting. The Fifteenth, Nineteenth, Twenty-Fourth, and Twenty-Sixth Amendments limit the grounds on which the franchise could be denied, but no express constitutional provision confers an individual right to vote in Presidential elections. Indeed, the rules governing the Electoral College set forth in Article II and the Twelfth Amendment pretty squarely foreclose the claim that there is such a right, and the Supreme Court, even in the midst

---

5. Reva B. Siegel, *Dead or Alive: Originalism as Popular Constitutionalism in* Heller, 122 HARV. L. REV. 191, 236 (2008).

6. *See* Lawrence v. Texas, 539 U.S. 558 (2003).

7. *See* District of Columbia v. Heller, 128 S. Ct. 2783 (2008).

of an extraordinarily divisive battle over the outcome of the 2000 election, unanimously accepted that voting in Presidential elections is a matter of state legislative grace, rather than federal constitutional right.[8]

That interpretation seems right to us, given what the Constitution says. But we think it is also a fact of American political life in the twenty-first century that no state would, absent extraordinary circumstances, choose its Presidential electors except by popular election. (We include Maine and Nebraska in this statement, even though they currently apportion electors by district rather than on a winner-take-all basis.) If we were to be perfectly precise about such things, we would say that there is an unofficial, extra-constitutional norm requiring that citizens be given a chance to vote in Presidential elections. Yet we would not quibble too much with those Americans who want to say that the right to vote in Presidential elections is a *constitutional* right—one rooted perhaps in the Due Process Clauses of the Fifth and Fourteenth Amendments, the Ninth Amendment, or the very structure of the Constitution. Surely the Court itself has rooted constitutional judgments in no firmer soil.

"We are not final because we are infallible," Justice Robert Jackson famously wrote in 1953, "but we are infallible only because we are final."[9] In context, his point was sound: The fact that the Supreme Court has the power to resolve legal questions does not ensure that its resolution of those questions is necessarily correct in any fundamental sense. But Jackson nonetheless overstated the Court's power. Even when the Supreme Court interprets the Constitution, its decisions are never truly final. Social and political movements may sweep away the Court's work, by persuading the Justices themselves to change their minds, by replacing Justices through the appointments process, or, rarely, by constitutional amendment. Despite a great many obstacles to the exercise of our power, it is ultimately We the People who decide what the Constitution means, and even what it is.

---

8. *See* Bush v. Palm Beach County Canvassing Bd., 531 U.S. 70, 77 (2000).

9. Brown v. Allen, 344 U.S. 443, 540 (1953) (Jackson, J., concurring in the result).

Index

Abortion
   conservative opposition
      to, 47, 51
   equal protection
      and, 150, 213–15
   federal/state standards on, 6–7
   liberal opposition to limits on, 48
   public opinion, 213–14
   representation reinforcement
      and, 59–60
   substantive due process and, 208,
      212–13
   undue burden test and, 209
Adams, John, 126
Administrative agencies, 63, 104,
   117–19
Advisory opinions, 32, 120
Affirmative action
   exacting standards of, 55, 59
   federal/state standards on, 6–7
   liberal opposition to limits
      on, 47–48, 51
   race-based, 134–38, 144–46
   strict scrutiny test and, 141–42
   University of Michigan Law
      School and, 141–42
African Americans. *See also*
      Equal Protection Clause
   Civil Rights Cases and, 219–21
   disenfranchisement of, 128, 192
   Jim Crow segregation and, 77,
      125, 128–30, 133–34, 136

slavery and, 63, 76, 125–27, 132,
      136–37, 192, 218
   voting rights, 148–49, 192
Age discrimination, 144, 226–27
Age Discrimination in Employment
      Act (ADEA, 1967), 225–27,
      225*n*26
Alienage, 144
Alien detainees, 16, 20
Allgeyer v. Louisiana, 197–99
Amar, Akhil, 237
Americans with Disabilities Act
      (ADA, 1990), 225–27, 225*n*26
Anti-Federalists, 62, 74
Anti-subordination
      principle, 134–42.
      See also Equal Protection Clause
Aristotle, 95
As-applied litigation, 32

Berlin, Isaiah, 160
Bicameralism, 17, 98–101
Bill of Rights, 61. *See also specific*
      Amendments
   applicability to states, 6, 63, 217
   founding debates on, 153–56
   heightened scrutiny and, 58
   incorporation doctrine, 58, 156,
      191, 201–5, 203*n*52, 207, 208,
      217, 223
   originalism and, 132
   privacy rights and, 207–8

241

Bills of attainder, 153

Black, Charles, 129

Black, Hugo
  on executive power, 107
  on incorporation, 203–5,
    203*n*52, 207
  on use of natural law, 53

Black Codes, 127, 144

Blackmun, Harry, 172

*Board of Trustees of the University of
    Alabama v. Garrett,* 225–27,
    225*n*26, 230–34

Bobbitt, Philip, 67

Bodily autonomy, 209

Bolling v. Sharpe, 132–33

Bork, Robert, 131–33, 170, 187–88, 213

Boumediene v. Bush, 123

Brandeis, Louis
  on free speech, 159–60, 168–70
  on states as experimental
    laboratories, 74

Brandenburg v. Ohio, 169

Branzburg v. Hayes, 157

Brennan, William J.
  on congressional power, 220
  on states and individual
    rights, 77

Breyer, Stephen
  on anti-commandeering rule, 87
  on congressional power, 226

Brown, Henry, 129

Brown II, 130

Brown v. Board of Education, 33, 38,
    126, 129–34, 136–37

Buckley v. Valeo, 161

Bush, George W.
  assertions of preclusive
    presidential authority of, 111–12
  signing statements, 36–37
  unconstitutional activities
    under, 16, 123
  war on terror, 36–37, 111–12,
    122–24

Bush v. Gore, 60, 214

Calder v. Bull, 52–53, 187

Campaign finance regulation, 161–63

Canada, 37–38, 71, 230

Canadian Charter of Rights and
    Freedoms (1982), 37–38

Capital punishment. *See* Death
    penalty

*Carolene Products Co.,
    United States v.,* 58–59, 145, 201

Catholics, 171, 178, 184

Censorship, 11, 159, 163, 165,
    167–70. *See also* Freedom
    of speech

Chase, Samuel, 52–53

Checks and balances, 16–17, 95–97,
    102–4, 117. *See also* Separation
    of powers doctrine

*Chevron U.S.A. Inc. v. Natural
    Resources Defense
    Council, Inc.,* 118–19

China, 139–40

Chisholm v. Georgia, 89

Cicero, 95

Citizenship, 92, 127, 192, 196

City of Boerne v. Flores, 173,
    223–25, 227, 230, 234

Civil jury requirement, 204

Civil Rights Act (1875), 218–19, 221

Civil Rights Act (1964), 81

Civil Rights Act (1965), 228

Civil Rights Cases, 219–21

Civil rights movement, 77, 125,
    129, 133

Class action suits, 120

Clear and present danger test, 167–69

Clear-statement rules, 9, 91–92

Clinton, Bill, 34, 173

Cloture, 103

Color-blindness principle, 134–42.
    See also Equal Protection
    Clause

Commandeering, 86–88

Commander in Chief Clause, 105,
    111–13

Commerce Clause doctrine.
    See also Interstate commerce
    dormant Commerce
        Clause, 92–93, 197
    economic/noneconomic
        activity, 82–83, 220–21
    interstateness and, 80
    other Congressional powers
        and, 84
    private suits against states
        and, 225n26, 233n53
    states and, 6
    Tenth Amendment and, 85–86
Common law, 54–56, 65–66,
        189, 211
Congress
    anti-commandeering
        principle, 86–88
    clear-statement rules, 9, 91–92
    commerce power, 79–84
    conditional preemption, 87–88
    constitutional interpretation
        and, 43–47
    enforcement as deterrence/
        prevention, 84, 173–74, 218,
        221, 228–34
    executive powers and, 5, 95, 97,
        102–4, 104–9, 109–17, 119, 123
    on federal court jurisdiction, 9,
        29, 30–31, 122
    foreign affairs and, 106, 110–11
    judicial review and, 13, 22–23,
        24–26, 27–28, 31, 35–36
    Ninth Amendment and, 189
    non-delegation doctrine
        and, 108, 117–19
    rights enforcement, 220, 222–28,
        225n26
    spending power, 43, 84, 87–88
    state action requirement, 218–22
    unified government and, 102–3
    war powers, 1, 105–6
Congruence and proportionality
    test, 230–34

Conservatives
    on color-blindness of
        Constitution, 134
    opposition to particular
        doctrines, 47, 51
    originalism and, 136
    states' rights and, 77–78
Constitution. *See also* Bill of Rights;
        Federalism; Separation of
        Powers
    Article I, 2, 4, 6, 43, 78–79, 92, 105,
        110–11, 117, 125, 153–54, 191
    Article II, 34, 105, 107–9, 238–39
    Article III, 28–29, 30–32, 89, 106
    Article IV, 6, 26, 29–31, 86–87, 92,
        125, 192–95, 206
    contemporary consent
        validation, 63
    judicial review and, 7, 11–12,
        14, 21–22
    negative rights vs. positive
        rights, 18–19
    omissions, 153–55
    structural limits on
        government, 4–6, 154
    Supremacy Clause, 6, 26–28,
        29–30
    on writtenness, 22–26, 28
Constitutional courts, 10, 12, 31,
        32, 238
Constitutional interpretation, 41–68
    eclecticism and, 65–67
    extra-judicial, 235–39
    judicial restraint and, 50–52
    natural law and moral
        reading, 52–57
    originalism and, 61–65
    representation
        reinforcement, 57–61
Constitutional law, overview, 1–10.
        See also specific doctrines
    applicability, 1, 4
    federal/state allocation of
        power, 4–5, 6–7

Constitutional law, overview (*cont.*)
   fundamental rights, 3
   neutrality requirements, 8
   procedural requirements, 9
   tiers of scrutiny, 2–3
Constitutions, of other countries
   affirmative rights, 19
   enforcement of social/economic
      rights, 10
   judicial review and, 12, 14–15
   length of, 44
   parliamentary supremacy, 25–26
Contraception, 53, 207, 213
Cooper v. Aaron, 33–35, 227
Copyrights, 90
Corfield v. Coryell, 192–95
Counsel, right to, 202, 203
Countermajoritarian
   difficulty, 11, 59
Covert heightened scrutiny, 148

Death penalty, 7, 47, 51, 54
Debs, Eugene, 168
Decentralization, federalism
   and, 71–72, 74–75
Declaration of Independence, 125
Democracies, judicial review
   and, 14, 21, 38
Democracy and Distrust (Ely), 58–60
*Democracy and the Problem of Free
   Speech* (Sunstein), 212
Departmentalism, 32–34, 235
Disability discrimination, 126, 144,
   147, 148, 225–27, 225n26, 231,
   234
Discrimination. *See also specific types*
   history of, 146
   immutability and, 145–46
   suspect classifications and, 3,
      134–35, 144–46, 149, 150,
      225–26, 232
District of Columbia v. Heller, 64,
   188–89

Divided government, 102–4
Dormant Commerce Clause
   doctrine, 92–93, 197
Douglas, William O.
   on obscenity, 167
   on privacy rights, 207
Dred Scott v. Sandford, 33, 127, 192
Due Process Clauses
   in Fifth Amendment, 54, 125–26,
      132, 150, 203
   in Fourteenth Amendment, 53,
      54, 150, 192, 197–98, 202–3,
      204–5, 206, 208, 217–18, 223
   Lochner era and, 190–91, 200
   Magna Carta and, 198
   voting rights and, 239
Dworkin, Ronald, 54–56, 66

Eclecticism, constitutional
      interpretation and, 65–67
Economic vs. noneconomic
      activity, 82–84, 220–21
Eighth Amendment, 15, 54, 214
Elected officials. *See also* Congress
   constitutional interpretation
      and, 23, 47, 50, 57–61,
      235–39
   departmentalism
      and, 32–34, 235
   judicial review and, 1, 11, 16,
      20–21, 31–38
Elections, 14, 17, 69, 128, 161–62,
   238–39
Electoral College, 69, 128, 238–39
Eleventh Amendment, 70, 89–90
Ely, John Hart
   Democracy and Distrust, 58–60
   on substantive due
      process, 202–3
Emancipation Proclamation, 127
*Employment Division
   v. Smith*, 172–78, 223
Enforcement power. *See* Congress

Engel v. Vitale, 180–82
England, 25–26, 95
Enumerated powers
    constitutional interpretation
        of, 43–45
    economic activity and, 82–84
    federalism limits on, 35, 78–86, 99
    internal vs. external
        commerce, 79–80
    pretext test, 81
    state vs. private actors and, 85–86
Enumerated rights. *See* First
        Amendment
Environmental Protection
        Agency, 118
Equality, concept of, 125, 150–51
Equal Protection
        Clause, 125–51. *See also*
        Fourteenth Amendment
    abortion and, 213–15
    anti-subordination vs.
        color-blindness and, 134–42
    Brown and, 129–34, 136–37
    concept of equality, 150–51
    Plessy and, 128–31, 134, 136
    purpose and effect of, 2, 35,
        148–49, 165, 166, 217–18
    race-conscious student
        assignments, 55
    slavery and, 126–28
    states and, 6
    tiers of scrutiny, 141–48, 224
    under-enforcement and, 190
    voting rights and, 228–30
Espionage Act (1917), 168
Establishment Clause, 178–85.
        See also First Amendment
    government funding of religion
        and, 183–85
    religious displays and, 179–80
    religious speech by government
        and, 181–83
    school prayer and, 180–81
    school vouchers and, 184

Smith and, 174–76
Ethnicity, as suspect
        classification, 144
European Convention on Human
        Rights, 37
Executive branch. *See* President and
        presidency
Ex post facto laws, 153
Expressive association right, 206

Facial litigation, 31–32
Fallon, Richard, 66
False statements, 165
Family and Medical Leave Act
        (FMLA, 1993), 232–34, 233*n*53
Federal courts. *See also* Supreme
        Court
    jurisdiction of, 9, 29, 30–31, 122
    political question doctrine, 34–35,
        120, 121–22, 236
Federal government
    Bill of Rights and, 6
    individual rights, 6–7
    separation of powers and, 5
    structural limits on, 4–6
Federalism, 69–93. *See also*
        Constitution
    benefits and costs, 71–78
    clear-statement rules, 9, 91–92
    commandeering and, 86–88
    economic activity and, 82–84
    enumerated powers, limits
        on, 78–92
    internal vs. external
        commerce, 79–80
    pretext test, 81
    sovereign immunity, 89–90
    states, limits on, 92–93
    state sovereignty and, 85–86,
        214–15, 222
Federalist Papers
    on bills of rights, 153–54
    on federalism, 75

Federalist Papers (*cont.*)
  on judicial review, 22
  as polemical, 62
  on separation of powers, 75
  on tyranny of majority, 75–77,
    145, 155
Fifteenth Amendment, 125, 137,
    148–49, 192, 217, 238
Fifth Amendment, 54, 125–26,
    132–33, 198, 203, 204, 239
Fighting words, 164–65
Filibusters, 103
First Amendment, 153–85. *See also*
    Establishment Clause
  freedom of speech, 4, 11, 35, 45,
    156–57, 159–71, 176–77
  freedom of the press, 11, 45,
    156–58, 157*n*14
  free exercise of religion, 145, 157,
    171–78
  inference-authorizing view
    on, 45–46
  invalidation of laws and, 35–36
Flag burning, 163–64
Fletcher v. Peck, 46
Formalism, 97
Fourteenth Amendment. *See also*
    Equal Protection Clause;
    Privileges or Immunities
    Clause
  adoption of, 61, 125, 127, 135,
    144
  Due Process Clause, 54, 198,
    202–3, 218
  enforcement provision, 84,
    173–74, 196, 217–34, 225*n*26
  incorporation doctrine, 6, 58,
    156, 191, 201–5, 203*n*52, 207
  minority rights and, 17
  private actors and, 218–22
  sodomy and, 238
  state citizenship and
    commerce, 92
  states, limits on, 6

  substantive rights provisions
    of, 192
  voting rights and, 239
Fourth Amendment, 54, 64, 150,
    188, 202, 238
Framers. *See also* Constitution;
    specific Framers
  diverse ideologies of, 61–62
  on federalism, 75, 222
  influences on, 95–96
  originalism and, 61–62, 65
  on political parties, 102
  writtenness and, 25
France, 71, 154
Frankfurter, Felix
  on constitutional
    interpretation, 106
  on executive power, 114
Franklin, Benjamin, 126
Freedom of contract, 190–91,
    197–200, 211–12
Freedom of speech, 159–71
  campaign finance regulation
    and, 161–63
  censorship, 11, 159, 163, 165, 167–70
  clear and present danger
    test, 167–69
  content-based laws/policies
    and, 159, 164, 176–77, 181–82
  core political speech, 160–61
  dissent and, 158
  electoral process and, 156–57
  fighting words, 164–65
  flag burning, 163–64
  hate speech, 165–66
  incitement test, 164, 169
  libelous speech, 38, 165, 167
  as means vs. end, 160–63
  new technology and, 45–46
  obscenity, 36, 165, 166–67
  original Constitution and, 153
  Pledge of Allegiance, 181
  public fora/private
    viewpoints, 164, 179

Freedom of the press, 45–46, 153,
    154–55, 156–58, 157n14, 160,
    202, 206
Free exercise of religion, 171–78
    federal government and, 157
    neutrality and, 8, 178
    original Constitution and, 153
    ritual animal sacrifice
        and, 171–72
    strict scrutiny test, 172–77
Functionalism, 97
Fundamental rights, 3, 192–95,
    208–9, 213

Gay rights. *See* Sexual orientation
Germany, 71, 75
Gibbons v. Ogden, 79–80
Gramm-Rudman-Hollings Act
    (1985), 5
Grand jury requirement, 204
Gregory v. Ashcroft, 71
Griswold v. Connecticut, 207–8,
    212–13
Guantanamo Bay Naval Base,
    20, 123
Guarantee Clause, 86–87
Guest, United States v.,
    219–20, 221
Guinn v. United States, 148–49
Gun control
    federal/state standards on, 7
    liberal opposition to limits
        on, 48
    originalism in decisions on, 64
    Privileges or Immunities Clause
        and, 196
Gun Free School Zones Act
    (1994), 78, 83
Gunther, Gerald, 141

Habeas corpus. *See* Writ of habeas
    corpus
Hamdan v. Rumsfeld, 112

Hamdi v. Rumsfeld, 122
Hamilton, Alexander
    on bills of rights, 153–54,
        156, 189
    on judicial review, 22
    on national bank, 43
Han Chinese, 139–40
Hand, Learned, on free speech, 171
Harlan, John Marshall, on
        color-blindness of
        Constitution, 134
Harlan, John Marshall II
    on incorporation, 208
    on meaning of liberty, 206–8
Hate speech, 165–66
Hayes, Rutherford B., 128
Hippies, as unfavored group, 147, 148
Holmes, Oliver Wendell, Jr.
    on free speech, 159–60, 168–69,
        170, 171
    on judicial review, 13, 30
    on labor laws and
        capitalism, 199–200
    on strict scrutiny, 142
House of Representatives. *See also*
        Congress
    impeachment trials, 34, 121
    party loyalty, 102
    separation of powers
        and, 98–99, 102
Human Rights Act (UK), 37

Impeachment, 2, 34, 121
Incitement test, 164, 169
Incorporation doctrine, 58, 156, 191,
    201–5, 208, 217, 223
    Black on, 203–4, 203n52, 207
    jot-for-jot method, 204
India, 44, 139
Individual rights. *See also specific*
    rights
    constitutional interpretation
        and, 3, 45, 57–61

Individual rights (*cont.*)
enforcement of, 20, 221
federal/state standards on, 1,
6–7, 77
inference-authorizing view
on, 47
separation of powers and, 108–9,
122
under Ninth Amendment, 188–89
Industry subsidies, 93
Inference-authorizing
view of constitutional
interpretation, 45–47
Institutional reform
litigation, 120
Intermediate scrutiny
standard, 141–42, 144, 233
Interstate commerce. *See also*
Commerce Clause doctrine
congressional deference and,
58–60
Hamilton on, 43
Marshall on, 80–81
neutrality requirement, 8, 197
Intrastate commerce, 8, 79–80,
81, 82
Iredell, James, 52–53
Israel, 71, 140

Jackson, Andrew, 35
Jackson, Robert
on authority among branches,
5, 123
on executive power, 105, 107–10,
112, 113–15, 116
on finality of Court, 239
on framers' intent, 105
Jefferson, Thomas, 43, 126, 154
Jews, 140, 178, 179, 184
Jim Crow segregation, 77, 125,
128–30, 133–34, 136
Judicial activism, 50–52, 53, 211,
214–15

Judicial exclusivity, 34, 224,
228, 235
Judicial restraint, 50–52, 224–25,
226–27, 236
Judicial review, 11–38
Article III on, 28–29, 30–31, 32, 42
Article VI on, 28–30
court jurisdiction and,
31–32, 224
definition of, 12
elected officials and, 9, 16, 20–21,
58–60, 113, 123
judicial supremacy and, 33–34
legislative supremacy and, 27
purpose of, 12–21, 53, 56, 154
writtenness and, 22–26, 28
Judiciary
political question doctrine, 34–35,
120, 121–22, 236
separation of powers
and, 119–24
standing doctrine and, 32,
119–21
Judiciary Act (1789), 22, 30–31
Jurisdiction, of courts, 9, 28–29,
30–32, 106, 122
Justice Department, 133

Kansas-Nebraska Act (1854), 127
Katzenbach v. Morgan, 228–29, 230
Kennedy, Anthony
on due process for enemy
combatants, 20
on gender discrimination, 233–34
Kennedy v. Louisiana, 54
Kerry, John, 162
*Kimel v. Florida Board of
Regents*, 225–27, 225*n*26, 230,
233–34

Labor laws, 81, 85–86, 199–200,
232–34. *See also specific laws*
Lawmaking process, 99–100

Left/right political ideology, 47–49
Legislative supremacy, 14–15,
    14n5, 27
Legislators. *See* Elected officials
Levinson, Daryl, 101–2, 103–4
Libelous speech, 38, 165, 167
Liberals
    on equal protection as anti-
        subordination principle,
        55, 134
    opposition to particular
        doctrines, 47–48
    race-based classifications
        and, 137, 141
    states' rights and, 77–78
Libertarianism, 19–20, 59, 75–77,
    99–100, 131, 199, 211
Liberty interest, use of term, 208–9
Liberty of contract and property, 18.
    See also Freedom of contract
Lincoln, Abraham, 16, 33, 34, 127
Line item veto, 5
Literacy tests, 149
Localism, 72
Lochner v. New York, 18–19, 190–91,
    199–201, 204, 210–12, 214–15
Locke, John, *Two Treatises of
    Government*, 95–96

Madison, James
    on bills of rights, 154–56, 189
    on checks and balances, 16
    on minorities, 145
    notes on Constitutional
        Convention, 61–63
    on separation of powers, 95, 100–
        104, 114, 116–17, 123–24
    on tyranny of majority, 75–77, 155
Magna Carta, 198
Majoritarian process, 61
Majority rule, 17
Mali, 171
Marbury v. Madison, 11, 15, 22, 24,

    26–28, 29, 33–34, 38, 42, 46,
    121, 222
Marketplace of ideas, 162
Marshall, John
    on constitutions, 41, 42
    on enumeration, 43–44, 79
    on interstate commerce, 80, 81
    on judicial review, 15, 22, 24,
        26–28
    on unconstitutional statutes, 46, 50
Marshall, Thurgood, on context-
    specific scrutiny, 146–47
McCarran-Ferguson Act (1945), 197
McCulloch v. Maryland, 35, 41–47,
    50, 78–79, 81
Medical marijuana, 1, 77
Meese, Edwin, 33
Minority rights, majority rule
    and, 17, 21, 76–77
Missouri Compromise, 126–27
Montesquieu, Baron de, *The Spirit of
    the Laws*, 95–96, 100
Moral reading, of Constitution, 54–57
Moral realism, 56
Morrison, United States v., 220–22
Musharaff, Pervez, 16

National banks, 35, 43–46, 79
*National League of Cities v.
    Usery*, 85–86
National origin, as suspect
    classification, 2, 126, 144
Native American Church, 172
Natural law, 52–57
Nazism, 75
Negative freedom, 160
Netherlands, 14–15, 14n5, 21–22,
    24, 27
Neutrality requirements, 8, 178–85
*Nevada Department of Human
    Resources v. Hibbs*, 232–34
*New York City Transit Authority v.
    Beazer*, 143–44

New York Times v. Sullivan, 165, 167
New York v. United States, 87
New Zealand, 72
Nineteenth Amendment, 238
Ninth Amendment, 154, 156,
    187–90, 203, 239. *See also*
    Unenumerated rights
Nixon v. United States, 2
Non-delegation doctrine, 108,
    117–19
Noneconomic vs. economic
    activity, 82–83, 220–21
Notwithstanding Clause
    (Canada), 37–38

Obscenity, 36, 165, 166–67
O'Connor, Sandra Day
    on congressional
        enforcement, 227
    on due process for enemy
        combatants, 20
    on endorsement of religion, 180
    on federalism, 71–75
    on free exercise of religion, 172
    on separation of powers, 122
Opposition rights, 104
Original intent, 61–63
Originalism, constitutional
    interpretation and. *See also*
    specific Originalists
    changed circumstances
        and, 64
    original intent, 61–63
    original public meaning, 62–63
    race-based affirmative action
        and, 136
Original public meaning, 62–63

Pakistan Supreme Court, 16
Palestinian Arabs, 140
*Parents Involved in Community
    Schools v. Seattle School District
    No. 1*, 55

Parliamentary supremacy, 25–26,
    95–96
Peckham, Rufus Wheeler, on
    meaning of liberty, 198
Philadelphia Convention
    (1787), 61–62, 70
Physician-assisted suicide, 77, 208
Pildes, Richard, 101–2, 103–4
Pledge of Allegiance, 181–82
Plenary power, 4–6
Plessy v. Ferguson, 128–31, 134, 136
Poe v. Ullman, 206–7
Police power, 4–5
Political actors. *See* Elected officials
Political correctness, 165
Political morality, 54–55, 66
Political parties, 5–6, 76, 101–3
Political question doctrine, 34–35,
    120, 121–22, 236
Political safeguards view, 69–70
Polybius, 95
Pornography, 59, 166–67
Posner, Richard, 67
Presentment, 17, 98–101
Presidents and presidency. *See also*
    specific presidents
    as Commander in Chief, 1, 36,
        105, 111–13
    election of, 69, 125, 128, 162,
        238–39
    foreign affairs and, 110
    judicial review and, 13, 31, 35
    military affairs and, 111–12,
        115–16
    overlapping congressional powers
        and, 104–9
    political parties and, 102
    separation of powers and, 98,
        104–17
    signing statements, 36–37
    tiers of executive power, 108–15
    Vesting Clause, 105, 110, 111
    war powers, 106, 111–12
Press. *See* Freedom of the press

Printz v. United States, 87
Privacy rights, 205–15
  bodily autonomy, 209
  family formation, 209
  parental rights, 1, 3, 207, 209
  same-sex marriage, 213–14
  sexual expression, 166–67, 209, 210
  sterilization, 207
  strict scrutiny test and, 208–9
  substantive due process doctrine and, 208–14
Privileges and Immunities Clause, 6, 192–95, 206
Privileges or Immunities Clause, 6, 190, 191–97, 201–2, 203, 217
Procedural requirements
  clear-statement rules, 9
  constitutional basis for, 8–9
Process theory. *See* Representation reinforcement
Public figures, libelous speech and, 165, 167
Public opinion, 155, 213–15, 238

Race
  affirmative action and, 48, 51, 134–38, 141, 144–46
  segregation and, 77, 128–30, 133–34
  student school assignment and, 55, 56
  as suspect classification, 2–3, 141, 144–46, 149
Racial equality, 76–77
Racial favoritism, 138–39
Rational basis test, 143–48, 200–201, 224–28, 232, 236–37
R.A.V. v. City of St. Paul, 165–66
Reasonableness review, 200
Red Scare era decisions, 159, 168
Regulatory competition, 71–73
Rehnquist, William

on abortion, 208–9
on defining of constitutional guarantees, 227
Religion. *See also* Free exercise of religion; Establishment Clause
  neutrality and, 8
  strict scrutiny test and, 145
  as suspect classification, 144–45
Religious displays, 179–80
Religious Freedom Restoration Act (RFRA, 1993), 173–75, 223
Reporters' privilege, 157–58, 157n14
Representation reinforcement, 57–61
Reverse discrimination, 139
Right-answers thesis, 56
Right of expressive association, 171, 206
Right to counsel, 202, 203
Right to travel, 6, 193, 196, 206
Roberts, John, on common-law system, 65–66
Roe v. Wade, 209, 210–14
Romer v. Evans, 147–48
Rosenberg, Gerald, 133

Sager, Lawrence, 189–90. *See also* Under-enforcement thesis
Same-sex marriage, 213–14
Santeria, 171–72
Scalia, Antonin
  on free exercise of religion, 172–73, 174, 175, 177
  on originalism, 64
Schnapper, Eric, 135–36
School prayer, 7, 47, 59, 180–82
School vouchers, 184
Second Amendment, 64, 188–89, 214, 227–28, 238. *See also* Gun control
Senate. *See also* Congress
  election of, 67
  equal representation of states, 69, 74

Senate (*cont.*)
  filibusters, 103
  impeachment trials, 2, 34, 121
  party loyalty, 102
  role of, 74
  separation of powers and, 98–99
Separate-but-equal doctrine. *See*
    Equal Protection Clause
Separation of powers
    doctrine, 95–124
  executive branch and, 104–17
  federal government and, 5–6
  function of, 97–104
  judiciary and, 119–23
  legislative branch and, 117–19
Seventh Amendment, 204
Sex/gender. *See also* Women
  application of immutability
    to, 145–46
  employment discrimination
    and, 233–34
  same-sex marriage, 213–14
  as semi-suspect
    classification, 2–3, 136, 141,
    144, 145, 150
  violence and, 78, 82, 83, 220–21
Sexual expression, 166–67, 209, 210
Sexual orientation, 47, 59, 126, 144,
    146–48, 150, 213–14
Signing statements, 36–37
Sixth Amendment, 202
Slaughterhouse Cases, 190, 194–97,
    202–3, 217
Slavery, 56, 63, 76, 125–27, 132, 135,
    136–37, 172, 192, 218
Social change, 238, 239
Social issues, 6–7, 213–14. *See also*
    specific issues
Sodomy, 209, 210, 238
Sovereign immunity, 89–90, 225*n*26,
    233*n*53
Speech. *See* Freedom of speech
Spirit of the Laws,
    The (Montesquieu), 96
Sri Lanka, 139

Standing doctrine, 32, 119–21
State action requirement, 218–22
State courts
  advisory opinions and, 32
  free exercise of religion and, 173–74
State governments. *See also*
    Federalism
  anti-commandeering principle
    and, 86–88
  Bill of Rights and, 6
  clear-statement rules, 9, 91–92
  Commerce Clause and, 6
  Equal Protection Clause and, 6
  horizontal federalism
    among, 92–93
  individual rights, 6–7
  plenary power, 4–6
  Privileges and Immunities Clause
    and, 6
  regulatory competition
    among, 71–73
  sovereign immunity, 89–90,
    225*n*26, 233*n*53
  state sovereignty and, 85–86,
    214–15, 222
  Supremacy Clause and, 6
  unconstitutional legislation, 36
State sovereign immunity, 89–90,
    225*n*26, 233*n*53
States' rights
  liberal opposition to protections
    for, 48, 51, 77
  racial discrimination and, 76–77
Steel Seizure Case. See Youngstown
    Sheet & Tube Company v.
    Sawyer, 5
Stevens, John Paul
  on context-specific
    scrutiny, 146–47
  on definition of economic
    activity, 83
Stone, Harlan F., on suspect
    classes, 145
Story, Joseph, on federal court
    jurisdiction, 30–31

Strict scrutiny test
    affirmative action and, 141–42
    free exercise of religion and, 145,
        172–73, 176–78, 223
    privacy rights and, 208–9
    on race-conscious remedies, 149
    on racial classifications, 136–42
    suspect classifications
        and, 144–46
Substantive due process
        doctrine, 191, 198–203,
        207–14. *See also* Incorporation
        doctrine; Unenumerated rights
Sunstein, Cass
    *Democracy and the Problem of
        Free Speech*, 212
    on freedom of contract, 211–12
Super-majoritarian process, 61,
        98–99
Supremacy Clause, 6, 26–28, 29–30
Supreme Court. *See also specific
        cases and Justices*
    on administrative law, 118–19
    on authority among branches, 5
    on congressional deference, 34,
        142–44, 197–98
    conservatism and individual
        rights, 77
    on First Amendment, 35–36
    fundamental rights and, 3
    on general laws and free exercise
        rights, 172–78
    on government funding of
        religion, 183–84
    on incorporation, 204–5
    on non-delegation doctrine, 108,
        117–19
    partisanship in decisions, 60
    on right of expressive
        association, 206
    on ritual animal
        sacrifice, 171–72
    on same-sex sodomy, 209,
        210, 238
    social change and, 238

    on standing, 32, 119–21
    on structural provisions, 19–20
    on unconstitutionality of Bush
        Administration activities,
        16, 123
    on unconstitutional statutes, 191,
        191*n*11, 223–24
    under-enforcement
        thesis, 189–90, 227, 237
    war-on-terror decisions, 16, 20,
        122–23
Suspect classifications, 3, 134–35,
        144–46, 149, 150, 225–26, 232.
        See also specific classifications
Suspension Clause. *See also Writ of
        habeas corpus*, 20, 123
Sweeping Clause, 78–79, 117–18
Swift Boat Veterans for Truth, 162

Tamils, 139
Tenth Amendment, 1, 86, 89, 188
Thayer, James Bradley, 27, 51
Thirteenth Amendment, 125, 127,
        192, 197, 217
Thomas, Clarence
    on federalism, 4
    on interstate and intrastate
        commerce, 80
    on race-based affirmative
        action, 137
    on use of natural law, 53
Tibetans, 139–40
Tiers of scrutiny
    equal protection context
        and, 2–3, 142–48
    fundamental rights and, 3
Tocqueville, Alexis de, 9
Torture, 16, 36–37, 111–13
Totalitarianism, 160
Travel, right to, 6, 193, 196, 206
Truman, Harry, 107
Twelfth Amendment, 238–39
Twenty-Fourth Amendment, 238
Twenty-Sixth Amendment, 238

Two Treatises of Government (Locke), 96
Tyranny of majority, 75–77, 155

Under-enforcement thesis, 189–90, 227, 237
Undue burden test, 209
Unenumerated rights, 187–215
    incorporation of Bill of Rights, 58, 156, 191, 201–5, 203n52, 207, 208, 217, 223
    Lochner Era, 196–201
    Ninth Amendment on, 156, 187–90, 203
    privacy rights, 205–15
    Privileges or Immunities Clause, 190, 191–96, 201–2, 203
Unified government, 102, 103–4
Unitary systems, 71, 72, 73–74, 75–76
United Kingdom, 37, 71
United States v. See name of opposing party
University of Michigan Law School, 141–42

Vesting Clause, 105, 110, 111
Veto gates, 17, 98–101
Violence Against Women Act (VAWA, 1994), 78, 83, 220–21
Voting rights, 148–49, 228–29, 238–39
Voting Rights Act (1965), 137

Wagner Act (1935), 41–42
Waldron, Jeremy, 15

War on terror (Bush), 16, 20, 36–37, 111–12, 122–23
Warrantless surveillance, 16, 111–12
Washington, Bushrod, on privileges and immunities, 192–95
Washington, George, 43, 126, 192
Weimar Germany, 75
Westen, Peter, 150
West Virginia State Board of Educ. v. Barnette, 181–82
White, Byron, on substantive due process rights, 210
Whitney v. California, 159–60, 169–70
Women. *See also* Sex/gender
    Ely on abortion rights and, 59–60
    equal protection and, 145, 150, 213
    gender stereotypes and, 145, 220–21, 233–34
    sex as semi-suspect classification, 3, 144, 145
    violence and, 78, 83, 220–21
Writ of habeas corpus
    as a fundamental right, 193, 196
    clear-statement rules, 9
    enemy combatant detainees and, 20, 123
    for noncitizen enemy combatants, 123
    Suspension Clause, 20, 123
Writtenness, 22–26, 28

Youngstown Sheet & Tube Company v. Sawyer, 106–10, 114–15

Printed in Great Britain
by Amazon

41878490R00149